SKIING
with
HENRY KNOX

A Personal Journey Along Vermont's Catamount Trail

Other Outdoor Books by Islandport Press

Making Tracks
By Matt Weber

Evergreens
By John Holyoke

Backtrack
By V. Paul Reynolds

Ghost Buck
By Dean Bennett

A Life Lived Outdoors
By George Smith

My Life in the Maine Woods
By Annette Jackson

Nine Mile Bridge
By Helen Hamlin

In Maine
By John N. Cole

Suddenly, the Cider Didn't Taste So Good
By John Ford

Leave Some for Seed
By Tom Hennessey

Birds of a Feather
By Paul J. Fournier

These and other Maine books available at
www.islandportpress.com

SKIING
with
HENRY KNOX

A Personal Journey Along Vermont's Catamount Trail

SAM BRAKELEY

ISLANDPORT PRESS

ISLANDPORT PRESS

Islandport Press
PO Box 10
Yarmouth, Maine 04096
www.islandportpress.com
info@islandportpress.com

ISBN: 978-1-944762-76-6
ebook ISBN: 978-1-944762-86-5
Library of Congress Control Number: 2019931594
Printed in USA

Dean L. Lunt, Publisher
Book design by Teresa Lagrange
Cover photo by TommL/iStock

For Elizabeth

Artist Unknown, *Hauling Guns by Ox Teams from Fort Ticonderoga for the Siege of Boston, 1775.*

Table of Contents

The author on the trail.

Author's Note

This book combines two very different stories.

One takes place between 1775 and 1776 in New York and Massachusetts, and features Henry Knox, then an unknown but ambitious volunteer in the newly minted Continental Army. Knox volunteers to undertake a challenging and dangerous mission to Fort Ticonderoga, which at this point in history is a twenty-year-old French military base in northern New York. There, he is to assess the heavy artillery and return to Boston—where George Washington has the British bottled up—bringing along any pieces of equipment that are in workable condition.

The second takes place in the winter of 2015, in Vermont, where I undertake to thru-ski the Catamount Trail—a rambling 330-mile cross-country ski trail that travels the length of Vermont—in a single expedition.

At first glance, they don't have a lot in common. But the two resonate closely for me, for various reasons—not the least of which is that long winter journeys such as we both undertook have many of the same challenges and obstacles, regardless of the terrain being covered or how they are accomplished. We both battled intense cold, heavy snow, poor trails, thaws, and many of the other physical conditions that Mother Nature and a rural landscape can throw in one's way.

Henry Knox was twenty-five at the time of his expedition, and just beginning a military career that would culminate with his role as secretary of war. Additionally, Knox had recently married Lucy Flucker, whom he loved dearly and missed while on the trail. They kept up a running correspondence that would continue throughout their lives, since this was only the first of many long separations.

I, too, at the age of twenty-seven, was facing a separation. My longtime girlfriend had decided to move across the country to pursue her career in medicine, and I needed to make a decision as to whether or not I would join her. Henry's and Lucy's thoughts on their separation provided me with some perspective on my own impending one, and I've taken advantage of their voluminous correspondence to reflect on my own decision-making process. I'm a passionate—albeit, untrained—armchair historian, particularly of the Revolutionary War era, and have frequently found lessons and experiences that are meaningful for me as I navigate the twenty-first century (which is how I stumbled across a description of Knox's journey in the first place). For all of these reasons, I've chosen to interweave my story with his, into one larger narrative.

Knox's story is told in the past tense—it happened in 1775 and 1776, after all. My own, in 2015, I've chosen to tell in the present, both to emphasize when I switch between the telling of one story and the other, and to dispel confusion, not cause it. I hope that I've achieved this result.

Throughout the telling of Knox's story, I have made liberal use of quotations from a variety of primary sources. As any reader of eighteenth-century history knows, journalists and memoirists of the time were far more creative in their spelling than we are today. I have chosen to preserve as much as possible their unique styling of the English language, and have chosen not to overpopulate their words with "[sic]." Any misspelled words or poor grammar within quotations can be understood to have been the original author's mistake and not mine.

Sam Brakeley

As always, I am indebted to the numerous historians who have written about Knox and the Ticonderoga Expedition before me. I encourage interested readers to explore my Notes section for further reading.

And finally, while every effort has been made to ensure factual accuracy, it is possible that an error has been made. If so, it is no one's fault but mine. Please forgive it.

THROUGH THIS PLACE PASSED
GENERAL HENRY KNOX
IN THE WINTER OF
1775 — 1776
TO DELIVER TO
GENERAL GEORGE WASHINGTON
AT CAMBRIDGE
THE TRAIN OF ARTILLERY
FROM FORT TICONDEROGA USED
TO FORCE THE BRITISH ARMY
TO EVACUATE BOSTON
ERECTED BY THE COMMONWEALTH
OF MASSACHUSETTS 1927

General Henry Knox monument, Wilbraham, Massachusetts

Historical Background of Henry Knox and the Ticonderoga Expedition

Henry Knox was born July 25, 1750, in Boston, Massachusetts, to William and Mary Knox. He was the seventh of ten children, but quickly found himself the eldest son in the house. William and Mary (like Henry years later) were plagued by the deaths of some of their brood, and only four of their ten children survived into adulthood. Henry's two surviving older brothers left home early to pursue lives as seamen and never returned, leaving a small household in Boston of William, Mary, Henry, and Henry's younger brother, also named William.

The elder William, a prosperous shipbuilder and merchant, immigrated to the British colonies in 1729 from Ireland. There, he quickly started a business that would grow to include a wharf, a construction yard, and the two-story home where Henry and his brothers would be born. William found himself out of work in 1756 during an economic downturn, however. Rather than face the economic hardship, he deserted his family for the West Indies in 1759, leaving Henry, at age nine, fatherless, and the sole provider for the now-smaller family. His father would die soon thereafter.

Faced with few options, Henry's mother, Mary, pulled Henry from the Boston Latin Grammar School where he had been studying and put him to work in the bookstore of Messrs. Wharton and Bowes. Nicholas Bowes was as much of a father figure as Henry ever had during most of his childhood, and was instrumental in shaping Henry's future career. For it was here, as Henry put food on his family's table by stocking shelves and packaging books for shipment, that he began a lifelong love affair with books and learning.

Even at this young age Henry was conscious of his lack of formal education, and he sought to make up for it in rare moments between tasks in the bookstore. No doubt Bowes guided his reading, as Henry took on Roman classics such as Plutarch. He also began learning French. But nothing excited his interest more than the study of military history and engineering. Artillery, in particular, captured his attention.

Henry was not your typical scrawny bookworm with his nose in a novel day in and day out. A strapping youth, who soon grew into a six-foot-plus frame, he more than held his own on the piers and streets of Boston. His natural inclination toward athletic endeavors was obvious, as was his sense of adventure. An oft-related tale from his boyhood tells of one such escapade. An old friend wrote to him years after the episode, recalling those prior carefree times. "I have often thought of our attempt to imitate the man who flew from the steeple of the North Church," penned Reverend David McClure in 1788, "when we were sliding down an oar from the small building in your father's yard at Wheeler's Point—and by our letting fly little wooden men from the garret window on strings." Knox in response agreed "our juvenile sports and the joyful sensations they created are fresh in my mind."[1] This attraction to adventure would permeate all of Knox's life.

Perhaps inevitably, rival factions developed between local neighborhoods and groups of friends. Never one to shy away from a fracas, Henry was an eager participant in the frequent melees that occurred between parties, and is said to have emerged champion more often than not from any tilt he involved himself in.

One such incident occurred on "Pope's Night," celebrated each year on the fifth of November. One gang of boys would drag a Pope figure around town while another, the replica of the Devil. They would parade around the streets in mock homage to their respective idols, and a lively fight would occur when these competing processions met. On this particular year, the wagon carrying Henry's effigy lost a wheel. Rather than allow that to ruin the night's festivities, Henry bent beneath the axle and marched onward, his shoulder replacing the broken wheel, to the admiring cries of his compatriots.

From these few anecdotes, we have a picture of a strong, joyful youth, already bearing the responsibilities of manhood and family, yet facing each day with a sunny outlook and upright posture. Equal to any challenge, he could have been forgiven for exhibiting a bit of haughtiness, yet this didn't seem to be part of his demeanor. Colleagues of the time universally note his even-keeled temper, contagious exuberance, and quiet sense of fairness and loyalty. John Adams described him as having "pleasing manners and [an] inquisitive turn of mind." Later, a French general wrote that Knox was "a man of understanding, a well-formed man, gay, sincere, and honest. It is impossible to know, without esteeming him, or to see without loving him."[2] Henry pursued life with zest, energy, and a strong sense of personal moral ethics. By the age of twenty, he was a powerful young man with rising prospects and a bright future.

But all was not well in his hometown of Boston, Massachusetts. The French and Indian War came to a close in 1763, leaving the British victorious but deeply in debt. Because much of the war with France took place in North America, Britain deemed it proper that the English colonies should help to pay off some of the debt. In 1765 Parliament passed the Stamp Act, establishing a small tax on all paper goods, including everything from newspapers to playing cards. It was the first direct tax on the colonists passed by Parliament.

The colonists were unimpressed. Protesting on the grounds that this was "taxation without representation," they argued that their rights as Englishmen were being stepped on. (Simultaneously, and not a little disingenuously, they also refused representation due to the distances and time involved to get to Parliament.) Benjamin Franklin voyaged to Great Britain in 1766 and testified before Parliament that the colonies had already contributed more than their fair share to the war effort, including soldiers, equipment, and money. His testimony, combined with a new government in power, led to the repeal of the Stamp Act later that year, but the damage to relations would remain permanent. In an attempt to save face, Parliament reaffirmed their right to make laws and tax the colonies.

One short year later, Parliament was at it again. They passed the Townshend Acts, taxing common goods such as glass, tea, and paper. Colonists once again organized boycotts and demonstrations, and the nascent Sons of Liberty stepped up their systematic harassment of customs officials. In response to the unrest, King George III deployed troops to Boston, noted for its particularly radical leanings, and led by individuals such as John Hancock and Samuel Adams. Those he sent were not the cream of Britain's military (the more elite and hardened forces were saved for the European theater). Many colonial troops were average citizens recruited from British streets and rougher neighborhoods. Their crude, uncouth, and confrontational demeanor only exacerbated the growing tensions. Small scuffles seemed to become more frequent between soldiers and citizens, and their size and import only grew in the retelling. Boston was a cask of gunpowder placed too near an open fire. All it needed was one particularly active ember to ignite a much larger conflagration.

It was into this charged and emotionally fraught atmosphere that Henry Knox strode on the afternoon of March 5, 1770, a date that would soon be memorialized as the Boston Massacre. It all began with a young apprentice taunting a British sentry for not having paid his bill to the apprentice's master. When the sentry replied civilly that perhaps more respect was due a British soldier, the apprentice responded with a vile epithet. The now-enraged Redcoat then struck the apprentice on the head with his musket, causing the boy to race down the street, screaming for assistance.

The boy's yelling brought a crowd of eventually more than fifty Bostonians to the sentry's position. Someone began ringing the church bells nearby, normally a signal for a fire, which brought even more people rushing to the scene. A nasty confrontation began. Townspeople yelled names and threw rocks, snow, and ice at the sentry, all the while taunting him to fire his weapon. The officer of the watch, Captain Preston, hearing the noise and being alerted by a runner, arrived with eight other soldiers to help his besieged private. With fixed bayonets, they kept the angry crowd at bay, which only enraged the mob further.

Henry, walking home from work at the bookstore, arrived on the scene and coolheadedly waded through the crowd, using his bulk to reach the British soldiers. Upon discovering loaded weaponry, he entreated Captain Preston, "For God's sake, take your men back. If they fire, your life must answer for the consequence."[3] Preston acknowledged this to be true, but made no move to retreat, instead ordering the mob to disperse. He might as well have ordered the Charles River to stop flowing.

The straw that broke the proverbial over-weighted camel's back was an object thrown at one of the privates, knocking him to the ground. Having faced taunts and projectiles all afternoon, this soldier had reached his breaking point and pulled the trigger of his musket. A ragged volley from his compatriots soon followed, and bullets tore the crowd apart. Eleven men were hit; three died immediately, and two in the ensuing hours. The crowd, amazed and aghast that the British had actually opened fire, broke almost immediately, leaving the shocked soldiers standing alone in the snowy street, now dotted with red.

The outcry in the aftermath of the event was instantaneous. While Captain Preston and the eight soldiers were put under arrest, and later, on trial, numerous descriptions of the shootings, some heavily biased, were published throughout the colonies and Great Britain. This would only speed the downward trajectory of British–colonial relations, and persuade some fence sitters that perhaps the King and Parliament were not as paternal as had been hoped.

Knox's experience and failed attempt to sway Captain Prescott may have been the deciding moment for him. He was now faced with firsthand evidence that the British were unwilling to reason or negotiate with colonists, and would rather fire into a crowd than back down. His sympathies from this moment on remained with the Patriots. However, by all outward appearances, Knox seemed unmoved by the outcry from the event. Rather than take a radical stand for or against one side or the other, he quietly pursued his own interests while remaining friends with Loyalists and Patriots alike.

Knox left the employ of Bowes and began his own bookshop in 1771, catering to both colonists and the British alike. His evenhandedness was fortuitous, both for his business and social life, for it was around this time that he met Lucy Flucker, daughter of well-known Tory Thomas Flucker. It was the beginning of a lifelong love affair.

As the Royal Secretary of the Province of Massachusetts, Thomas Flucker was a fierce Loyalist to the Crown. His daughter Lucy was born in 1756. Raised in an upper-class, thoroughly Tory environment, she participated in the busy social scene of wealthy Boston. Described as "a woman of much tact, quick and ready sympathy, and good judgment, combined with great good-nature and a love of fun," Lucy was a popular guest and sought-after date.[4]

The men and women of this circle were frequently Tories, solidly loyal to Britain due to their close business ties with the mother country. Perhaps Lucy, too, would have remained loyal, but for her love of literature. She joined the many Tories who shopped at Knox's new store, and soon found reasons for stopping by that did not include purchasing new books. The "uncommonly good-looking" (for he was handsome in addition to being jovial and fair-minded) man behind the counter and stocking shelves soon caught her eye, and she would corner him between the stacks for private conversations.[5]

For Knox's part, he never seemed to shy away from the attention. Perhaps the best indication of his feelings is shown by the fact that he always seemed to be miscounting her change when she did make a purchase. His mind was apparently on other things besides pennies.

Lucy's parents were not in favor of the match. Not only was Knox merely a tradesman selling books, but he was also becoming known for his patriotic leanings as well. Knox and Lucy would often resort to fervent love letters and secret meetings in order to communicate. Many of these letters have been preserved and testify to the depth of their passion. "My only consolation is in you," Knox wrote, "and in order that it should be well grounded, permit me to beg two things of you with the greatest ardency: never distrust my affection for you without the most rational and convincing proof—if you do not hear from me in a reasonable time, do not lay it to my want of love, but want of opportunity; and do not, in consequence of such distrust, omit writing to me as often as possible. Don't distrust the sincerity of your Fidelio."[6] In an era where so many marriages lacked love, Lucy and Knox would care deeply for each other until death.

All that remained was to overcome Lucy's parents' hesitations to the marriage. "What news?" Knox asked breathlessly in a 1774 letter. "Have you spoken to your father, or he to you, upon the subject?"[7] They considered elopement until, like so many fathers both before and after, Thomas Flucker finally gave in to his daughter's wishes and permitted the marriage. They were wed on June 16, 1774, and immediately set up a home under the watchful eyes of Lucy's parents, who forecast only poverty and hunger for the young couple with revolutionary leanings.

Knox had joined The Train, the local militia's artillery company, in 1768. Now, as if Knox did not have enough to keep him busy between wooing Lucy and managing a bookstore, he cofounded the Boston Grenadier Corps in 1772, an offshoot of this first foray in the military. Why the artillery? Their resplendent uniforms no doubt appealed to him (they certainly appealed to Lucy, who admired the handsome man astride his large steed). The romance and social standing would have been attractive, as well. When he later formed the Grenadier Corps, they issued a rule that all members must be at least five-foot-ten, a standard that added prestige to those who were able to join the select group. Finally, the intricacies and challenges of moving literally tons of equipment over battlefields must have appealed to him.

As a member of The Train, he not only learned to load and shoot cannons, but also quickly realized the importance of understanding military tactics and technique. He now redoubled his efforts to learn all he could, ordering books on the subject and raiding the local library. The Train was led by Adino Paddock, and was well known for its expertise, having been trained by the British themselves when an artillery regiment became snowbound in Boston one winter. Knox made use of this incumbent knowledge and expanded upon it with his own readings. The education he received here would stand him in good stead throughout his career.

Knox continued to maintain a neutral stance as best he could throughout his day-to-day life in Boston. As a small business owner, he had to. Many of his customers were loyal to Britain and wanted nothing to do with the rebels stirring up revolutionary fever in the colonies. At the same time however, as a member of Boston's working class, he couldn't help but continue to empathize with Patriot concerns. He felt more and more drawn to their cause as time passed and tensions rose, but with a new wife, a just-opened bookstore, and a younger brother for whom he felt a more than average sense of responsibility, he no doubt felt his hands were tied. Could he leave all this promise and take up with the Patriot cause?

On the morning of April 19, shots were fired in Lexington and Concord as British soldiers marched to capture Patriot arms and gunpowder. The day's fighting would result in three hundred casualties for the British. The conflict had begun. Knox now had no option but to pick sides.

For Knox, it wasn't so much a choice as it was a coming to terms with the facts. His sympathies were irrevocably with the colonists, and always had been. His bookstore he would leave under the care of his younger brother William, the only family remaining to him (his mother had died in 1771). Lucy would come with him, forsaking her own family who remained staunchly Tory and entrenched in Boston, protected by the British army. Knox would join the American cause.

His persistent friendliness with radicals such as Samuel Adams had by now brought him to the attention of the British. (Paul Revere would occasionally visit Knox's bookstore and the two would commiserate about Britain's mulishness. If a British soldier chanced to walk in while they were deep in conversation, they would immediately begin a fake quarrel complete with mock insults and barbs over fictional work Knox had commissioned from Revere. Supposedly their ruse was so successful that Revere, then unknown to the British as a rebel, was approached for information about Knox.) Boston was locked down by this point, with soldiers entrenched upon the narrow strip of land that connected the city to the mainland. Knox feared arrest and trial for treason if he attempted to leave. (Most of his artillery company had already departed for Patriot lines at his urging.) So, under cover of darkness, not long after the beaten British soldiers had straggled back into Boston from Concord, Lucy and Knox made their escape into the night, heading to Cambridge and the Patriot army.

Years afterward, Washington Irving would write, "Henry Knox was one of those providential characters which spring up in emergencies as if formed by and for the occasion."[8] The momentous decision that Knox and Lucy made to leave all they were familiar with and strike out into unknown territory would prove to be a fortuitous one for George Washington and the budding Revolution. The future unknown to them, Knox and Lucy must have trembled with the audacity of their actions. With no option of return, they had set out on a grand adventure. None could know just what it would bring.

The author and Elizabeth on a few of their shared outdoor adventures.

Prologue

I shiver and inch a hand up through the minuscule opening in my sleeping bag to check my watch. It's six a.m. on a frigid winter morning in January of 2015. It's pitch black in my tent, and God only knows what the temperature is. My sleeping bag is damp from the moisture from my body and my exhalations, and I stink to high heaven.

I pull the hand back into the bag with me and warm it up in my crotch. Then, inching it out into the frigid temperature again, I check my ski boots, positioned next to my sleeping bag. Frozen solid. Sighing, I pull them into my bag and hold them against my chest for the next twenty minutes. The buckles are so cold they burn my skin, but I only clench them tighter. I need them to thaw to get anywhere today.

As I lie here and let them defrost against my chest, adding to the moisture and rank odor of the sleeping bag, I wonder to myself for the thousandth time since starting this trip, "What the hell am I doing out here?" But within the hour, having finally managed to slide my ski boots on and eat a breakfast of oatmeal and coffee, I hit the trail.

Almost immediately I begin to descend through an open hardwood forest. The snow stands several feet deep and consists of the

1

lightest powder. Birches, maples, and beeches whiz past as I take big swooping turns around boulders and over fallen logs. Snow whooshes up into my mouth and eyes with each maneuver, and I feel as though I'm floating down a cascading river of snow. Not a breath of wind stirs the branches, not a sound disturbs the snowy woods.

Except for me.

I yell for the sheer pleasure of it, the delight of this wonderful descent on this mountain. Not words, just nonsensical hoots and hollers of pure joy.

This is what the hell I'm doing out here!

Months before this blissful morning, the whole premise had sounded a lot more impulsive and foolhardy than brave or audacious when, the previous fall, I'd told my girlfriend, Elizabeth, of my resolution to ski the length of the Catamount Trail.

"I thought that was just a pipe dream," she had said, a little disbelievingly. "Something you've been talking about. I didn't know you were actually planning it."

Her brown eyes had looked hard into mine, hoping to see the glimmer of some joke she wasn't getting. But I wasn't kidding, in spite of her incredulity.

"You don't even like to cross-country ski all that much."

"That's not true," I remember saying—even though it was sort of true. I didn't particularly enjoy chasing her around in circles, so I parried. "I like to cross-country ski just fine. I'm just not that good at it." She was nice enough not to agree with me.

She did have a point. She knew far more about winter travel and cross-country skiing than I did, and up to this moment, I hadn't shown her a lot of enthusiasm when we'd gone out together. Elizabeth was an excellent XC skier who had raced during her school years. She loved to speed along a groomed course, and she'd also guided multi-week winter expeditions through the mountains of northern New England.

I was much less experienced in winter-camping, and I had to struggle to keep up with her on those same groomed courses. She would lap back and forth in front of me, much like a dog will do with its owner on a walk, her thin, muscular form eating up the distance, me far behind, seeing the back of her winter hat and brown ponytail sticking out below it. She wished (often out loud) that I could pick up my pace.

I had always felt that I was holding her back on excursions like those. But when we were off the track, trekking through the woods and ducking branches as we carved our own path, I felt a greater sense of fulfillment, finding that I could keep up with her through the deeper, untracked snow.

The unspoken truth of that conversation was that Elizabeth was trying to convince me how bad an idea the trip was because she was deeply concerned for my well-being. Bad things can happen fast in the freezing cold, far from help. A solo winter journey through deep snow and subzero temperatures is dangerous. She knew that in the course of a single day I could get lost, get frostbite or hypothermia, or die.

"You get these ideas in your head, and you just can't shake them," she said. "Once you dream up a trip, you can't let it go until you do it. Just because you *think* it doesn't mean you have to *do* it." At this point she tucked herself into the crook of my arm, fitting snugly into my shoulder, and squeezed me tightly.

This was patently true, and we both knew it. I'm a dreamer, and once my imagination seizes hold of a new adventure, it's very hard to let it go. I get caught up in the fantasy, the excitement of traveling to an unknown place.

This isn't my first trip, and it won't be my last. Each and every time, the pure potential—the newness of an expedition—seizes hold of me, not to release its grip until I'm actually under way and setting out on the journey.

But what's wrong with that? In response, I just smiled. We both knew she was right.

I also knew then that what she was really saying was that she loved me. Deeply. The Catamount Trail in midwinter was, and is, a dangerous journey for anyone to undertake. The risks are real, and the chance of hypothermia and death, while not probable, are at least present.

But more than my physical safety, she knew I had a lot on my mind, and a worried mind doesn't always make the most pragmatic decisions. We were at a serious crossroads at this point in our relationship, and I needed to find the emotional space to figure out what would come next, for us, in life.

Being in the wild is actually one of the ways I focus my mind—away from all the distractions and headaches of "civilization." I knew that regardless of the risk, an escape into solitude was exactly what I needed at that moment. So, as I often do whenever life throws a curveball at me, I was turning to the outdoors to help me figure it all out.

This wouldn't be my first solo foray into the woods. I've hiked the Long Trail in Vermont and the 2,100-mile Appalachian Trail along the Eastern Seaboard. I've paddled thousands of miles through New England and Canada and backpacked for long distances around the world. I'm a wilderness EMT, and intimately understand both the risks and hazards of outdoor living as well as the potential consequences, and have treated hundreds of injured individuals through work as a ski patroller and as a member of several search-and-rescue teams. So while this will be my first *long-distance* winter journey, I'm supremely qualified to be spending long periods of time outdoors. I've been doing it my whole life.

Beginning with family camping trips to northern New England in the 1990s, somehow the outdoors has always been the place where I've felt the most comfortable. No matter the time of year, no matter the weather, we were always outside. Playing rousing games of pickup football in the fall or hockey on the nearby pond in the winter, my parents made sure we grew up outdoors, even in the spare hours after school. No TV for us—it was forbidden—and there certainly wasn't a PlayStation or Xbox or any other gaming console under our roof. Weekends were punctuated with long family hikes, camping trips, or ski expeditions to the mountains.

And when Mom and Dad weren't directly involved, as kids, my brothers, our friends, and I would head out to the woods behind the house and create vast, sprawling fantasy lands of trails, forts, and imaginary villages and personas. Somehow, it always felt right, "living" in the trees back there, playing out an imaginary existence in the woods. It was always tough to go back inside when Mom finally called us for dinner.

When I reached adulthood, I structured my life around the outdoors, always finding seasonal jobs that would allow me to not only work there, but also to provide sufficient time to play in the outdoors, as well. I've taken full advantage of my wilderness skills throughout my life—fortuitously so, because I've always found the time I spend outdoors essential to re-center myself, to ground me and allow me to move forward with more equanimity and mental composure.

I felt more than physically prepared to face an adventure like this one. I certainly had better equipment and warmer clothes than

American revolutionary Henry Knox, who made a similar trek more than 240 years ago.

I first learned about the Catamount Trail on a day trip to Camel's Hump, one of Vermont's taller peaks. It wasn't even winter. The May sun shone across bluebird skies while feathered fliers celebrated the weather with a haphazard chorus of sound. We could see for miles around from the treeless summit, but it wasn't until I had descended back through the open hardwoods and inches-deep muck on the trail—Vermont, of course, is well known for its mud season—that I spotted the blue diamond nailed squarely to a beech tree. "Catamount X-C Ski Trail," it read, beneath an oversize paw print, although no path was visible.

Peering into the forest behind the blaze, I spotted another sign, but between the two lay untrodden leaves, downed branches and twigs, and a quilt of undisturbed greenery. Clearly this wasn't a trail used in the summer. An Internet search that evening revealed the details. That blue medallion was one of many, guiding skiers from the Massachusetts border to the Canadian, tracing a spine along the north–south axis of the Green Mountain State ("The Length of Vermont on Skis" was their motto).

Adventure it certainly was, but not being much of a cross-country skier myself (I prefer the faster, downhill variety), I dismissed it out of hand. Besides, it simply sounded too cold.

Several years later, while researching a book about Benedict Arnold and his three-hundred-mile wilderness paddling expedition,

I continued to find references to another remarkable Revolutionary War expedition.

Only months after Arnold had arrived at his destination, another general named Henry Knox set off on his own journey through wintry New England. Bookseller turned military engineer, Knox traveled to Fort Ticonderoga, from which he set off on his own three-hundred-mile trip back to Boston.

In a strange coincidence, Fort Ticonderoga had recently been taken from the British by Arnold and Ethan Allen, the near-mythical leader of the upstart Green Mountain Boys of Vermont, who were active both before and during the Revolutionary War. The fort was built in 1757 by the French during the French and Indian War, and occupied a strategic narrows on Lake Champlain, an essential travel route for any army traversing northern New England in an age when armies often relied on waterways to supply their needs.

While winter travel through eighteenth-century New England was no easy feat, this journey wouldn't have made the history books except for the baggage Knox carried with him: nearly sixty tons of cannons and armaments. Lauded as one of the greatest feats of logistics and fortitude of the era, Knox covered the three-hundred-mile distance with what is known as "the noble train of artillery" in just eight weeks. Battling poor weather conditions—namely, snow—submerged cannons, and dozens of mutinous teamsters, he and his fellow travelers reached Boston in January 1776.

The British, unaware of the newly arrived artillery, thought their troops were safely sequestered in Boston—until the morning of March 5, that is, when they were amazed to find their position under siege. They evacuated less than two weeks later, returning the city to the Patriot cause.

Knox's feat contributed directly to the British loss of Boston, and therefore, to the American victory and the conclusion of the Revolutionary War. If not for Knox's successful journey, it is far more likely that Americans would be speaking with a British accent today.

But this wasn't what truly piqued my interest. What intrigued me most was the image of Knox fighting snow, wind, and ice along what I imagined to be an open expanse. Knox was the original American winter traveler whose expedition during the first winter of rebellion inspired awe and reverence among the nascent army. Storm-swept, his men leaned into the wind, lashing oxen and horses onward into the squall, fog whipping their frozen faces, cannon-laden sleighs in tow. I could see the icicles hanging from their mustaches and the frost in their eyelashes, barely visible for the fur hoods wrapped tightly around their heads. As they dragged the cannons through mountain passes, I could almost feel their exhaustion—and their determination. I could picture them stopping for a few stolen moments, stomping their feet and beating their hands in a vain attempt to regain circulation. As for the nights, that was beyond my imagination.

It turns out, of course, that my imagination went a little beyond the truth. The men were held up for days on several occasions due to unseasonably warm temperatures (the cannons could only be moved by sled and, without snow, they were stuck), and they were frequently able to stay indoors overnight. Given the choice between mountains and roads, the teamsters, of course, always chose roads. And while storms did occur, they can't exist in perpetuity. Inevitably over the course of eight weeks, some of the days must have been beautiful.

That said, it remains an amazing example of endurance and resilience, and would be the first of many feathers in Knox's cap.

I wanted to live that—all of it. I wanted to face the wintry landscape with the wind in my face and a pack on my back. I wanted to feel (or not feel) the cold and starkness of winter. I wanted to experience the same journey as that noble train of artillery.

But how? Knox had followed the existing roads of his day as well as he could, a route that has now become a part of major state and federal highways. While stone roadside monuments mark his path and provide momentary interest for car travelers, this was no way to truly experience the same challenges he faced. I had no desire to rub shoulders with tourists along an exhaust-filled thruway. It seemed as though I'd missed my opportunity to follow in Knox's footsteps.

As time passed, Knox's journey remained in the back of my mind. Leaning back from my desk and stretching my arms skyward, it would come to me, as though altering the axis of my head had caused old thoughts and memories to resurface. There I was, working at my computer on a trail proposal or a budget for a stone wall, and suddenly I'd be far away, crunching through a crust of snow and cursing with sled drivers. Or perhaps on a blustery January day, as I trudged through the snow to and from the woodpile, he'd return to me. I'd picture Knox and his men huddled around a fire, backs to the cold and hands held to the flame, staving off frostbite and hypothermia. Could I do that, I wondered; could I have made that journey? Did I have it in me?

I didn't put the two ideas together until one specific night. Driving home from work, singing along to Eric Clapton on the radio and letting my mind drift, Knox suddenly entered my thoughts. Perhaps a particularly deep pothole had rearranged the equilibrium of my brain to cause that exact notion to jump to the surface. Regardless, I realized that Knox hadn't been traveling on roads as we think of them now. The word *road* today so often connotes two (or more) lanes of pristine asphalt stretching linearly into the distance. It gets travelers from point A to point B, and for many, speed is of the essence.

But that pothole got me thinking. Paving and asphalt were simply not in existence in 1775. The "road" Knox had traveled on would barely qualify as such in the twenty-first century, having seen no steamrollers, dump trucks, or graders, and certainly no asphalt. No, what Knox traveled on in 1775 was a trail. Wide, no doubt fairly flat, but with enough ruts and rocks to rule out all but the most formidable of today's motorized vehicles. To experience Knox's journey as he did, I would need a trail.

Another pothole brought the Catamount Trail to the forefront of my thoughts. A trail designed for winter travel, traversing three hundred miles of New England—Knox's three-hundred-mile winter journey through snowy New England. Here, at last, was a way to perhaps experience as best I could some of Knox's trials and tribulations!

Excitedly, I mulled over the prospect, Clapton forgotten in the background. Full of the kind of exuberance that no pothole could dislodge, I decided then and there that I would ski the Catamount Trail with Henry Knox.

As for my own history, I met Elizabeth at freshman orientation at my college in Maine, in 2006. Like many northern New England colleges, the administration deemed outdoor trips to be the best way to break in new students. Their thesis seems to be that pooping in the woods and fighting off mosquitoes and snakes together builds intimacy. Perhaps unsurprisingly, they're often right. Many close friendships arose from these four-day expeditions.

It was virtually our first collegiate experience. Day one we got our keys, moved into our rooms, and found the dining hall. Day two, we were up early and on a bus, loaded with tents, stoves, camp food, and bug repellent. Barely twenty-four hours after arriving on campus, we were leaving again.

My orientation trip included ten of us—eight freshmen and two upperclassmen, who served as our leaders. The first two days were fairly uneventful. We traversed several mountains, hiked through a jumble of boulders that nearly broke two ankles, and successfully set up tents that had almost all of the necessary components (never trust a tent that was more than likely last used by someone with zero outdoors experience). I got to know my fellow trippers, and we successfully navigated a spaghetti spill and a tragic case of missing pepperoni (such are the challenges of a camping trip). We even managed to discuss pooping in the woods like adults, with only minimal giggling and double entendres. But I didn't fall in love with any of them.

The third night was different. We joined another group, which included Elizabeth, at a mutual campsite, doubling our numbers. At first we remained on separate sides of the campfire—only three days of living, hiking, and eating together can create a surprising clannishness—but soon we found enough in common to intermingle.

That night the bugs quieted enough that seven of us slept outside under the stars. Elizabeth didn't join us. She had been relatively subdued throughout the evening—not shy so much as observant, as though she was quietly watching the goings-on and keeping her conclusions to herself.

We both agree on these events thus far; however, our stories differ from this point forward as to what actually happened next.

The night after we returned to school, our second on campus, there was a dance. Typically collegiate, it involved a DJ, pop music, and kegs of beer (for those of age, of course). I was enjoying a beverage and chatting with a new pal when Maggie, one of the girls from Elizabeth's trip, who'd spent the night under the stars with me and the others, walked by.

"Have you talked to Elizabeth? She's looking for you," she told me.

Immediately, my eighteen-year-old heart started beating a little faster. Nothing excites a teenager like hearing that a girl is looking for him. Especially a beautiful girl like Elizabeth; don't think I hadn't noticed her on the trip just because she was on the quieter side. To the contrary—I'd admired her unobtrusive self-possession.

Elizabeth has a slightly different take on this part of the story. She avows that she wasn't looking for me in particular; she'd been looking for me, or Chaz, or Rachel, or anybody else from my group that she'd met during our trip.

I know better. It remains obvious to me that she had fallen hard for me at first sight.

I wrapped up my conversation as quickly as I could and went on the hunt for Elizabeth. I soon tracked her down among a group of others from our two orientation groups.

"Would you like to dance?" I asked, figuring an up-front approach was best.

Demurely, she nodded. Much less demurely, she took my arm and led me to a space on the dance floor. There, amid the gyrating bodies, each of us sweating profusely, we laughed and danced and tried to hold a conversation over the ambient noise of the crowd.

Slowly, with much repeating and screaming into each other's ears, we got to know each other a little bit.

After what seemed like hours, she proposed we get a breath of fresh air. I knew what that meant and eagerly agreed, resulting in another hotly contested point in our mutual history. She insists that romance was the furthest thing from her mind when she asked me to join her outside—it was simply a chance to cool off. I know otherwise; this was yet another manifestation of the fact that she'd clearly fallen for me.

Regardless of which of us had romance on the mind, I was the one who led us to a bench where we flopped our spent bodies and gratefully inhaled the nighttime air. I pointed out all the constellations I knew (three), and we shared our first kiss with their reflected light shining down on us. I was a goner.

What followed was a tumultuous, on-again, off-again relationship throughout college. The vagaries of dorm life and my teenaged short-term outlook resulted in several breakups throughout our time there. We also took semesters off from school at different times, resulting in more than a year of separation and causing yet another split. We just couldn't seem to stay together.

Yet we kept coming back for more. For when we were together, it was amazing. True to how we'd met, we went on long hikes together, racing each other to the tops of the trails. I took her winter camping on one of our first dates; she loved it and wanted more. As we cooked breakfast over a small fire the following morning, she kept giggling as I shivered and struggled with the oatmeal. Her spirited peal of laughter was one of the things that had initially attracted me to her, and I couldn't help but grin along with her at the burnt oats. Her laugh was like no one else's in the world, leading me to fall in love anew every time I heard it.

For her birthday I bought her a pair of hockey skates. Thinking it wasn't romantic enough, I stuck a rose through the laces of each skate. We went out to the local pond that night where I skated circles around her. She shuffled across the ice, getting used to the lack of a toe pick. Naturally athletic and a quick learner, she was soon passing a puck back and forth and joining me for pickup games with friends, just as I'd done as a kid.

The first Valentine's Day we spent together I reserved us a table at one of the fancier restaurants in town. A February blizzard cut short those plans, but eating take-out Chinese food while snuggled up together, large snowflakes pelting the windows outside, more than made up for it. We dipped apples in melted chocolate chips for dessert and fed them to each other. I felt on top of the world, and so in love that I could have burst a blood vessel just thinking about it.

After graduation we went our separate ways. Confused about what I required out of life, I wanted to leave college with no strings attached. After all, I was young and reckless and ready to take the world by storm. The possibilities were overwhelming. Not wanting to miss a thing, I needed to be free of anything that might tie me down. Elizabeth was one of those considerations, and I didn't want her grounding me in one location. There was simply too much to do.

I jumped from seasonal job to seasonal job, always in outdoor recreation, and always in New England. I had no interest in looking past the Northeast. Elizabeth took a position as an instructor and guide at an alternative education organization for a year before being accepted to medical school in Hanover, New Hampshire. We stayed in touch and visited each other occasionally, but both of us were seeing other people by this time. When I drove up for a visit, I anxiously anticipated the sight of her, but somehow my expectations never lived up to reality. Time together seemed fraught with painful memories of happier times.

Elizabeth had always dreamed of becoming a doctor. Photos of her as a toddler frequently show her playing this role with her sisters. She applied to and was accepted at Dartmouth Medical School on the New Hampshire–Vermont border. I, between jobs and at loose ends yet again, proposed that I join her. I missed her laugh, her sparkle, her joie de vivre. No one else had had the same effect on me, and I was hoping to give it another shot at making it work in adulthood. To my surprise, she accepted, and in August of 2012 I moved in with her.

It would be the best decision of my life.

In a house set amid hundreds of acres of forest at the end of a dirt road, removed from the scenes of our previous dysfunction, we thrived. We reveled in sharing our respective cooking skills with each other. An expert at peanut-butter-and-jelly sandwiches, I demonstrated how my father had added sprinkles and chocolate chips when Mom wasn't home and he'd been in charge of lunch. Unimpressed, she taught me how not to overcook asparagus and how to make a successful roux.

I countered with a proposal that we learn how to brew beer together, and soon we were fermenting our own in a five-gallon bucket. Feeling braver, I experimented with yeast breads, and was soon baking fresh loaves for those same peanut-butter-and-jelly sandwiches. I even decided that chocolate chips belonged elsewhere, and restarted my family's tradition of Sunday-morning pancakes.

We went hiking on the weekends, and chased each other on long jogs through the picturesque landscape. We attended the surprisingly good theater nearby, where we laughed uproariously along with our fellow theatergoers (all of whom were at least three decades older than us). Finished with school and officially adults, we fell in love all over again.

She continued to succeed in her chosen medical career, and I started a small business designing and constructing hiking and biking trails, as well as stone walls and patios, throughout the area. This was a dream come true for me, allowing me the flexibility and time outdoors I craved. Perhaps more importantly, I discovered that I loved the permanence and timelessness of what I built. My team and I had begun to specialize in stone construction, and when I contemplated a finished structure and considered that it was likely to remain there for dozens—if not hundreds—of years, I found immense joy in the beauty of its immutability.

In a location seemingly custom-built for our interests and passions, we thrived. Sure, there were the inevitable disagreements and petty disputes that arise between partners. I refused to retreat on my stance that dishes headed for the dishwasher didn't require pre-rinsing, and she never remembered to wring out the sodden sponge when she was done cleaning up.

I also began to sense hints of a broader conflict in our priorities as she continued the single-minded pursuit of her dream of doctorhood, starting to explore what would come next after medical school, no matter where it took her, while I focused more and more on building a space and community where I could find a permanent life, and home. Despite my habit of seasonal jobs and love of travel, I discovered that it meant a lot to me to have a place I could call home—especially one where I could look around and point to walls, patios, staircases, and other installations that I'd created.

But for the most part, these three years were filled with peace, friendship, love, and affection.

Throughout this period I continued to take long trips throughout eastern North America. I hiked the Appalachian Trail along the Eastern Seaboard and canoed across New England, from New York to Maine. By living in and slowly moving across a landscape, I became one with it, knowing its every root and rock, twist and turn. By living outdoors, regardless of the weather, I grew confident in my own body and abilities, learning that I could thrive in whatever type of circumstances nature threw at me. These long-distance trips completed and rejuvenated me, refreshing my outlook and allowing me to tackle anew the challenges of everyday life.

It had to end sometime, I guess.

Following medical school comes residency—a prolonged internship for recently graduated doctors lasting anywhere from three to seven years, where placement is determined by a computer program. The winter before graduation, students input a ranked list of location preferences across the country, while residency programs input a list of openings. The computer program then finds the best possible match, and that's where you go.

Elizabeth did ask me where I would prefer to be when she applied, and I told her that I wanted to stay in New England, among my family, on the land I love. If she wanted to go to Maine, Vermont, New Hampshire, or Massachusetts, I would follow, but I was not interested in venturing further afield. This place meant too much to me to leave it.

She nodded, silently taking in the information. Then, my pleas notwithstanding, she opted for Denver and Salt Lake City as her two top choices. The residency machine settled on Salt Lake City.

From her perspective, it made sense: Salt Lake offers one of the best residencies for her chosen specialty of OB/GYN, and Elizabeth, in her unwavering pursuit of perfection, would have nothing less. She would move to Utah in June.

I was aghast. Not only was she leaving, but she was giving me a sort of ultimatum. "I'm going to Utah whether you like it or not," she seemed to be saying to me. "And I know you don't like it."

What did this mean for me? Did she even care about what I wanted, having so flagrantly circumvented my own preferences? Did she still love me?

"Of course I still love you," she said. "But I have to do this. For me. Can you understand?"

And, of course, I could. I knew her—knew what drove her. Knew that being a doctor, the best doctor she could be, was her life's goal. Her drive was one of the things I most admired about her, one of the things that had attracted me to her right from the beginning.

"But what about me?!" I selfishly wanted to holler at the top of my lungs. Do I now have to leave all I know and love to follow you across the country, leaving family, friends, and my own small business of four years behind? Isn't there some sort of compromise here? Why on earth do I not get more of a say in this?

More than ever, I needed the outdoors to help bring clarity to my muddled mind. Our past had built up to this exact moment, when I decided to mentally commit to skiing the Catamount Trail with Henry Knox. The trip would be challenging and exciting, no doubt, but it would also get me away from Elizabeth, from our home and the scene of all this turmoil, to sort this out.

I was confused and scared and unsure and insecure and yes, *torn*, between the people and places I cared about. I knew that I loved Elizabeth, more than anything. But I also loved my family and New England and my home, too, and it had always been an additive equation. I wanted to have them all.

But that fall, I had to face reality: I could see two roads into the future, and the Catamount Trail seemed as good a path as any to help me decide which one to take. This was my essential question as I set out on the trail. Although my trip may not have been as noble or important as Henry Knox's, it was as momentous to my own trajectory as Knox's had been to our nation's.

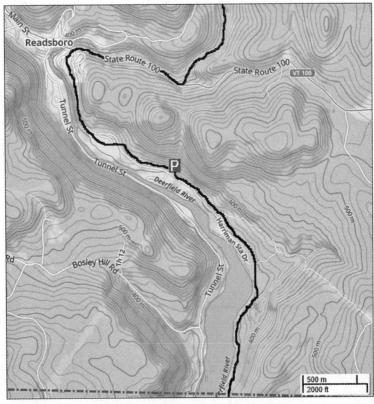

The Catamount Trail from the Massachusetts border to Route 100

1. *No Trouble or Expense Must Be Spared*

Staring out the window on our way south, driving from our house in Norwich, Vermont, toward the beginning of the Catamount Trail on the state's southern border—more than 240 years after Knox's journey—these crucial questions still raced through my head. Do Elizabeth and I have a future together? And if so, where will it be?

I don't have the answers right now. But with three hundred miles of snowy trail in front of me, copies of Knox's journals and letters in my backpack, and Henry Knox with me in spirit, maybe I can find a solution to this dilemma.

Elizabeth has endured and even embraced these adventures of mine, chauffeuring me around New England to ease the logistics.

"Do you ever want to do something like this together?" I asked her the first time she provided her car (and her time) to pick me up at the end of Vermont's Long Trail, after a thru-hike of seventeen days.

"No," she had said emphatically. I appreciated her clarity.

"Besides," she deadpans now, "I'd only slow you down."

"Ha ha," I say.

I'm glad she's not coming. Not only am I sure that our currently fragile relationship would not survive three weeks together in the cold and snow, I also plan to use this time to sort through my own feelings and future. A solo trip is what I need, and the steady silence of gliding across the snow will hopefully provide a counterbalance to my mind racing every which way. Even as I sit in the passenger seat and watch the highway guardrails pass by, my thoughts continue to turn over and around that big question. I know two truths: I love Elizabeth and don't want to lose her, and I love New England and my family and don't want to move. The fact that those truths are polar opposites of one another have placed me in hell. I am hoping this expedition will help me find a way out.

We lapse into silence as she pulls off the highway and turns onto a secondary road. It twists and winds along a river, hazy through the gently falling snow. I turn the car heat up another notch, treasuring the manufactured warmth for the final half-hour before we reach the head of the Catamount Trail. In the days to come I will try to recapture these moments of being peppered with stale air from the car's heating system, sitting next to the woman I love.

As passenger, I know that I am also the navigator, and I dutifully point out the way to Elizabeth. She never wears glasses except when driving—her only vanity as far as I can tell—and she peers through them a little nearsightedly at the road signs as we pass them. Noticing me watching, she gives me a mock glare and self-consciously hitches them back up the bridge of her nose. I just smile.

When people ask, I tell them that we started dating seven years ago. Using that particular sentence structure deftly hides the fact that if one were to sum up our total time of being officially "together," it would barely amount to four years. Like I said before: We've had our moments. But four years is more than enough time for us to have gotten to know and, for the most part, love each other's little quirks. Like being self-conscious of her glasses. It's an old joke between us. "Stop staring at me," she says into the windshield. "You're making me nervous." I laugh and face forward once again.

To an outside observer, our teasing of each other can sometimes seem like insensitivity. But she grew up with two sisters and me, with two brothers; teasing and jibing were how we demonstrated affection. We didn't know any other way. With every verbal jab we swap we are simply telling each other, "I love you. I care about you. I'm invested in you." I know this, and so does she. It's a way we've learned to express ourselves without having to be forthright and overt in verbalizing our feelings. And over the length of our relationship, we've discovered that if something important is looming over us, or challenging us, it's even more important to begin with a little lighthearted teasing. It's a way to ease the tension.

Now, still looking forward, I tell her what I'm really feeling. "I'm scared." I say it quietly. "For us." Above all else, I don't want to lose her. We've built too much, loved too much, endured too much for it to end.

She chuckles briefly to try to lighten the moment but then turns somber.

"I know. I am too. But I love you, and we'll figure it out. No matter what you decide to do, I'll always love you."

I've come to rely on her patience and uncompromising love over the years, through everything. "I love you too," I tell her, reaching over to squeeze her hand.

I continue to hold her hand as I direct us to the final turn that will take us to the southern boundary of Vermont, or as close to it as we can get via automobile. Northbound skiers like me must ski three miles south to the actual border before turning around and beginning the long northward trek, since no roads actually cross the border near here.

The Catamount Trail is brand new. It started as the brainchild of three Vermont students in 1984 who researched the route as part of a thesis project. Public land is not ubiquitous in New England, and so, with much of the route traversing private land and therefore requiring specific permission, the Trail itself wasn't fully completed until 2007. Since then, some sixty-odd individuals have completed the route, mostly in a series of multiple day trips across several seasons. (Later I would hold an e-mail conversation with the organization, asking about other thru-skiers. It turns out that they don't keep track of them, as so few have set out to take on the whole trail.) I am aiming to become the first of the 2015 season to complete it, and one of the few to do it in its entirety, in a single trip.

As we round the final curve in the road, a power station appears from behind an outcropping of trees. We park in the small lot nearby.

"I think we're here." I pause hopefully, then heave my lanky frame up out of the seat and into the cold. A quick survey of the graveled area reveals a small sign, which states that indeed, this is parking for the southern terminus of the Trail.

"I hope I have everything," I announce, if only to say something.

"Me too," agrees Elizabeth. Then she lapses back into teasing me. "Did you remember your ski boots?"

"*Hardy* har." I grimace in her direction. "Yes. And you're not funny."

We had ventured out on a day ski trip just a week before to break in my equipment, and after an hour's drive to the start of our planned trip, had discovered that I'd neglected to pack my boots. We went for a hike instead, but I knew it would be a while before I would live this down. Clearly it hasn't occurred yet.

I shiver slightly. "What if we just turn around and go home? It's cold out here!"

"No way, buster," she says, wagging a finger in my direction in faux remonstration. "I carted your tuchus down here. You can get it back up north by yourself!"

"Fine," I respond. "But if I freeze to death, you'll have no one to blame but yourself. I expect a big bouquet of flowers at my funeral from you."

"Ha," she snorts. "As if."

I change tack, taking a more-serious tone. "I'm going to miss you. Really."

"I know; I'll miss you too. But I know you need this. So go and do it. If you need anything, call me." After a pause, she amends, "Even if you don't, call me. Check in. I'll need to hear your voice."

Then, to avoid too much mawkishness, she returns to teasing again.

"Now, who is going to keep me warm for the next couple of weeks while you're gone? Maybe I'll get a temporary boyfriend until you come back. If you come back." She grins nastily and sticks her tongue out at me. I take a fake swat at her.

We both know she's kidding. So much for sentimentality.

Extracting all my gear from the trunk of the car, I pack my food into the top of my pack from the grocery bag it had been sitting in and change out of my sneakers into ski boots. Brand new and only superficially broken in, I hope they won't give me blisters in the coming days. After strapping on my pack and adjusting the straps, I turn to her.

The immensity of what I want to say to her overwhelms me at this moment.

That I can't put into words how much she means to me. That it is impossible to quantify her importance to me, to my sanity and my life. That I don't know where I'd be—physically, emotionally, or psychologically—without her. That I love her with a power that scares me. And that I'm terrified at having to make such a momentous choice.

But since I've never been one who easily broaches tough topics or verbalizes emotions, I simply settle on a platitude. It's not enough, but it's all I can do in the moment.

"I think I'm ready."

"I love you," she repeats in response, trying to bridge all that is being left unsaid. She opens her mouth as if to say more, clearly grappling with some of my same emotions, but quickly closes it again. Words, or at least the power to express them, clearly escape her as well. She settles for action, and with a quick step forward, she buries her face in my shoulder.

"We'll figure this out, right?"

She's upset now, and I briefly flash on the possibility of just saying I'd follow her anywhere. But I'd be lying.

"Yes, dear. We will. I love you too."

The words feel stilted and all too brief, but I don't know what else to say at this juncture that won't sound hollow or forced. I don't actually know if we'll figure it out. I don't know if what we feel for one another is strong enough to survive either outcome. But that's what I'm trying to accomplish on this trip. I'm hopeful that the ensuing three hundred miles will lead me to some conclusions.

Elizabeth grabs her camera and snaps a couple pictures of me standing in the parking lot. With the cold—the temperature is in the teens according to the car thermometer—already seeping through my layers and snow accumulating on my hat and shoulders, I'm anxious to get going. Jiggling my legs and thrashing my arms to get the blood flowing, I ski over to her and give her a kiss.

"Be safe," she says. "I'll see you when you're done. Know that I love you. A lot." She repeats herself: "A lot a lot."

"I know. See you soon."

I turn and ski across the parking lot. This current storm has dumped two inches thus far, which is just enough to permit me to do so with minimal scrapes from protruding gravel. I duck-walk up a short slope and find an old roadbed with blue blazes nailed to trees along the side.

The car starts up behind me and I turn to watch the reverse lights flicker briefly as she shifts into gear. Then the car moves off slowly—I can see her hunched slightly over the wheel, peering forward through the falling flakes—and turns the corner to disappear down the road. I turn, too, take my first stride on the Catamount Trail proper, and begin to ski southward, tottering slightly as I find my equilibrium on these unfamiliar skis, and embarking on my own thru-ski, and the decision-making process that will dictate the rest of my life.

Back in 1775 Knox had already made his decision. As he and Lucy made their way through the cold April night, what were they thinking? They had left all they knew behind, deserting business and family to embark on their own life-changing adventure. It was a giant

Stuart, Gilbert. *Portrait of Henry Knox*. Courtesy of the Museum of Fine Arts, Boston. Image courtesy of The Athenaeum.

step for their little family, and a fortuitous one for the American Revolution.

Before Knox could even consider joining Washington's army and the Revolution, he needed to see to Lucy. They had friends in Worcester, and it was there that he brought her, amid protestations that she wanted to stay with him. Knowing that a piecemeal army encampment was no place for his wife, he refused and settled her away from the center of conflict. Then he returned to Cambridge solo and joined the besieging army, if "army" it could be called.

Hoit, Albert Gallatin. *Portrait of Lucy Flucker Knox.* Courtesy of the Knox Museum, Thomaston, Maine.

In Cambridge he found a hodgepodge of militias made up of myriad individuals who had answered the call to arms. Men from across the colonies and all different walks of life had flocked to Boston to join the rebel army, everyone from farmers to shopkeepers to ne'er-do-wells. Discipline was poor and sanitation poorer. Rumors ran rampant through the troops, each wilder than the next (including one that Knox had been "discovered to be active in exposing our works to the enemy" and arrested as a spy).[1]

Few of the men had any military experience, and the man in charge, Artemus Ward, was desperately trying to create some sort of order from the chaos. He offered Knox a post as a lieutenant colonel, but Knox, in what would become a typical display of pride, declined. (This marked a second straight demurral: His father-in-law, Thomas Flucker, had offered him a commission in the British army, which he had also declined for obvious reasons.) Knox believed that he warranted a full colonelcy, and decided to remain a volunteer until such a commission was proffered. In spite of being entirely self-educated in artillery and military matters, Knox had a strong sense of his own worth, and refused to accept any position that he felt was beneath him.

Rank would be a sensitive subject throughout his life, and perhaps one of two vanities. The first was a mutilated left hand missing two fingers—the result of a hunting accident when he was twenty-two. He kept a handkerchief wrapped around it for much of the rest of his life, to disguise the injury. The other was his standing in the army. Later in the war Knox would threaten resignation (an admittedly common tactic for the many quick-tempered eighteenth-century officers) over an affair with a Frenchman named du Coudray. Du Coudray had arrived from France with a letter stating that American commissioners there had guaranteed him leadership of the American artillery, which was Knox's position by then. A touchy matter—the colonies were wooing France at the time—became touchier when Knox attempted to coerce Congress into seeing his side of the matter. It was only resolved with the untimely (or timely, from Knox's point of view) death of du Coudray when he drowned while crossing a river.

Still later, Washington and Knox's friendship took a serious blow during the Quasi-War with France in 1798. This quarrel centered on who was to be second in command to Washington: Alexander Hamilton, Charles Pinckney, or Knox. Knox, who had been absent from national affairs for several years, seemed to be getting the short end of the stick when the conflict deflated with the end of hostilities. Throughout his life, Knox was acutely conscious of how others perceived him.

But now, in 1775, Knox was content to remain a gentleman volunteer. With his physicality, he had no trouble making his presence known regardless of his rank. Knox had by this point in his life ballooned to 260 pounds, and at age twenty-five, could aptly be described as pear-shaped. In an age when carrying extra weight was a mark of respectability and wealth, Knox was still much larger than the average man. He carried it well, however, and it never seemed to detract from his energy or verve. Lucy kept pace with him, weighing in the mid-200s for much of her adult life. Universally known for his joie de vivre and even-keeled good humor, "no man better enjoyed a hearty laugh," although "when thinking, he looked like one of his own [artillery] pieces."[2, 3] His booming voice and sunny disposition would fast become a mainstay of the Continental Army.

Instead of the lieutenant colonelcy, Knox suggested that he aid in strengthening the defenses surrounding Boston. Ward, recognizing that Knox would be an asset, concurred, and soon Knox was racing about, improving the fortifications. Quickly acknowledged as the authority on artillery matters, men such as John Adams wrote to Knox for advice on books on military matters. "[Is there] a complete set of books upon the military art in all its branches in the library of Harvard College, and what books are best upon these subjects?" penned the future president.[4] Clearly the young artillery prodigy was making waves.

In the meantime, events were quickly moving forward. On May 10, Benedict Arnold and Ethan Allen took Fort Ticonderoga on Lake Champlain. A coup for the rebellion, the fort not only controlled all water traffic on Lake Champlain—and therefore, all troop movement in the northern war theater—but it also held a wealth of cannons and artillery for the under-armed Continental Army. Even so, it was located three hundred miles away from Cambridge over rough roads. Transport of these arms to anywhere else would have to be put off indefinitely.

Closer to Boston, the British became restless as Knox continued to fortify the heights overlooking the city proper. While severely lacking in cannons, guns still trickled in as militias from across New England arrived to join the army. On June 17, the British finally struck, crossing the Charles River and assaulting Breed's Hill. In what is now known as the Battle of Bunker Hill, the British successfully surmounted the slopes at the cost of over one thousand casualties. Their expensive victory, however, would discourage them from making further attacks against American lines.

The army's injured morale after the defeat soon got a lift when George Washington, appointed by Congress as commander in chief of the Continental Army, arrived on the scene to take over for Artemus Ward. Washington's stately appearance and unflappable disposition, along with the experience he'd gained throughout the French and Indian War, reassured the troops, and his enthusiasm for strict discipline soon began to make sense of the rabble army. Knox, encouraged with the new leader's energy, wrote to Lucy, "General Washington fills his place with cast ease and dignity."[5]

Knox would soon get a chance to know this dignity intimately. The two men met in early July, and Washington was quickly impressed with Knox's ability. Washington and his aides walked to the Roxbury Heights fortifications, whose defenses Knox had overseen during the Battle of Bunker Hill. After the inspection, Knox wrote to his brother

William that "When they viewed the works, they expressed the greatest pleasure and surprise at their situation and apparent utility, to say nothing of the plan, which did not escape their praise."[6] Washington would soon take the young volunteer under his wing, as he would many others, including Alexander Hamilton and Nathanael Greene. Their first meeting would become the opening act in a lifelong friendship, the closest male relationship either man would have.

Knox had another reason to be thrilled. A visit to Lucy around this time was met with the news that she was pregnant. Knox and Lucy both desired a large family, and this would be the first of thirteen pregnancies.

But now was not the time for Knox and Washington to be getting to know one another or to be dawdling around their respective wives, pregnant or otherwise: There was a war to fight. Colonel Richard Gridley was in charge of the artillery at this time, but with his failing health, he could not see to his duties. Agreement coalesced among the officers that Knox should be next in line, despite never having held a commission, a testament to widespread agreement that his ability and knowledge exceeded all others. In November, Washington wrote to Congress to recommend that Knox take over the artillery regiment from Gridley and be promoted to full colonel. It would be a large step for a man who was still only a private citizen.

Knox's response was typical. His growing intimacy with Washington allowed him to jokingly ask just where exactly the artillery was that he had just been recommended to command. It was a pointed joke. The Continental artillery at Cambridge consisted of just one regiment of 635 men with only about twelve cannons.[7] Not that Knox had much more respect for the opposition's artillery, either. After watching a bombardment by the British of colonial lines, he wrote, "[T]hey fired 104 cannon-shot at [our] works, at not a greater distance than half point blank shot—and did what? Why, scratched a man's face with the splinters of a rail fence!"[8] No doubt Knox vowed to do much more to the British in return than send splinters flying through the air.

But where to get additional cannons? The meager twelve or so pieces were nothing compared to the might of the British army. The colonies had no foundry to produce their own cannons, and had actually been forbidden to do so. Now that they were in open rebellion, of course, the rules had changed, but they would need time to build a foundry and train workers—and the army needed artillery *now*.

It's unclear exactly who thought of the idea first. Benedict Arnold certainly was in favor of moving Fort Ticonderoga's artillery, if it could be done. And Washington undoubtedly felt the want of heavy cannons throughout the first year of the siege. Knox pushed for the march to be made, and is often credited as being its source. Regardless of whose idea it actually was, in late October of 1775, Congress sent a letter to Washington in Cambridge approving the idea, as well as its associated expenses. Knox was going to Fort Ticonderoga to return thenceforth to Cambridge, with badly needed cannons in tow.

Washington issued his formal orders on November 16, 1775. Knox was directed to go to New York City first, to discover if any cannons resided there. Afterward, if not enough were to be found in the city, Washington said: "You must go to Major-General Schuyler and get the remainder from Ticonderoga, Crown Point, or St. Johns; if it should be necessary, from Quebec, if in our hands." Washington had just dispatched an expedition under Benedict Arnold to travel through Maine and attack Quebec City, held by the British after they'd taken it from the French during the French and Indian War. If

Knox felt he needed to, he could travel that far to get the necessary cannons, so important was the need. "The want of them is so great," continued Washington, "that no trouble or expense must be spared to obtain them."[9]

Washington knew all too well the dire need for heavy artillery. He had the British bottled up in Boston, but with no way to remove them, he was stuck. Knox was to provide the answer.

As I strike out southbound through the woods in 2015, I am avoiding the hard questions for now. Knox must not have been thinking about Lucy the *entire* time he was settling into his role in the Continental Army, I figure, so I certainly have some time before I must face my own dilemma. I have set out on this expedition at least partially to find some sort of resolution, but that can wait. I haven't planned and worked so hard for the past couple of weeks to simply fret the entire time. I'm also here to embrace the outdoors.

Travel is my lifeblood. Although I love my current careers—combining skiing in the winter with constructing trails and stone walls in the summer—I need the periodic escapes these long-distance trips provide. I live for these forays, these brief intervals of tripping. There is something utterly freeing and rejuvenating about leaving it all behind and simply traveling with what I can carry on my back, beholden to no one and nothing.

That freedom washes over me now as I set out, and it's a magnificent feeling. I have felt this way since I was a child. In fact, I cannot remember a time when I wasn't downhill skiing. In the late 1980s, before I could even strap on a pair of boots and skis by myself, I was *schussing* down the slopes. My father, an avid skier and former racer himself, would carry me in a carrier backpack as he skied at our local mountain, putting it on for each run and setting it next to him for the lift rides back up to the top. No, he wasn't tearing through the trees or racing through a mogul course, but we were taking gentle turns down the trail together.

He still likes to tell the story of me "zonking out," as he calls it, in the backpack during the day. I'd provide a steady chorus of toddler snores as background music for the rest of his afternoon on the snow. Later, he would carry both of my younger brothers in turn. By the time the third boy came around he was chasing me down the mountain, with my middle brother learning between his legs, and the youngest still in the backpack on his back. All three of us boys grew up passionate about skiing. I suspect we couldn't have helped it; after all, many of our first dreams occurred literally on the side of a ski mountain.

Arrival back at home was not met with rest and relaxation, however. Instead, we'd head straight to the neighborhood pond for a pickup hockey game. My childhood was always one activity after another; Dad's philosophy has forever been that any moment not engaged in some physical endeavor is a moment wasted and lost forever. Since skiing only occurred on weekends and hockey took place (seemingly) daily, weather played different roles in the two sports. The mountain remains perpetually sunny in my remembrances. The pond does not. Some days were bitterly cold. Not an obstacle to my activity-driven father ("There is no such thing as bad weather, just bad clothing," he'd say as we bundled up).

Out we trundled to the pond, leaving ribbons of snot along our cheeks as the wind whipped past. Tugging on frozen skates with frozen fingers before attempting to lace up frozen laces often took far longer than it should have. This was only the beginning, however. The wind whipped far worse on the open pond than it did in the trees, and toes quickly became numb. With fingers that seemed as though they belonged to someone else, I'd halfheartedly pass to Dad who was skating laps around me, cajoling me to greater speeds. I was only praying it would be over quickly.

Now, at the outset of my 2015 expedition, my first tentative movements soon turn to a more confident but still slightly awkward progress. I am not a fluid cross-country skier. At least, not yet. I chuckle to myself as I think back to when Elizabeth tried to teach me. It was our first winter at school, and I had bought a pair of cheap, waxless skis. They were much wider than her racing skis, and a little too short for me. Using complicated words like "kick" and "glide," she tried to teach me the basics. I was a mess, flailing all over the place and becoming more frustrated by the minute. Finally, I challenged her to a short race. Literally running while strapped to my skis, tails slapping against the snow with every step and arms pumping furiously, I beat her by a length and felt much better. But I still wasn't a good distance skier.

My clumsiness doesn't seem to matter out here now, where I'm alone. As I navigate a short hill down to a road, I spread my legs, knees locked, and hold my arms and poles stiffly out from my sides in the classic beginner's stance. Picking up a little speed, I hoot with glee. This is fun even if I don't look good!

I'm using a backcountry Nordic ski built by Madshus. Wider than a typical Nordic ski, they have metal edges and scales underfoot on their bases. They're waxless as well, eliminating both a time-consuming and delicate daily chore. They'll allow me to float better in deeper snow, hold my position on icier sections, and easily ski up gentle hills with the scales helping to maintain traction. I have decided to forego climbing skins—pieces of fabric cut to match the skis' footprint that attach to their underside, giving the user an even stronger grip on the snow. They would be used for steeper uphills, but most of the Catamount Trail is pretty well graded (so I believe), and I figure I can herring-bone or side-step up any of the steepest sections.

With flakes falling softly around me, I slowly ski along what appears to be an access road for the reservoir. Sherman Reservoir is to my right, stretching into Massachusetts. For the first several dozen miles of the trail I will be weaving in and out of a series of reservoirs along the Deerfield River. Hydropower seems to be a popular energy source down here.

The trail is mostly flat, and I make good time southbound to the Massachusetts border and the official start of the Catamount Trail, silently saying thanks to whoever sent this current snowstorm. Two inches of snow blanket the woods here; without it, I suspect I would be walking. Even now I scrape against the occasional piece of gravel. But by taking gentle strides and gliding evenly, I can stay on top of the snow and ski. I even enjoy the faint sting of snow as it lands and melts on my cheeks and eyelashes, the burn of the cold air as it moves in and out of my lungs, the tickle of my sweat as it dribbles down my lower back. I hope Elizabeth is safely making her way back home; she's not an excellent winter driver, and I'm a little worried, but there is nothing I can do for her out here.

Besides, she's leaving me and heading to Utah—one of the snowiest places in the United States. She'd better learn, and learn quickly, how to drive in winter.

Before I know it, a small granite obelisk appears in front of me. Topped with snow and set amid a patch of saplings, it's an unprepossessing start to a three-hundred-mile journey. But with "VT" etched on one side and "MA" on the other, there is no doubt that this is the beginning. It's time to head north, to Canada, and toward a decision that will transform the rest of my life.

Knox's leave-taking was similar to my own. Lucy was not thrilled that her husband was heading off into the wilderness without her—for Fort Ticonderoga in 1775 was certainly situated in much more of a wilderness than it is today. Since she was pregnant with their first child, she had excellent reason to want her husband by her side.

Per Washington's orders, Knox took full stock of the current armaments and then headed off to Worcester to say good-bye. No doubt there were many protestations of love and promises to communicate regularly. He, too, met with a storm, the "most violent northeast storm" he'd ever seen, before proceeding on to New York City.[10]

He was not alone. He brought his brother William with him, who had escaped himself from Boston. William would prove to be a great asset throughout the endeavor as an individual on whom Knox could rely, but would later become a bit of a charity case. After British forces left Boston in 1776, William would try to resurrect Knox's bookstore, but importing goods from England remained challenging given the hostilities; add to this the fact that many of the wealthy Tories and former patrons of the store had already left the city. William traveled to Europe, returned to join Knox for part of the still-ongoing war, and then ventured back across the ocean to England, where he began to exhibit signs of insanity. He had a period of recovery during which he worked briefly under Knox as a secretary in the War Office, but periodic relapses meant that William spent his last days in a hospital for the insane. It would be an ignoble end for a devoted brother and aide.

All that, however, was in the distance; the outlook for the near future must have appeared bright as the two ventured south. In New York City they met with Colonel Alexander McDougal, to whom Knox presented a letter from Washington requesting "all the assistance in your power."[11] McDougal offered some small pieces of cannons, but could not part with the larger guns; New York needed to see to its own defenses as well.

In spite of that disappointment, Knox took some time to tour the city. "Their churches are grand," he wrote in the first of many letters home to Lucy, "their college, workshop and hospitals most excellently situated and also exceedingly commodious; their principal streets much wider than ours." But he was less inspired with the city's citizens. "The people—why, the people are magnificent; in their profaneness, which is intolerable; in the want of principle, which is prevalent; in their Toryism, which is insufferable, and for which they must repent in dust and ashes."[12] Lest their vices wear off on himself or William, the brothers departed after only several days. Without New York's heavy artillery available, they would have to travel to Ticonderoga and examine the cannons there.

Back in Philadelphia, while Knox was en route to Fort Ticonderoga, John Hancock was signing Knox's commission as a full colonel. Until now, although nominal head of the Continental Army's artillery, he had remained a civilian. Now, as "Colonel of the Regiment of Artillery . . . he is to be obeyed as such."[13] Knox wouldn't hear of the promotion for weeks, however, and as he battled another snowstorm in his travel northward, it likely wasn't at the forefront of his mind.

Reaching Fort George in the early afternoon of December 4, William and Knox decided to spend the night and cross Lake George the following day. In doing so, they managed to cross paths with an individual who would later be involved in one of the most infamous instances of treason in the history of the United States. John André was a captured lieutenant in the British army and was on his way south for an exchange. By chance, Knox and André shared a small cabin and spent a very pleasant evening together, discovering that they shared much in common.

Their second meeting would not take place under such convivial circumstances. André was caught near West Point on his way to a rendezvous with American general Benedict Arnold. (A close friend of both Henry and Lucy's, Arnold would later write Lucy a letter asking for "intelligence" on his wooing of one Miss DeBlois, as well as Lucy's assistance in presenting a trunk of gowns to the "heavenly" and "charming" lady.)

Arnold managed to escape to British lines, but André was court-martialed by a board of general officers, which included Knox.[14] Knox's displeasure at participating in the proceedings was no doubt outweighed only by his disbelief at Arnold's treachery. "The strangest thing in the world has happened," he wrote incredulously. "Arnold has gone to the enemy."[15] André was sentenced to be hanged, and no doubt Knox harbored grave misgivings about sending to death the man with whom he'd spent such a memorable evening some years before.

Now, however, Knox had only pleasant thoughts about André as he crossed Lake George to Fort Ticonderoga the next day. The weather cleared up enough for him to write that "having an exceeding fine passage [we] reach'd the landing place belonging to Ticonderoga about half past five and immediately went up to the fort Ticonderoga."[16] It was December 5.

It was not an impressive sight. Built in 1755 by the French, it was already falling into disrepair by the time Knox arrived in 1775. Benedict Arnold, Ethan Allen, and the Green Mountain Boys had captured it from the British in a surprise attack, without a single shot fired, but since then, little effort had been made to restore its defenses.

John Becker, a teamster who drove one of sleighs carrying cannons and penned a memoir of his career, wrote a description of its appearance just a few short months after Knox's arrival there. "We arrived at Ticonderoga, which presented but a sorry sight; the glories of Ti were rather on the wane; the fortune of war and a change of masters had not in the least benefitted its military appearance. Its ditches were nearly filled with rubbish, and its ramparts were dismantled and ruinous."[17] The British retook the fort again in 1776 (upon which Knox would write that its defeat held "the most disagreeable consequences of anything during the war"), but by then, Knox was long gone.[18]

An inventory of the cannons present revealed that much of it was too worn to be worth transporting across New England. Fifty-nine pieces weighing nearly 120,000 pounds were deemed serviceable, however, and they, combined with a barrel of flints and 2,300 pounds of lead, would round out the massive amount of iron and brass to be carted across the countryside. While some mortars weighed only 100 pounds apiece, it's likely some eyebrows were raised upon hearing that Knox proposed to take the three 18-pound cannons, each one eleven feet long and weighing 11,000 pounds.

None of it seemed to daunt him. The day after his arrival, Knox merely noted in his journal that he was "Employ'd in getting the

Cannon from the fort on board a Gundaloo [likely gondala] in order to get them to the bridge."[19]

His return journey to Boston had begun.

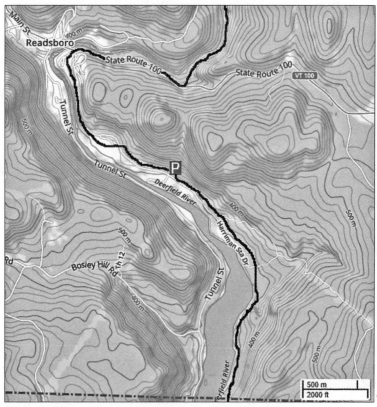

The Catamount Trail from Route 100 to Stratton Pond

2. *It Is Not Easy to Conceive of the Difficulties We Have Had*

From the parking lot where Elizabeth dropped me off, I ski south along the Trail for three miles to the true Vermont border, where I find the small stone obelisk marking the boundary and the official beginning of the Catamount Trail. From there, I retrace my steps northward, happily grumbling to myself about the fact that no one had seen fit to build a road directly to the start of the Trail.

Soon, I am forced to pause briefly to examine my feet. Hot spots are already appearing on my right heel, and knowing I have a long journey in front of me, I want to address them before they become a real problem.

Balancing on one foot is not the easiest of jobs, and doing so in a snowbank while wearing ski boots I'm only vaguely familiar with makes it no easier. I tip over initially, catching myself with my bare hands in the snow. This small distraction frustrates me unnecessarily—perhaps because I feel so uncoordinated as I struggle back to my feet and then continue to attempt this balancing act. Somehow I finally manage to slap some duct tape on the back of my foot, re-zip and buckle the boot, and step back into the binding. It feels much better, and a slight reorganization of my pack at the same time to better balance the weight only improves it further. In the end, blisters will not be my main foot problem on this trip; the cold will be.

Arriving back at the parking lot, the car's tire tracks are already blurred by the new-fallen snow. The Trail continues to parallel the access road until reaching Jarvis Hill Road. From there I walk north to Route 100 and turn right to walk along the breakdown lane (what little there is of it), through the dirty slush that inevitably accumulates alongside a thoroughfare. Cars whiz by as I trudge with skis over my shoulder, and I grin at one in response to a friendly toot of the horn.

Back on skis just past a guardrail, I turn north again and ski down the snowbank to a small cluster of people beneath a banner. It announces a snowshoe race, and the fact that the Trail is packed down with snowshoe prints is testament to the number of participants.

"Just keep an eye out for the racers," one organizer warns me. "They should be returning soon."

"I'll certainly step off to the side," I reassure her before pushing on, striving to demonstrate my best form as I pass the watching group. I doubt they buy it.

It takes a bit longer to reach the frontrunners, but I finally spot a flash of color through the trees ahead, tramping toward me. The trickle becomes a flood, and I spend ten or fifteen minutes to the side of the Trail, enthusiastically cheering the racers on. More than one gives my oversize pack a sidelong glance, and one woman spares enough breath to ask my destination.

"Canada," I grin proudly.

"Wow," she pants. "Good luck!"

"You too," I holler after her retreating back.

Once the racers have passed, I make good time for much of the rest of the day. The Trail remains relatively flat as it twists and winds alongside the Deerfield River, and while several short, steep pitches add some interest to the day's travels, it mostly remains a gentle, peaceful ski.

I pause throughout, snacking on peanuts, chocolate, and granola bars. Instead of a meal, I've decided to spread lunch across several hours, using mostly these snacks to fulfill my caloric needs during the day. I have no idea how many calories I'll actually burn, but there's no way I could reasonably carry enough to compensate for what I'll lose. I've just resigned myself to losing weight and feeling hungry throughout.

When planning, I had struggled to settle on a lunch option. Peanut butter and jelly, meat, and so forth would all freeze. I certainly wasn't going to stop and set up a stove to heat something up. It was Elizabeth who gave me the idea to snack instead of eat a regular lunch. She had done it throughout her time as a winter guide and highly recommended it. Even this first granola bar is a little frozen, and I have to tear at it with unusual force to get a bite off. Still, I silently applaud her advice—anything else would have been frozen harder still.

I cross the Deerfield River on Harriman Dam, enjoying the sight of the snow-swept reservoir. The Trail remains flat but rocky. I take a break where it briefly merges with an old railroad bed. To cross through a steep ridge, the rail engineers had blasted a passage through the rock, and the resulting steep walls on either side make for a neat ski. After gliding along all day through open hardwoods, I can't help but move more slowly and quietly through the miniature chasm. The sound of the dripping icicles that hang from projecting rocks on either side metronomically punctuate the otherwise-silent cleft in the rock. While the effect is not as awe-inspiring as, say, echoes within the Grand Canyon, it still gives me pause.

The rest of the afternoon passes by smoothly. A wet seep dripping down from the hillside forces me to stop and walk briefly, and as I emerge onto a multiuse trail, I struggle to keep my skis moving straight. Amid all the various types of prints and tracks, they seem to slew sideways almost as much as they move forward. This pales in comparison to my biggest frustration: Near midafternoon temperatures reach their warmest of the day. It must be above the freezing point, because as I leave the shores of Harriman Reservoir for the last time, my speed begins to slow beyond what my tired legs say it should. I stop, and then stop again to scrape the snow from the bottom of my skis, but it's no use. The snow is too sticky. I trudge onward, exasperated, my glide limited now to mere inches.

To avoid the power station the Trail takes me up a steep hill and through a brushy field. Returning briefly to the Deerfield River, I cross through an old apple orchard and then hike up the side of an embankment to peer through the guardrail at the traffic humming by on Route 9, contrails of snow swirling in their wake. The Trail makes use of the state bridge here to cross the Deerfield, so I walk along the road once again before returning to the relative quiet of the woods on the north side of the road.

It's getting late by this time, and once back among the trees I begin to look for a spot to camp for the night. With limited campsites, the Catamount Trail organization encourages users to find public land on which to spend the night, or to at least get permission to use private land, but I'm not picky. By camping on snow I will leave little permanent trace of my passing, and as long as I find a quiet, out-of-the-way place, I know I won't bother anyone.

One such spot presents itself near Vose Brook. Thankful, I ski off the Trail a ways, shrug off my pack, and step out of my skis. It feels good to have made eighteen miles on my first day, but it also feels good to stop. Really good.

Vose Brook is open, so water is not a problem. I cook up two Knorr rice packets on my WhisperLite stove (these packets are fast-cooking, easy, and pre-flavored—quite artificially, of course). I add some additional cheese and pepperoni to increase the caloric value, but I have trouble eating it. My stomach doesn't feel quite right, and finally I dump almost half of it out. Am I exhausted? Dehydrated? Or sick? Hopefully it's one of the two former options, since I can deal with those, but for now I'll just have to wait and see.

I drink a lot of water and one cup of piping hot tea, which feels simply wonderful going down, and crawl into my sleeping bag. It's only six o'clock, but it's already quite dark, and when alone, there's not much to do once dinner is done and chores and cleanup are finished.

I've decided to use my summer tent for this trip—the only tent I have. I wasn't interested in investing in a new one, and this one will hopefully fit the bill. It's light and durable and easy to set up. The fly should trap warmth within and keep any snow off.

I settle into my soon-to-be-nightly routine of writing in my journal before reading for a little bit. Not only do I want to document this trip so I'll be able to look back on it in years to come and remember what I did and felt in detail, I also hope to use it as a sort of sounding board as I explore my feelings for Elizabeth, the decision I must make, and what it means for my—and, potentially, our—future. I've got Knox's 1775 journal with me, too, from which I intend to read excerpts each night, as well.

The author's tent in action

But, tired, I finally just close my eyes and fall asleep—although not before unzipping my sleeping bag. It's probably 20 or 25 degrees outside, and I'm far too hot in my negative-20-degree-Fahrenheit bag. As I drift off to sleep, snug in my tent on my first night in the wintry woods, I hope that all nights are this warm.

While I was winding my way in and out of southern Vermont's lakes on the first leg of my twenty-first-century journey, Knox, on his first leg, was setting out across the only lake he had in his path.

Fort Ticonderoga sits on the narrow spit of land between Lake Champlain and Lake George and guarded the main thoroughfare for north–south travelers, making it an essential stronghold for any eighteenth-century army hoping to control the region. The best immediate route south to Boston, therefore, was across Lake George's often treacherous waters to its southern tip, where the cannons could then be loaded onto sleighs on the main road. After dragging the cannons from Ticonderoga—first, briefly, by boat on Lake Champlain, and then to the north shore of Lake George, by oxen and cart—Knox took on the unpredictability of the big lake. With ice already forming along the fringes of the shore, he couldn't afford to dawdle at Ticonderoga, although at the same time he needed the temperatures to drop and a heavy snow to fall to allow the rest of the journey to progress smoothly, with the cannons loaded on sleighs.

Lake George lived up to its reputation. After loading the cannons onto three boats, a "Scow, Pettianger [pirogue or a shallow draft boat with a mast] & a Battoe [bateau]," they set off. "At 3 o'Clock in the afternoon [we] set sail to go down the lake in the Pettianger, the Scow in coming after us run aground." Knox was too far ahead to help, but William managed to re-float the boat and continue southward. The wind died soon after, however, and it was only "with the utmost difficulty [that we] reached Sabbath Day Point about 9 o'Clock in the evening." There, some "civil Indians" shared a dinner of roasted venison with the tired men.[1]

While not the most auspicious of starts, they had made more than ten miles on the lake and, perhaps more importantly, had made positive progress in their journey south.

The next day provided no relief from challenges. Knox set off in the lightly laden bateau to make a beeline for Fort George and the south end of the lake. He had lightened his boat in an effort to arrive before the others, to plan the next leg of the journey. However, no sooner had they begun to make steady progress than the wind turned and "sprung up very fresh & directly against us. The men after rowing exceedingly hard for about four hours seem'd desirous of going ashore, to make a fire to warm themselves."

Knox agreed, knowing their exertions, and they made for land, where they fortuitously found a large stack of cut wood with which they built a bonfire. "We warm'd ourselves sufficiently & took a Comfortable nap, laying with our feet to the fire." It wasn't long before they rose and set forth again. After "six hours & a quarter of excessive hard pulling against a fresh head breeze we reach'd Fort George."[2] Knox, ever the laconic diarist, notes no celebration or pride in their success, and simply describes their struggle without comment.

Meanwhile, the trailing scow continued to run into trouble, this time finding a submerged rock. After breaking all their own ropes, William and the crew sent back to Ticonderoga for additional ropes and men with which they eventually managed to free the heavily laden boat. They managed to reach Sabbath Day Point themselves, but the same heavy winds that forced Knox to shore wreaked even more havoc upon the scow. "The wind being exceedingly high the sea had beat in her in such a manner that she had sunk."[3] Only a silver lining saved the expedition. Luckily, the boat was "so near the shore that when she sank, her gunnel was above water and yesterday we were able to bail her out," William reported in a letter to his anxiously waiting brother, who was now at Fort George.[4] With the next north wind, William told him, the scow would join the others at the south end of the lake.

Knox was not idly twiddling his thumbs at Fort George while William struggled with the scow. Demonstrating a trait that would become a hallmark of Knox's life, he was already planning ahead for the next leg of the journey, as well as the ensuing siege at Boston once the cannons had successfully arrived. Working with General Philip Schuyler—commander of the Northern Department of the Continental Army, and based in Albany, New York—Knox began collecting sleds, oxen, horses, and drivers to take the cannons the rest of the way. He also sent letters to towns along his proposed route, begging their Committees of Safety to set aside food and shelter for his men upon arrival. In a letter to Colonel McDougall in New York, he ordered shells to be sent to Washington outside Boston. Nothing was to be left to chance.[5]

In a letter to Washington on December 17, Knox reflected on the journey thus far and predicted easier times for the remainder of the journey. "It is not easy to conceive the difficulties we have had in getting them over the lake, owing to the advanced season of the year and contrary winds; but the danger is now past. Three days ago it was very uncertain whether we should have gotten them until next spring; but now, please God, they must go."[6]

Crossing the lake was only the first small part of the journey, however. The ensuing leg and vast majority of the distance entailed utilizing local roads that were often in a state of disrepair. On December 5, Knox had written Washington that "without sledding, the roads are so much gullied that it will be impossible to move a step."[7] He'd used carts to get to Lake George over the relatively short and well-kept road from Lake Champlain, but now that he had passed Lake George, winter was actually the best time to be transporting heavy loads over poor roads and dangerous river crossings.

In the same letter of December 17, Knox also informed Washington of his preparations. "I have had made 42 exceedingly strong sleds, and have provided 80 yoke of oxen to drag them as far as Springfield

[Massachusetts], where I shall get fresh cattle to carry them to camp . . . I have sent for the sleds and teams to come here, and expect to begin to move them to Saratoga on Wednesday or Thursday next."

This was all contingent upon cold weather and snow, for which he was praying now that the waterborne leg of his journey was complete. All he could do was "trust that between this and then we shall have a fine fall of snow, which will enable us to proceed further, and make the carriage easy." And forecast an easy trip, he most certainly did. "I hope in sixteen or seventeen days' time to be able to present to your Excellency a noble train of artillery."[8]

It was to be a gross underestimate of the time and energy required.

On the first morning of my trip, I am more rested than perhaps I've ever been in my life after twelve hours in my sleeping bag. Still horizontal, I, too, do some math in my head. I skied nearly nineteen miles yesterday. If I average twenty per day, I can do the Trail in fifteen days. I only need to go a little farther today than I did yesterday!

This is how I approach all of my trips. I plan very little of the itinerary and just let the terrain and events dictate my progress. It doesn't mean that I don't look ahead; it just means that I try not to commit to being at any one place at any given time. This day-to-day approach gives me a lot of latitude to respond to the myriad unknowns of a trip. Beautiful spot or friendly people? I can dawdle a while. Challenging terrain and slow going? No rush; I can take it as it comes. As long as I have a little extra food and coffee, I can be flexible.

I crawl out of the tent into the dawn hours and cook instant oatmeal and coffee. I down the piping hot beverage with pleasure.

Its bitterness feels awfully good in my stomach on this cold morning, and contrasts pleasantly with the sweetness of the instant oatmeal packets.

I break camp, rolling up my sleeping bag and pad, stowing my stove and pot, and carefully organizing everything from my toothbrush to my down jacket in my backpack, to both minimize wasted space and balance the weight. I do note my slightly damp sleeping bag as I pack it up, specifically spots where my body heat melted snow during the night. Something to keep an eye on. A damp sleeping bag on a summer trip is an inconvenience; a wet sleeping bag in the winter can be deadly. Moisture not only sucks essential heat away from one's body, but also can limit a sleeping bag's capacity to insulate. If temperatures dip too low, this dampness could be the difference between a snug, secure night and potential hypothermia.

The morning's ski along the Deerfield River is as pretty as yesterday's. I am forced to navigate a couple of blowdowns (fallen trees across the Trail), and take a small pride in clambering over them without removing my skis. It's an intricate challenge, swinging a leg attached to a six-foot ski up and over a large trunk and in between long branches, and it takes several minutes to work myself through each one. But with someone's tracks in front of me and no new-fallen snow, I continue to make good time.

Just before I reach the next reservoir, the Catamount Trail briefly joins one of many snowmobile trails. A group of perhaps seven machines go growling and crawling by as I snack on a granola bar on the side of the trail. *Cold, noisy, and slow*, I can't help but think to myself, watching the bundled riders huddled behind their windshields. How can that be any fun? They're just creeping along eating each other's exhaust! Yet thousands do it every year.

The Catamount Trail hugs the east side of the Somerset Reservoir, and a stiff westerly breeze means that I have to navigate a number of deep snowdrifts. The wind has packed them down enough to create a slight crust on top, but I'm able to force my way through. Eventually the trail turns deeper into the trees, and I find better protection from the elements.

At the north end of the reservoir I pass through the Grout Pond Recreation Area. A network of ski trails here spreads outward from the Stratton-Arlington Road, and I pay close attention to blazes to avoid a wrong turn. As I stand thoughtfully at an intersection, double-checking my next turn, I spot a threesome coming toward me through the trees—my first encounter with other skiers. It looks like a father and his two sons, one perhaps ten, and the other, around eight.

The older boy greets me with an enthusiastic "Good morning!"

"Good morning to you too!" I respond with the same energy, always pleased to meet an exuberant kid. "Where'd you spend the night last night?" I ask.

The father—confirmed once I hear the boys calling him "Dad"—who is pulling a sled full of gear, tells me there's a lean-to around the corner. They are just out for one night, so they're working their way in a roundabout fashion back to their car.

The younger son is simply sitting in the sled, seemingly getting towed by his father.

"You can't be tired already?" I tease.

He smiles shyly, and his father answers for him.

"He's my brake man. He hops in the sled on the downhills and keeps it from hitting my tails. And doing a fine job of it, he is."

I laugh, bid them good-bye, and continue on. It's always nice to see a family enjoying themselves together in the outdoors. It seems to happen less and less in the twenty-first century.

Soon after, back on a snowmobile trail, I meet a walker. His heavy snowmobile pants and jacket, complete with brand names emblazoned across his chest and legs, can't hide his large belly, and this, combined with his shuffling, wandering gait, tells me he's not used to, nor prepared for, a walk in the snow.

I greet him with a question. "Where's your rig?"

"Broke," he answers simply. "Luckily it's next to the truck. My son still wants to ride his, though, so I figured I'd go for a walk. You know, get some exercise."

With a smile, I agree and continue on, shaking my head.

I had hoped to make it to the Stratton Pond shelter for the night, where the Catamount Trail crosses the Long Trail for the first time. It's the only shelter on the Trail, and I thought it'd be nice to take advantage of it. But the final two miles from the road crossing to the shelter prove to be more challenging than I'd anticipated. Following an old logging road for a while, I am forced to push my way through dozens of sagging birches, bent over with the weight of snow and ice. Birches like to grow up along the edges of these old roads where there is more room and light than in the interior of a forest. But winter wreaks havoc on their fragile trunks, breaking many and bending the rest. What appears to be an open path in the summer turns into an obstacle course in the winter.

As I drag myself through yet another birch top and enjoy the experience of ice and snow falling down my back for the umpteenth time, I can't help but compare myself to a vehicle going through an icy car wash.

My frustration only grows, and the trail feels interminable. It's a tough challenge at the end of a long day, and I think back to Robert Frost's opening lines on birches.

When I see birches bend to left and right
Across the lines of straighter, darker trees,
I like to think some boy's been swinging them.

I can't help but change the last line to "I like to think I have a chain saw to cut them all down." A little less poetic, perhaps, but it makes me feel better.

Exhaustion has certainly begun to set in as I finally reach the shelter. I set my stuff down and then ski to the water source, chop a hole in the creek, and get some water. Returning, I try to take my skis off but can't seem to unclip the binding. I finally take my boots off while still attached to the skis and then spend some time chipping away the ice that has built up on the bindings before finally being able to unclip them. Not ideal.

I whip up some more pasta for dinner and again, have to force it down. I simply don't seem to be hungry. Am I too tired again? Am I pushing too hard? I'm not sure, but I do know I need to eat more—I'm burning thousands more calories out here than I would in normal life.

I crawl into bed, too tired to do much, and snuggle into my sleeping bag as best I can, tucking my water bottle in beside me so that I'll have unfrozen water for breakfast in the morning. My body heat will keep it a liquid. It is much colder than last night—perhaps because I've chosen an open shelter instead of a protected tent—but I decide to tough it out. It's the only lean-to on the trail, after all.

In spite of his overly optimistic timeline for the return journey, Knox had done everything he could to plan ahead. This forethought is indicative of just how his mind worked. Throughout the Revolutionary War, Knox's mind was often one or two steps ahead of current events, and he always planned far into the future.

Case in point: Soon after the march from Ticonderoga, Knox wrote to John Adams, arguing for an organized and modern military academy. Adams agreed, writing, "I am fully [in agreement with] your sentiment, that we ought to lay foundations, and begin institutions, in the present circumstances of this country, for promoting every art, manufacture and science which is necessary for the support of an independent state."[9] In the midst of a war whose sentiments rebelled against some of these very ideas of a trained, standing army, this was a visionary argument.

Knox would expand upon these ideas soon after in a letter to his brother, William, from whom he was now separated. Knox, fighting the British in an ill-fated defense of New York City, lamented the lack of adequate officers. "The bulk of the officers of the army are a parcel of ignorant, stupid men," he railed, "who might make tolerable soldiers but [are] bad officers . . . We ought to have academies, in which the whole theory of the art of war shall be taught, and every other encouragement possible given to draw persons into the army that may give lustre to our arms." He summed up his proposal with a ringing indictment of the existing revolutionary force: "As the army now stands, it is only a receptacle for ragamuffins."[10]

Congress, moving far too slowly for a forthright man of Knox's temperament, finally adjudged his ideas worthy of merit, and investigated the matter in 1776. Determining that there was substance to Knox's complaints, they requested a plan for a future military academy. Entitled "Hints for the Improvement of the Artillery of the United States," it also included some of Knox's own particular needs for the artillery corps.[11]

A school would not be built until 1779, the delay likely due to fears of a standing army. A precursor of West Point (later founded in 1802), the Pluckemin Artillery Cantonment centered around a large hall that could hold several hundred students. Knox taught most of its classes, lecturing on subjects that included battle tactics, logistics, engineering, planning, and the use of every type of weapon within the American arsenal. West Point's founding several years later can also be directly attributed to Knox's zeal in lobbying for a permanent military institution.[12]

But now, still cooped up at Fort George and awaiting the landing of the scow under his brother William's supervision, Knox's thoughts also strayed toward home. After seeing to the transport of the incoming cannons by contracting with a local militia captain for the service of forty sleds, with a potential payload of 5,400 pounds each, his mind turned to another sort of transport, one a little closer to his heart.

"Had I the power to transport myself to you," he wrote Lucy, "how eagerly rapid would be my flight." Distance and time had not dimmed the power of his ardor. Upon further consideration, however, he couldn't help but laugh at the image of himself racing across the snowy terrain to his love. "It makes me smile to think how I should look—like a tennis ball bowled down the steep."[13] All the delays and mishaps in the world couldn't dampen his self-deprecating sense of humor.

On December 16, William and the scow finally reached Fort George. With a full complement of cannons once again, they were ready to start the next leg of the journey.

Like Knox, my thoughts often turn to my own love, who I've left at home. As I toss and turn, trying to find a comfortable position on the wooden bunk and attempting to snuggle deeper into my bag, I, too, wish to transport myself homeward to Elizabeth. It would be a lot less cold, at the very least.

More than the physical warmth, it's the sense of confidence and comfort I feel when she's around. Exuding a calm self-assuredness, she seems easily secure in who she is, and where she fits in the world. Her father is a doctor, a family physician who works far longer hours than most humans should ever want to work, remaining on call for his patients at all times of day or night. Growing up in his shadow, Elizabeth learned about self-sacrifice, what it truly means to give up part of your own life for others. It's a burden most choose not to bear, but one that her father carries with uncomplaining equanimity. Since she was old enough to know what "growing up" meant, she knew she wanted to become a doctor someday.

Now in her fourth year of medical school, she has her own long days in the hospital, and longer nights spent studying. At this moment, she may be snuggled up in the rocking chair in front of the woodstove, reading an enormous textbook rife with unpronounce-able words (at least for me), preparing herself for the following day's workload. She, like her father, endures the arduous training with-out complaint, adopting a sort of serene acceptance of its trials and tribulations with the same composure she's learned from her father. She knows it's just part of her journey toward becoming a doctor, her dedication to the health and happiness of others.

This selfless drive only enhances Elizabeth's beauty and attractiveness. Drawn to this woman who applies herself so wholeheartedly to her dreams and goals, I immediately became yet another ward under her thoughtful eye. From careful support during times of sadness to playful yet heartfelt reminders that some of my riskier adventures were perhaps not conducive to bodily health, she has looked out for me throughout all of our years together. She has always been, in a very real way, that pillar of support for me to lean on in times of need, as she will to so many others in her professional life.

And so I lie awake in my tent, thinking about her impending departure to Salt Lake City. When she'd opened the envelope that day, my watching, hoping, dreading eyes upon her, she had immediately burst into tears upon reading the words "University of Utah Hospital." Tears of joy at the great potential opening up before her; tears of dread at the vast changes that would be a necessary part of this new road. She'd looked at me through brimming eyes before falling into my arms. For once I was the one comforting her, although secretly I was nursing a heavy heart.

So far, on the second night of the expedition, the burden of my decision—whether or not to join her—has not lifted.

A sudden creeping sensation of wetness stirs me from my heavy thoughts. The quick moment of inertia where I hope it's simply the cold is quickly overcome by the sudden memory that I'd placed my water bottle next to me inside the bag. I grab at it and right it—but not before several ounces of water have soaked into my sleeping bag. In the dark, with ice caught in the threads of the lid, I had somehow neglected to cap it properly. Now I'm paying for my lack of oversight. My sleeping bag is all that keeps me from freezing at night. I clamber to my feet, cursing my stupidity as I grab my headlamp. A damp spot the size of a bread box covers one side of my bag. Mopping at it with an extra pair of socks absorbs only the tiny puddle that remains on top of the fabric. Shaking my head and shivering already, I viciously throw the water bottle across the shelter.

Temperatures are in the teens and a stiff breeze is whipping through the shelter. I'm already existing in a situation where one small mistake can lead to terrifying consequences, and I've just come within a hair's breadth of making a bad one.

Examining the wet spot, I send up a fervent *Thank you* to whoever up there deserves it. The spot is not that big, and it won't ruin my sleeping bag, or its insulating capacity. I climb back in and gingerly try to avoid the dampness, all too aware of my (perhaps undeserved) good luck. I furiously vow to never keep water in the bag again, and as my anger finally subsides, I manage to drift off into a fitful sleep, broken only by periodic rude awakenings when a shift in position brings me into contact with the icy splotch.

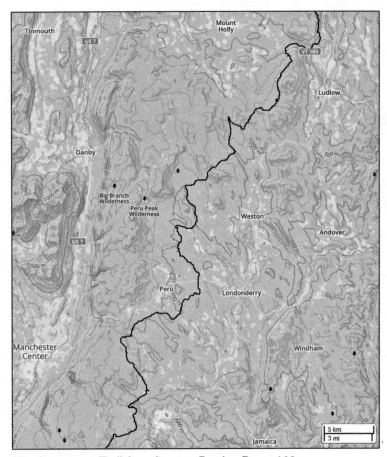

The Catamount Trail from Stratton Pond to Route 103

3. I Almost Perished with the Cold

Knox was relieved upon the arrival of the rear boats. Ice was already forming on the shores of Lake George, and had the lake been frozen, the mission would have been postponed until spring. Now, with all cannons on the south shore, they could move forward.

Whereas he had prayed for warm weather to cross the lake, Knox now prayed for snow. His prayers remained unanswered, however, as day after day passed without precipitation. Finally, not able to bear the wait for snow any longer, he again skipped ahead of the main expedition to make his way to Albany and General Schuyler. Even if the expedition couldn't move forward yet, he could still make sure that all was in order for their arrival so that there would be no delay once they finally hove into sight.

When I wake on the third morning, it is to stiff muscles, a sore back, and very cold temperatures. I stumble to my feet in my down booties—a winter camper's best friend—and try to beat off the ice that had frozen to my sleeping bag throughout the night. Last night's spilled water remains stiff, and I only semi-successfully remove the rime that's built up around the opening for my head. When sleeping, I pull the drawstring as tight as possible, allowing only the barest outlet for my breath. As a result, the natural moisture in my exhalations immediately freezes to the hemmed edge of the sleeping bag. It also does not want to detach from the fabric.

I am forced to ski down to the water source again to get water for breakfast, taking some time to beat my re-frozen water bottle against a tree before I can remove the lid to fill it up. But I finally manage to return to the shelter, light the stove, and get oatmeal and coffee cooking. I take all actions as a disparate sequence of steps, frequently interspersed with periods of beating my hands against each other and my body as I hop from foot to foot to warm myself.

I decide to not carry water from here on out. It only seems to freeze in my water bottle, making drinking impossible anyway. Instead, I'll move from water source to water source, drinking a lot at each stop but not carrying anything with me in between. Vermont has enough water sources that I don't expect this to be a problem. Nor do I bother to treat it. I'm a fervent believer that giardia is an overhyped scare in New England. I wouldn't drink straight from Lake Champlain itself, but I consider these mountain streams to be perfectly safe. And I have a small hatchet, so that even if a stream is frozen over, I can hack through to the running water below. This will not only prevent another accident like what happened last night, but it will also shave a couple of pounds off my heavy load. Resolution gives me a sense of accomplishment, and having made these decisions, I find renewed purpose and energy.

Back on the trail, after the night's travails, it all seems worth it. Gone are the overhanging birches and icy logging road, replaced by widely spaced evergreens. Clearly swampy in warmer months, the trail through here is a skier's dream in the winter, and I wear a perpetual smile on my face as I glide along, enjoying the sun's glint as it fragments against the crystalline snow. Monitoring the faint rub of my heels in my boots, I decide to ignore it. It seems minor, and my feet feel good.

Even better is the long descent down to Kendall Farm Road. I practice my telemark turns, dropped knees included, as I swish down through the snow. Several inches of freshly fallen snow from the night before provide just enough cushion and resistance to make it enjoyable, and I whoop repeatedly in pleasure. Still getting the hang of downhill skiing on touring skis, I take several falls. But with no permanent damage, they're all part of the fun.

And indeed, falling becomes such an integral and inevitable part of each day that I can't help but keep count. With three tumbles on each of the first two days, and two falls simply accessing the water supply this morning, I know that my third day will produce a bumper crop of miscues. (Sure enough, I top out at five for the day, the most of any twenty-four-hour period on the Trail.)

Once on the road, I am able to ski along the snowbanks abutting the plowed pavement, where I quickly catch up to a woman walking her dogs.

"How was the descent?" she asks.

My grin is likely a sufficient answer, but I extoll the virtues of spending the morning in the hills.

She laughs, and offers to give me a lift back to my car.

"No, thanks," I respond. "I'm skiing to Canada!"

This literally stops her in her tracks, something that surprises both me and her dogs, who are brought to an abrupt and no doubt painful halt via their leashes and collars. Having rarely seen this well-worn cliché occur in the flesh, I can't help but be very pleased with myself.

"No way!" she proclaims in disbelief. "Really? Good for you!"

The remainder of the afternoon is along open woods roads, worn snowmobile tracks, and through open trees. The churned snow underfoot makes for good progress, but sometimes challenging footing, especially when the trail is rutted and torn from numerous users.

I set up camp near Jones Brook, having surpassed my mileage goals for the day by skiing more than twenty-two miles. I am finally able to enjoy a full meal, and sated, tea in hand, I listen to the tinkle of the brook before crawling into bed, consciously leaving my water bottle empty and to the side, ready to fill up again when I wake.

The next morning, darkening clouds overhead threaten snow as I take care of human business and perform my morning ablutions. It's a quick affair, given the temperatures. Then, since the ground is too frozen to dig into, I simply kick some snow over the hole. Elizabeth had encouraged me to become a purist and use solely snow to wipe.

"Just form it into a slightly elongated snowball," she'd told me. "It works great! We did it all the time when I guided!"

I'd refused—it sounded like it would be far too cold on my nether regions—and rightfully so, as it turns out. This snow is (and will remain) too cold and fluffy to mold; I would have been trying to wipe with powder. So I bury my toilet paper with my waste and apologize to the Leave-No-Trace gods before returning to eat breakfast and break down my camp.

I begin the day by making my way along the trail past Little Michigan Road. Perhaps paying too much attention to the skies overhead and not enough to my feet beneath me, I stumble against a fallen branch, overcorrect, and tumble to the side, landing with a resounding crack on my right ski pole.

Broken.

I stare at it for a brief minute in disbelief, then curse myself out loud for not paying attention.

I realize that yelling isn't going to fix the problem, so I sit down, pull out some duct tape, and take a stab at fixing it, attempting to use sticks as braces, both within the hollow pole and on the outside. Of course this doesn't work. It's useless; the pole is broken.

It seems silly to turn back. I've crossed only secondary roads, and while my guidebook tells me there's a small cross-country skiing center nearby, it seems unlikely they would have a spare pole that they'd just give me, and I didn't want to buy a new set. Further examination of my maps tells me that I'm not going to pass near a town until I reach Route 103 near Ludlow, which is where I intend to resupply anyway. Fortunately, the pole didn't snap in half; I've only lost the bottom sixteen inches or so, so while I'll look a little funny with a short pole, it'll at least be of some use, even without a basket (the spoked ring at the tip of the pole).

Rising and re-donning my pack, I continue on, slowly learning that the short pole is best used on the uphill side and that it is totally useless to push off with. It still helps me to maintain balance and a good stride with momentum, however, so all is not lost.

The rest of the day progresses in fits and starts. I run into a morass of blowdowns with only sporadic trail blazes and spend some time thrashing about through deep snow, trying to find my way. Eventually I emerge onto a VAST snowmobile trail, where I make much better time. ("VAST" stands for Vermont Association of Snow Travelers, an organization that oversees, maintains, and grooms hundreds of snowmobile trails throughout Vermont. The Catamount Trail overlaps with VAST trails throughout, providing a pleasing contrast between the sometimes deep slogging of the backcountry with the quicker pace of a packed trail.)

The Catamount Trail organization blazes only very intermittently on these groomed trails, so sometimes I go for miles between blue diamonds. Blazes on long obvious stretches where one doesn't really need a blaze—except to confirm that no turns have been made—are called "confidence markers," so named because all they do is reassure trail users that they're on the right path. Since they are so few and far between, I cleverly dub them "no-confidence markers." Even I, an experienced trail user and builder, can sometimes feel the nervousness in the back of my throat. *Am I on the right trail?*

As I cross Route 155, the skies finally follow through on their threat. The ensuing three miles are still on a VAST trail, mostly through what appear to be brush-hogged fields. Amid flurries that grow steadier, I am but a minuscule being moving slowly through the winter landscape. A light breeze chills the air and dense clouds obscure the sun. In the open, surrounded by clouds and falling snow, I feel time is suspended, and progress seems unattainable. It's somewhere between vertigo and timelessness, like history has left me behind and I will awaken to find that, like Rip Van Winkle, I've lost twenty years of my life.

Finally spotting one of the elusive blue diamonds resurrects my sense of self, and I realize that it's getting late, I am quite cold, and I have few options for the night. I'm high on a ridgeline with running water unlikely and help too far away to be anything but a recovery mission if something goes wrong. Nervousness again seizes my throat—not because I'm afraid I've strayed from the path, but because I feel a very real anxiety about my prospects for security.

There are only a few requirements for a good wintertime campsite. There's certainly no need for flat ground; I'll just mash out a flat spot in the snow and set my tent up on that. Running water is a perk but not essential. There's water all around me in the form of snow, and I have enough gas to melt it on my stove without worrying about running out of fuel. What is most essential is shelter. This is even more important, given my flimsy tent. I need a spot that's protected by trees, out of the wind, where the wind chill isn't going to push temperatures even lower than they already are. If push comes to shove, I can always dig into the snow and construct a protective berm around my tent.

Although it shouldn't be too hard to find trees in Vermont, here on this open, wind-blasted ridge, the promise of shelter seems far off. The sense of exposure I feel is tying knots in my stomach as I contemplate what my evening might look like.

The Trail, now on the north side of Ludlow Mountain, at last turns to the right, off the groomed track. I quickly slow to a trudge through the deepening snow, winding between numerous alders and stunted birches. Finally, I cross a small stream and deem it perhaps the best I can do for the night. Stamping out a flat surface upon which to camp and prepare dinner, I set up my tent and light the stove. The small stream I've found is mostly covered with snow, but I stumble downhill fifty yards to where flowing water peeks through the pillows of white and access it there.

Dinner is instant pasta, and on this night I can't get enough—a good sign. Something, perhaps, about the artificial cheddar broccoli flavoring? Who knows. I crawl into the tent and my sleeping bag, at last able to gulp back the tension I'd felt all evening. The ice that forms around the rim of the sleeping bag threatens my nose with its freezing touch, the stack of clothes I'm using as a makeshift pillow bears no resemblance to my big fluffy white one at home, and the fact that I can't stretch my arms out within the tight confines of my sleeping bag certainly doesn't lend itself to luxury. Nor does the permeating stink of wet dog rising from my feet—no, my entire body. But snug in my space, I know I'm safe. On a cold winter's day high on a mountain, the difference between safety and peril can be pretty slim. And somehow that wet dog smell lends a certain *je ne sais quoi* to the evening's ambiance.

Leaving Fort George on December 24, 1775, Knox made his way south on foot before "Judge Dewer procur'd me a sleigh to go to Stillwater—after crossing the ferry we got with Considerable difficulty to Arch. McNeals Saratoga where we din'd & sat off about three o'Clock."[1] The difficulty was due to the snow that was finally falling in answer to his prayers. The trust he had put in "a fine fall of snow which will enable us to proceed further and make the carriage easy," as he had written to Washington the week before, had finally proven merited.[2]

"[It was] still snowing exceeding fast & it [was] very deep" when Knox reached lodging eight miles south of Saratoga, on Christmas Day. He went to bed thankful that night, and awoke the next morning to an overdue Christmas present. "In the morning the snow being nearly two feet deep, we with great trouble reach'd about two miles." Knox continued his struggle south, staying ahead of the cannons—now securely strapped to sleighs drawn by oxen—and finally reached Schuyler in Albany that evening, although not before "our horses tir'd and refus'd to go any further." He was forced to finish the day's progress on foot. "[I] almost perish'd with the Cold," he wrote, completing that day's journal entry.[3] But with snow on the ground, his cannon-laden teams could now make progress.

And progress the teams made, albeit somewhat slowly against the thick snow. As historian Alexander C. Flick describes, "Horses as well as oxen were employed. Instead of moving in a single cavalcade, the drivers were divided into companies which were often many miles apart. The largest group was of 14 sleighs."[4] This made logistics and lodging easier on the drivers; with fewer wagons in each group, they could move more quickly and efficiently.

The weather, along with the roads, river crossings, and associated logistics, were easily their biggest challenges. There was no danger of British interference, as the Redcoats remained holed up in Boston, successfully corralled by Washington and the Continental Army. Townspeople along the way were universally supportive and helpful wherever possible. Had moving this much artillery been easy, they would have skated through the journey. But it's not easy to move sixty tons of artillery across mountainous landscapes in deep snow and freezing temperatures without a few hiccups.

Flick goes on to describe some of them. "Some [sleighs] were drawn by two horses or oxen, and others by four or eight. The heavy cannons broke down the sleighs and hence delays were frequent. Extra horses and oxen were needed for snow drifts and steep hills."[5] On the steep grades, teams of animals would be doubled or tripled up to draw a single sleigh up the hill before returning to do the same for the sleighs left behind. Once on flatter terrain, the draft animals would resume their places at their assigned individual sleighs.

The journey was not without its pleasures, however. The wagon drivers were particularly spurred on by the amazement and awe of the local townspeople. Flick writes that "the people along the route were filled with pride and wonder at the huge guns which were being taken to Boston to defend their rights, and gladly gave assistance and entertainment to the patriots engaged in the enterprise." Traveling along "roads that never bore a cannon before and never have borne one since," the caravan of artillery was a unique sight, and the citizens turned out in droves.[6] As one of the teamsters, John Becker, wrote, "even then [we were] celebrated as an object of curiosity."[7] Word of their movements traveled faster than the sleighs, so their fame only grew.

All in all, it was only with extraordinary effort that the teams made any progress at all through the now-daunting piles of snow. According to Becker, they "reached Glen's Falls the first night," a distance of only ten miles from the south end of Lake George.[8] At this rate, it would be very slow sledding.

I wake to my own snowfall on the side of Ludlow Mountain. Unzipping my tent flap, I am deluged by drifting snow. It sifts into my tent, my gloves, my stove—everywhere. What a mess. And not good; it might melt.

I try to scoop it all out and then, struggling once again to don my frozen boots, I stumble into dawn's half-light and stamp a flat spot on the ground. It's only after wriggling my toes interminably and tugging, first on one side and then the other, that I can finally force my foot in.

It actually hurts as I do so, the hard, icy wrinkles in the boot's fabric dragging at my skin unnaturally. By the time I finally get my boots on, my toes are numb, and I spend the next ten minutes stamping up and down and flexing my toes in an attempt to restore circulation. Only then can I pause to take in the day and my surroundings.

And what a beautiful sight it is. Only the ridge of the tent peeks through the drifted snow, the light, airy fluff covering most of the sides. The grove of beeches where I am camped has taken on a startling new look. Branches stretch to three times their diameter and now bend earthward under their load. Sunlight filters through irregularly and shafts of light seem to shoot this way and that. I swing my arms, taking in the exquisiteness of the morning, punctuated by the occasional *pfff* as trees release their recent burden. What a day to be alive!

When I'm not actively moving on one of my trips, I'm addressing the many chores that crop up. Whether it's cooking a meal, finding water, repairing gear, or planning ahead, I find myself go-go-going from dawn 'til dusk. When I finally lie down at the end of the day, sleep comes quickly. I'm too tired to do more than scrawl a couple of pages in my journal before quickly turning off my headlamp. And so it is now—after admiring the scenery for a fleeting moment, I buckle down to the first meal of the day.

Breakfast—oatmeal again—is over quickly, and I strap on my skis, excited for the descent off Ludlow Mountain. It does not disappoint. The Catamount Trail zigs and zags back and forth, but for the first time on the trip I purposefully ignore the blazes and carve my own trail down the fall line. With nearly a foot of new and incredibly light snow, it is pure joy. With every turn I hoot in amazement. Rarely do I get to feel this weightless while skiing. Too often, especially on the East Coast, the snow is dense wet-pack, requiring aggressive, forceful turns. In contrast, today it hardly feels like there's any snow at all. The only indication that I'm not floating in the air are the periodic self-inflicted powder shots to the face. Choking on mouthfuls of snow, I experience something very close to ecstasy.

Of course, I can't go downhill all day, and the slope gradually evens out. I jump off of one last log and get back onto the blue-blazed trail to ski it out to the parking lot. From there, I walk out to Route 103. This is my fifth morning on the trail, and I'm out of food. So I stash my skis under a nearby tree, step out into the breakdown lane, and stick my thumb out.

Hitchhiking in Vermont is a time-honored tradition. During the summers especially, it is not uncommon when crossing the state's Green Mountain spine to spot a hiker or other outdoor enthusiast in need of a lift back to their car. In a state universally recognized for its community-oriented friendliness, it doesn't take long for someone to offer a helping hand. (In winter, that helping hand often takes the form of pulling a car out of the ditch—inevitably, one with out-of-state plates.) For someone like me who just needs a ride, the wait is short. Within ten minutes I'm scampering down the breakdown lane toward a car that has pulled to a stop in front of me.

"Sorry, but I'm a little snowy and wet," I say by way of introduction.

He waves a hand in dismissal and motions for me to climb in. The old hamburger wrappers and dirty receipts littering the floor let me know that my apology was unnecessary. The stained upholstery in his rusted, dented pickup truck further eases my concern.

"Where you going?" he asks. And then, with a second, more-appraising look at my ski boots and clothes, asks, "And where are you coming from?"

Focusing on the first question, I reply, "The grocery store. I think there's something this way, in a couple of miles." I had taken a cursory glance at a map before the trip and thought I had spotted a small market not too far away.

He shakes his head. "You want to go east, not west, toward Ludlow. That's the closest place. I'll take you." And amid my protestations that I didn't want to inconvenience him, he whips a U-turn to head back.

It is a half-dozen miles into town, so we get a chance to chat. The driver, sporting a scruffy beard and an old work coat, tells me he's transporting some sort of medical samples between hospitals. With his appearance and the condition of his car, I can't help but be dubious—he also mentions that he can't afford windshield wipers right now—but I don't question his story.

I tell him about my own adventure, and like most, he's thrilled at the thought of traversing Vermont on skis. Throughout my travels, I've found that people love to be a part of any trip, even if it's only in a small way. It allows them to step outside their own, everyday lives and be a part of something different, something unique.

My chauffeur today is no different. He immediately launches into a story of his own about the time he spent living in a cabin in the woods while reading Thoreau (a bit of a cliché, if we're being honest), which runs into another, more-original story, about another period of time he spent living in an igloo.

Finally drawing a breath, he concludes with the oft-expressed wish, "But now I'm a little old for that. I sure wish I had the time to do something like what you're doing."

We've arrived in town by this point, so I stiffly dismount from the cab while reassuring him, "You're never too old to go adventuring!" He nods in hopeful agreement and waves good-bye.

I stumble around the grocery store, grabbing food off the shelves as it strikes my fancy (a half-dozen donuts? Sure, why not?!) before settling down to make sure I have enough of the staples. Ski boots were not made for walking on tile floors, but I don't have much choice, so I skid a little bit as I walk around, thankfully without falling. At the checkout counter I get more questions. The cashier is also excited about my trip, "But I'm not sure I could do it," she says. "My fingers get cold pretty easily." I laugh. If only she knew.

My next stop is the sports store nearby. While in town I hope to replace my broken ski pole. The first store offers nothing, but they direct me across the street to a second ski shop (although small, Ludlow is a ski town, with Okemo Mountain Resort nearby). I walk in, set my pack down near the entrance, and stroll over to the rack of poles they have on display.

"Can I help you?" The larger of the two employees walks over, wearing a pleasant smile.

"Yes, please," I say, giving him my own in return. "I'm skiing the Catamount Trail and broke a pole yesterday. I was hoping you might have a spare one lying around. You know—maybe someone left it, because they only needed one, too; do you have something like that?"

He looks across the store to the other, smaller man, who gently shakes his head.

"I don't think so—sorry. Just what you're looking at here. But the Catamount Trail—wow! The whole thing?"

I explain my travels thus far, retelling the story of the broken pole and extolling upon the glories of my descent this morning. They lap it up, expressing their own desire to join me.

While I've got the floor, I continue to leaf through the hanging sets of ski poles, checking price tags. The cheapest set is $50, far more than I'd hoped to pay for just one ski pole. After going through them all, I indecisively start to flip through them again, hoping I've missed something.

The chattier, larger man shares a look with his fellow employee. "How much were you looking to spend?"

"Oh, I don't know. Not a lot. I was really hoping to get a random one. Maybe fifteen or twenty bucks?"

The two men swap another look.

"I'll give you this set"—motioning to the $50 pair—"for half price. Consider it a gift to help you on your way. You're doing a pretty cool thing, you know. And you're making good time. It'd be a shame to get held up now."

Gushing my thanks, we head to the cash register where he rings me up for $20. Spotting the discrepancy, I glance at him questioningly. He gives me a gentle smile while the smaller man shakes his head knowingly.

"Good luck" is all he says. "And enjoy. Have fun out there—for us."

I express my appreciation once more, and wave as I exit. It's nice to meet two such truly kindhearted and generous people. I can't help but think of Knox as the bell jingles on my way out. He, too, took advantage of such kindness on his journey; townspeople along his route offered aid and comfort whenever they could with food, drink, lodging, and even occasional labor—as we shall see.

Afterward, flush with my success, I cross the street to the local bakery. It's a long-standing tradition of mine to stuff myself with as many fresh baked goods as I can (the store-bought donuts I just purchased will be saved for later). So I settle into a chair next to the window, treasuring the artificial heat blowing in my face from the radiator, and chow down on a multi-grain morning glory muffin, blueberry scone, cinnamon donut, and a piece of pound cake. These should help me replace some calories. At the very least, the baker is impressed with my appetite.

And I'm impressed with her products. The butteriness of the scone in particular is phenomenal, compounded by that little spurt of juice as I crunch into a hot berry. My taste buds are wagging. I feel exquisite—this must be the height of luxury—and I finish them far too fast before sitting back in satiated splendor. I even leave a dust of cinnamon on my nascent mustache while I turn on my cell phone and plug it into the wall. It's time to check in on the outside world.

I call my father first.

"Yes, Dad, it's pretty cold . . . No, no frostbite yet. Yup, plenty to eat. Please, don't worry, I'm taking good care of myself. I love you, Dad. See you soon."

He's a little worried about this trip, it being my first long-distance winter expedition. I promise to check in whenever I can, and he seems satisfied with that.

My next call is to Elizabeth.

"Hi, honey," she answers, above the faint buzz of static. "Where are you?"

"Made it to Ludlow. Sorry I haven't called. Not too much service in the mountains, as you know."

"That's all right; I'm glad you're safe. Do you have all ten fingers and toes?"

The first time I left her for a long-distance trip was in 2008. I took a semester off from college to hike the Appalachian Trail. I'd promised to call as often as possible, much like I'd vowed for this trip. On March 8, my first day on the trail, a snowstorm hit Georgia. I hiked through it with little trouble, but that first night was fairly cold.

When I packed I had planned on at least moderate temperatures, so I'd spent much of that night in and out of sleep, shivering. The next day I ended up heading into town to purchase an extra liner for my sleeping bag, and called her from the store. Upon hearing my voice and explanation, she had promptly burst into tears on my behalf. Now, fully confident in my abilities to look out for myself, she just teases me mercilessly.

"Yeah, it's been pretty cold. But I'm making good time. Covered over eighty miles the first four days. I think it'll take me two weeks—maybe a little more? It depends. It snowed an awful lot last night, which might slow me down."

I ask her about school the last couple of days, and we chat about trivialities, carefully avoiding any mention of what will happen beyond this trip. The flat tone of her voice tells me it's in the back of her mind, but it doesn't come up.

Finally announcing that I'd better head back to the trail, we say our good-byes and she wishes me luck. While it's good to hear her voice, it also reminds me of the fear and confusion surrounding our future. I've managed to stave off thinking about the decision so far, as my mind has been occupied with immediate challenges. But I also don't really *want* to think about it, and talking with Elizabeth has forced me to do just that. I consciously suppress my thoughts, and decide to focus on skiing.

I finish the last piece of cake, don my layers, and step outside into the cold. Sitting has not improved my gait, so I stumble down to the road and stick my thumb out once again. While watching traffic go by, I think back to a passage I read last night, about Knox and his relationship with Lucy.

While still in New York City, before he'd even arrived on the shores of Lake Champlain, Knox wrote to his wife. "Keep up your spirits, my Lucy," he penned. "Preserve your health by every means in your power for the sake of the youth who values you above all earthly blessings." Later, on January 5, as he struggled to move the cannons forward, he wrote to her again. "Those people who love as you and I do never ought to part. It is with the greatest anxiety that I am forced to date my letter at this distance from my love . . . My Lucy is perpetually in my mind, constantly in my heart."[9] Worried about Lucy, and in love as only newlyweds can be, Knox would keep in constant contact with her throughout the Revolutionary War.

Despite missing his wife, Knox was called to serve his country. When he wrote that he and Lucy "never ought to part," he was expressing a wish, not making a promise. He and Lucy would spend much of the war apart. Although she would periodically try to follow him, it was often inappropriate for her to be in the army camps, near the front lines. "I thank Heaven you were not here yesterday," he wrote from New York City, his next posting after Ticonderoga. "We had a loud cannonade but could not stop [the British]. I was so unfortunate as to lose six men by accidents and a number wounded."[10]

Lucy had just left the city days before, following an uncomfortable incident for both of them. While enjoying a peaceful breakfast together, British ships had suddenly appeared in the distance, heading for The Narrows of the Hudson River. Knox, knowing he had to dash off to his station and his men, was torn between his duty to country and caring for his wife. "Everything in the height of bustle; I not at liberty to attend [to Lucy], as my country calls loudest. My God, may

I never experience the like feelings again!" he recalled later in a letter to his brother William. "They were too much; but I found a way to disguise them, for I scolded like a fury at her for not having gone [from New York City] before."[11] She left soon after.

Juggling the twin calls of duty to both country and family would be an ongoing struggle for Knox throughout much of his career.

Just as Knox and Lucy were often forced to make do with letters, I knew that I'd be forced to make do with phone calls if I chose to stay in New England while Elizabeth completed her residency. Would I be able to do as good a job as Knox, overcoming the obstacles and maintaining a happy relationship, or would the separation prove too much? We'd tried long distance before, in college, and it hadn't gone well. And with many friends who'd had similar experiences, I wouldn't expect to fare much better if we tried to repeat the experiment. Elizabeth and I had tacitly taken that option off the table, so it would be an either–or situation. Stay or go.

I laugh at myself. Just moments before I'd decided not to think about this, and now look at me. Oh, well enforced inactivity while waiting for a hitch will make you think.

I decide to examine it from another perspective. What is holding me here, in New England? It isn't duty to country, but instead, an investment in a business, in the community, and in my relationships with family, friends, coworkers, clients, and neighbors. It is the sense of place and belonging that I feel when at home in these Green Mountains of Vermont. It's my good old-fashioned New England stubbornness.

But does this meet the standard of something that has an indisputable, irrevocable hold over me? Do I actually love Elizabeth enough to change my life? Am I just being selfish in wanting what I want, without considering her career or her needs?

Probably, I decide. But I can't help it. I know where I want to be. Here. In New England. And while I don't have a single-minded drive toward a specific career, like she does, I do know where and what make me happy. And if that's selfish, well, so be it. I'm selfish.

I acknowledge that this would be a lot easier if Elizabeth was training to become a corporate lawyer or insurance salesperson or something a little less high-minded and selfless.

My thoughts are interrupted by a beat-up pickup truck swinging around in a U-turn in front of me, fishtailing a little. It was my ride from before, now returning from the hospital where he'd left the medical samples. Still heading in the wrong direction, he once again offers me a ride, and I gratefully climb in.

He regales me with tales of his own outdoor exploits, cautioning me to keep the medical sample I'm holding level. (This *cannot* be how medical samples are meant to be transported; I'll ask Elizabeth later.) Between the freshly baked treats, the Good Samaritan ski shop employees, and this generous driver, my morning could not get much better. Folks are certainly nice in Vermont—further cementing my desire to stay in New England.

Recovering my skis from beneath the tree where I'd hidden them, I strap them on. With three poles now—my old one, and the new set—I leave my spare at the trailhead. Perhaps somebody like me will find it when they themselves are in need. I decide to leave one of my new ones; somehow the aesthetic of having a different graphic and manufacturer's name on each pole, one old and one new, appeals to me. This, along with the fact that one is two inches shorter than the other—not enough to matter to a skier of my undiscerning abilities, but enough to be noticeable and invoke a slight smile at my own silliness whenever I think of it.

Then I begin climbing. Slowly. And then still more slowly. The new snow from the night before, while light and fluffy, is more than a minor impediment. Perhaps I, like Knox, when he wrote to Washington, was a little overconfident in my time estimate to Elizabeth.

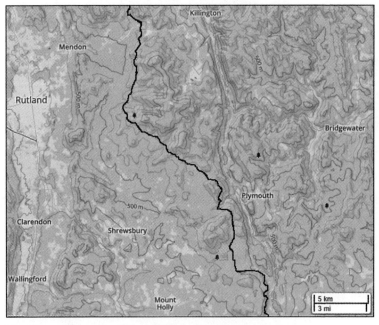

The Catamount Trail from Route 103 to Route 4

4. In the Manner of the Esquimaux

The climb from Route 103 seems interminable. I'm edging around the east side of a hill named Sawyer Rock, but the Trail feels as if it heads straight up for the first mile or so. The one thing the climb does do is keep me warm. The cold has not let up, and it must be in the single digits now. Eventually the Trail evens out, but it leads me into another obstacle: an open power line cut that it follows for perhaps a quarter of a mile. It takes me far longer than it should to cover that short distance. The stiff wind has formed a thick crust across the top of the snow throughout the clearing. With every step, I'm forced to thrash my leg with ski attached up and down several times in order to break through the crust. I then inch it forward, stamp down hard to thoroughly break through the crust, and repeat with my other foot. And then repeat again. And again.

This isn't skiing. This is walking—in skis. And it sucks.

Furthermore, I am forced to crisscross back and forth across the power line several times, searching for blazes and avoiding steep sections. At one point, I simply make for the woods to avoid the crust and wind for a little bit, but, fearful of missing the turn off the power line and finding that hugging the edge provides little relief from either wind or snow crust, I soon return to the open. Several times I am forced to stop, beat my hands together to warm them, and blow into my cupped, gloved palms to warm my cheeks. By the time I finally reach the woods again, I am thoroughly frozen and more than a little frustrated. But several fairly clear logging roads now make up the Trail, and I am again able to set a good pace.

I enjoy a brief descent down to Patch Brook Road, warmed again now that I'm protected from the breeze. While moving along, I reflect that Knox must have encountered similar drifts, which, while not caused by a power cut, likely plagued him as well. Upstate New York in the eighteenth century relied predominantly upon agriculture, and any fields alongside Knox's passage must have caused no end of trouble. The open space would have created endless drifts for the oxen and horse teams to struggle through with any new snow.

Like myself, Knox's teams began to settle into a routine after the first several days of the expedition. The teamster John Becker again provides an outline of life on the trail. Only a boy of twelve, he was already working alongside his father at the time of Knox's journey. With a level of responsibility that seems outlandish today, he was entrusted with his own wagon and team, not out of the ordinary during the Revolutionary War era. All aspects of what must have been one of his first trips remained with him for decades afterward, for he described the trip vividly when he penned his memoirs, at age sixty-six.

"Long before daylight we were on the move," Becker writes about the second day of the trip, noting that the artillery in tow was much heavier than the typical teamster's load. "I had [the] trouble of managing an extra pair of horses. We had taken on many more than the usual number in consequence of the service in which we were engaged."[1] Not only was the weather a trial, but the mere weight of the loads added an extra layer of complication.

Later Becker elaborates on the system they used of breaking the caravan into several smaller units, allowing them to move much more expeditiously. "The pieces were apportioned to our respective companies. My father took in charge a heavy iron nine pounder, which required the united efforts of four horses to drag it along. Others had the heavy resistance of 18s and 24s to overcome, which required the exertions of at least eight horses."[2] These were very heavy loads, especially for horses, and oxen quickly became the preferred draft animal. Although slower, their larger bulk and greater strength provided the necessary power to move the cannons.

Nights were still more of a challenge. Writing about a later expedition that took place nearby, Becker sheds light on what a typical evening on the wagon trail would have looked like. "Our sleighs were all driven together in a row. Our horses were rubbed, fed and blanketed, and tied to the sleighs. We were divided into messes of six men each, and went to work quite systematically to secure ourselves a comfortable night, notwithstanding the snow was three and a half feet deep. We dug it away in different places in the manner of the Esquimaux, and in our frozen apartments we likened ourselves to lodgers in a lower story."[3] As I discovered during my trip in 2015, it sometimes took a while to create a snug space for the night.

Becker and his companions did make use of fires to warm themselves, something I never availed myself of. "Some diligently collected fuel for the fires, and others stripped the walnut tree of its bark, which to the voyager is so well known in its quick kindling and for its resemblance to pitch pine. Our bags, containing the oats for our horses, were snugly stowed around our sleeping apartments, which were also made comfortable by a well replenished fire."[4]

I myself never found a fire to be desirous. Faced with the options of huddling outside around a small flame with frozen back and toes, exposed to the snow and elements, or snuggling into my warm goose-down sleeping bag out of the wind and in the tent, I always preferred simply heading to bed. With no one to keep me company or converse with, it rarely made sense to stay up and build a fire out in the cold.

All in all, a winter night seemed to be pretty appealing to Becker. "After eating a hearty supper, which, if not distinguished for its cookery, was well relished for its flavor, we sank into our beds, and soon forgot our troubles and our toils. Had they been of down, we could not have slept more sweetly and refreshingly—so strangely do circumstances control our feelings and moderate our desires."[5]

Sentiments I certainly echoed on my modern-day trip.

Becker makes it clear that this was not a regular occurrence, however. Prefacing the above description of the night's encampment with the sentence, "It was what in modern times would have been called our bivouac," he implies that often it was not required. Instead they were frequently able to find lodging at friendly homes, in local barns, or at an inn or tavern. Following his rather rhapsodic description of this night under the stars, he wrote that "[we] were glad to pass the next night under a comfortable roof, instead of the canopy of the skies." While sleeping "in the manner of Esquimaux" was romantic, he would have agreed that a sturdy, heated building was far more desirable in the winter.[6]

Sam Brakeley

While my own nights up until this point have been cold, I am now experiencing my coldest evening of the trip thus far. It must be in the single digits, if not lower. After climbing up and over another mountain, sweating significantly as I force my way through deep, untrammeled snow, I make another speedy descent, schussing through open hardwoods as I enjoy the beauty of the fading light playing across the snow's surface.

I'm chilled through by the time I reach the bottom as my sweat cools and begins to evaporate. It's the body's natural cooling mechanism—drawing heat away from the skin by first sweating and then evaporating when exercising. In the wintertime, however, this can have adverse effects and quickly lead to hypothermia. It's a cardinal rule of winter travel: Avoid sweating. Do what you have to—layer appropriately, add or subtract clothes as needed, move at a slower pace to prevent it, but avoid perspiration. It can kill.

Now I've broken that rule. And with darkness drawing near, my now-chilled body is in need of some food and warmth. I've got damp under layers and I need to select a campsite for the night and get some dry clothes on.

It's important to always have a reserve of inner strength in the winter. In summer, you can just flop down wherever, utterly spent after a long day on the trail. You can skip dinner, skip a tent, skip just about everything. A summer's night out in New England won't kill you.

That just isn't true in the winter, so while I'm tired at the end of a day, I certainly haven't used up all of my energy. I have more than enough left over to deal not only with the standard procedure of making dinner and setting up my tent, but also, should something go wrong, to address any emergency that might arise. Imagine, for example, that all I'd left myself in the tank was enough energy to set up camp. As I descend the final hill into where I hope to erect my tent, I take a tumble and sprain a knee. Or worse. What would I do then? These are the kind of catastrophes that can turn an adventure into a tragedy.

So as I cruise down the final hill of the day toward where I want to set up camp, yes, I'm a little sweaty, a little cold, and yes, I'm tired. But I've preserved enough strength to not only take care of my regular evening chores, but also maintained some in reserve, too. I have no interest in dying out here.

After some thrashing about, I select a small copse on the shores of Great Roaring Brook near Old Plymouth Road as a bivouac for the night. It's far too close to a nearby VAST trail and its noisy riders for my liking, but it's nearly five o'clock, and I want access to the water source—easier than melting snow. I find that the river is mostly frozen over, however, so my first task is to hack a hole in the ice to simply access the river. It doesn't take long; my ax is sharp, and the ice is thin where the current has boiled up beneath it.

I cook dinner quickly: more instant pasta. The flavor doesn't matter—what I notice most is that it's hot and salty and filling. Its burning heat as it slides down my throat and fills my stomach is an essential morale and energy booster at the end of each day. I eat as snowmobilers buzz by, their headlights carving cones of light into the darkening landscape.

Nestled as I am in this copse in a small valley, the cold of night seems to settle in quickly. I crawl into my sleeping bag as soon as dinner is finished. It's far too cold to do anything else. But since it's still early evening, sleep does not come quickly.

Staring at the webs of frost above me, I take stock of my situation. I can feel the filth and sweat of the previous days' work. Thankful that my nose isn't working particularly well in the freezing temperatures, it nonetheless feels like I'm stewing in my own juices. The clamminess—both in feeling and odor—of my unwashed body as it sticks to the unnatural polyester of the sleeping bag is a familiar sensation. Although life on the trail is a stinky and disgusting experience, I've grown accustomed to it. I recognize that although this part of tripping might not be all that enjoyable, it's the natural and unavoidable by-product of doing what I love.

Fortunately, my body seems to be holding up fairly well. The blisters on my ankles from the first day are forgotten, and my muscles remain strong. I no longer feel utterly spent at the end of the day. My hip flexors and IT bands (the long muscles connecting the hip and knee) have begun to act up due to all the duck-walking I've been doing to get up some of the steep hills, but I feel confident that they will grow accustomed to the work as well.

What seems to be the most important thing to keep an eye on is my own morale. Slogging through deep snow is a challenge, and doing it alone during the coldest part of a cold winter doesn't make it any easier. Whatever breaks I take during the day are short ones—enough to eat a snack and slurp some water before moving on. It's too cold to remain in one spot for long. I certainly don't sit down.

In camp, I go out about my chores and dinner preparation quickly and without a break. It's too cold to lounge over dinner or pause over my evening tea. Actions requiring fine motor skills without wearing gloves must be done in short bursts of activity, with pauses between each step in order to re-glove my hands and beat them together to restore circulation. Then the gloves come back off to perform another quick action before I toss them back on again to beat my hands together for warmth and circulation.

I could lose a finger out here, I remind myself. I have to be careful. Every action must be thought through with significant regard for its potential consequences. A lost finger could be the least of my worries. I've come close already: a leaking water bottle in my sleeping bag, exposed travel late in the day high on a ridge, and now negligence in monitoring my body temperature and perspiration. Amid all this constant vigilance, I'm still making mistakes. And all the while, I still need to monitor my emotional well-being, both in regard to my short-term trip and my longer-term future. It's all absolutely essential—and also exhausting.

The ubiquitous light and fluffy snow is a challenge in and of itself. While making for excellent skiing, it does seem to get everywhere. In my pockets, boots, gloves, tent, stove. Each move I make in camp needs to be methodical and premediated to ensure that I don't douse the stove with a deluge of snow or accidentally kick a pile into the tent. It would only lead to more moisture problems as it melts, with potentially far more serious ramifications down the trail. Donning and removing my ski boots each morning and night requires thoughtful preparation and swift exercise to protect my toes from both cold and snow. All of my actions need to be rapid yet careful. I write "Snow is everywhere" several times (with many exclamation points) in my journal.

Moisture in the evenings and during the night is also becoming an issue (and will remain so for the rest of the trip). My exhalations and sweat are building up on the interior of the tent, and when I take it down in the morning, I beat it to release the frost caked on its inside. Similarly, my sleeping bag (irrespective of the spilled water bottle several nights ago) has begun to attract more moisture as well, and when I unfold it in the evenings, I am forced to pull it apart. It's only when I settle into it and warm it with my body heat that the ice within melts and it becomes flexible. But then, of course, it is far damper than it should be, and is costing me precious insulation.

Simple things become far more elaborate processes. Velcro fails to work when frosted over. The same holds true for zippers. Yesterday, simply removing my crusty ski boots took ten minutes as I fought to loosen up the frozen material enough to be able to contort my foot and lift it out. Writing, never easy when on your back, becomes doubly hard in the cold. Looking back several pages, I can track my hand's temperature by my increasingly erratic scrawl. Suddenly the handwriting will improve where I've taken a break to put my hands between my legs for a bit. Patience seems to be even more of a virtue out here.

I roll over in my sleeping bag. It's still not even seven p.m. I'm spending upward of twelve hours a day lying in this filthy, crusty sleeping bag. Sometimes more. With only so much daylight to work with, it seems tough to get more out of the day. I can sense my body slowing down and quieting for the evening. My temperature finally regulates, and the intermittent shivering lessens. I vow to arise a little earlier tomorrow morning. I finish my laundry list of winter challenges in my journal and end the day's entry with "Such is the life!"

Knox had predicted making twenty miles per day and arriving in Cambridge by New Year's Day. Notwithstanding the uncooperative weather, this would have been an audacious timeline. Moving an army in even the best of conditions is a complicated process, and wintertime in northern New England and New York often precludes even marginal progress. Mother Nature was at her worst vis-à-vis Knox's ambitions. He had barely escaped the winter freeze on Lake George, been compelled to await snowfall at the southern end, and then been forced to wade through two feet of new-fallen snow. A change in circumstances was now in the offing that would place another obstacle in their path—one which I would thankfully never have to face.

As folks in the Northeast like to say, "If you don't like the weather, wait five minutes," and for Knox, the weather turned mild yet again. As he wrote to Washington from Albany on January 5, "The want of snow detained us some days, and now a cruel thaw hinders [us] from crossing Hudson River, which we are obliged to do four times from Lake George to this town."[7] Normally frozen over throughout the winter, enabling an easy crossing, the Hudson now presented a nearly insurmountable barrier. Without ice of sufficient thickness to cross, the cannons would once again be held up. As it turned out, it would be a near thing.

Teamster John Becker describes the methods employed to cross rivers. "As the ice was not uncommonly strong some precautions were taken to get across with safety. The method adopted was this: A rope forty feet long was fastened to the tongue of the sleigh, and the other end was attached to the horses. The first gun was started across in this way, and my father walked [alongside] the horses with a sharp hatchet in his hand, to cut the rope, if the cannons and sled should break through."[8] In this way, even if the cannons did crash through the ice, the horses could be saved from being dragged under.

Knox also ordered that "holes [should be] cut in the different crossing places in the river in order to Strengthen the Ice."[9] While the theory seems to be that the water bubbling up from the holes would spread across the remaining ice, re-freezing it and adding thickness, it did not work. The ice remained perilously thin for crossing the heavy cannons.

Alas, their suspicions proved well founded. "In the centre of the river the ice gave way, as had been feared," Becker narrates, "and a noble 18 sank with a crackling noise, and then a heavy plunge to the bottom of the stream." One last attempt was made to save the cannon before it fully sank. "With a desperate hope of overcoming its downward tendency, and just as the cracking of the ice gave the alarm, the horses were whipped up into a full jump," to try and rescue the cannon from the fracturing ice. It was "to no purpose," Becker writes.[10] The cannon was submerged.

Fortune seemed to favor the expedition, however. Like the scow on Lake George, the gun sank in fairly shallow water. The loose end of the now-cut rope "was used to secure a buoy over the place where the cannon was lying, and afterwards materially aided in its recovery."[11] Then a messenger was sent for Henry Knox, who was ahead of the caravan in Albany.

Knox was "much alarm'd by hearing that one of the heaviest Cannon had fallen in to the river at Half Moon Ferry." The news arrived "just as I was going to sit down to Dinner" (and therefore was likely doubly upsetting, for Knox enjoyed his meals more than most). He arrived on scene at dusk and voiced his displeasure and "excessive surprise at the Careless manner in which he carried the Cannon over, without taking those precautions which by his Instructions he was bound to have done."[12] As described above, however, the men had taken all conceivable precautions; the ice was simply too thin and the cannons too heavy. Knox was simply lashing out in his frustration at the weather, something he didn't typically do. Perhaps it was his empty stomach that shortened his otherwise mild temper.

His mood would not have improved once "it began to rain [and] the weather [began] changing." They were "forced to retrace [their] steps in some measure, and seek passage across the Mohawk."[13] Delay stacked up on delay, and Cambridge must have seemed farther away by the day.

With four river crossings between Fort George and Albany, progress was exceedingly slow—far too slow for the young Henry Knox on his first major assignment. In his January 5 letter, he wrote to Washington in aggrieved tones. "[T]hese inevitable delays pain me exceedingly as my mind is fully sensible of [the] importance of the greatest expedition in this case." Schuyler wrote a supporting letter reinforcing the fact that the weather, not Knox, was to blame for the delays, and that Knox was "exceedingly assiduous in this matter." All Knox needed was one "severe night [which] will make the ice on the river sufficiently strong; till that happens the cannon and mortars must remain where they are."[14] Regardless of the cause of the delay, it could not have been easy to sit and wait for colder weather. Knox wanted to be on the move.

I wake in the middle of the night. My watch tells me it's midnight, and I feel wide awake. It's not the cold that has awoken me.

I roll over. No, I'm not particularly uncomfortable (apart from the obvious factors of freezing temperatures, damp sleeping bag, frosty nose, and odiferous body). What on earth am I doing up at this hour? The same thing happened to me the night before—waking up feeling refreshed at midnight and not being able to fall back asleep for an hour or two. And it will happen to me each night for the remainder of the trip.

I am unnerved enough by the experience that, upon returning to civilization several weeks into the future, I research it. It turns out that my experience of sleeping in "two sleeps" is a well-documented phenomenon, one that most humans likely have experienced for millennia. It would not be until the advent of widespread artificial lighting—electricity—that humans would sleep in one long shift, what we all deem as "normal" now. But, as historian Roger Ekirch describes, "until the close of the early modern era, Western Europeans on most evenings experienced two major intervals of sleep bridged by up to an hour or more of quiet wakefulness."[15] My wakefulness in the depths of night is actually hard-wired into my system; I just overrode it with artificial light for the first twenty-seven years of my life.

Ekirch describes a division of the pre–Industrial Revolution night into "first sleep" and "second sleep." In between, individuals would often rise to smoke, think, urinate, write letters or read, perhaps visit a close neighbor, make love, pray, or sometimes just lie quietly and mull over one's dreams. Then, when sleepiness overtook once again, they'd return to bed and sleep for the remainder of the night.[16]

This was such a well-known phenomenon, Ekirch argues, that it rarely merited comment by diarists or memoirists—the reason it has largely escaped notice by historians. Since it is by and large no longer experienced today, it has received little serious examination.

But one study by Dr. Thomas Wehr in the late 1990s attempted to re-create "prehistoric" sleeping conditions and discovered that, given the opportunity, humans would quickly return to ancient sleep rhythms, including the "two sleep" phenomenon, if electric light was removed from their lives. It's only when we artificially shorten night's length that one's rest is condensed down to one continuous sleep.[17] I, with more than twelve hours of darkness each night, am performing a miniature study of my own, with myself as the star subject.

I rise and take a leak—the evening's tea has run right through me—and I hop and jump and shiver as I do so before tumbling back into my sleeping bag. I have some time on my hands now, for I'm truly wide awake. I do a little self-reflection on my dreams (throughout this trip they will remain quite vivid and outlandish), and then pull out my journal and write a little. Other nights I will read or simply lie quietly and let my mind float: my own version of prayer and meditation. This will be my routine for the remainder of the trail—an hour or two awake in a tent in the woods in the dark in the middle of winter. It does take a while, but eventually I manage to drift off into my second sleep.

The next morning I awake fully rested, in spite of not having slept the whole night through. Breakfast requires another hole in the ice, as my excavations from the night before have frozen over. A few simple hacks with my ax suffice to reopen the access. The meal is a hurried affair as I hop from one foot to another, stomping in an attempt to restore some semblance of circulation to my long-suffering toes. (My desire to get an early start was foiled when I emerged from the tent and found that I couldn't get my boots on. They were too frozen. Cursing them robustly, I had to return to my sleeping bag and hold them close for fifteen minutes to loosen them up enough to allow my feet access.)

Hence, my awkward dance as I scarf down my grits and coffee.

After further delay—I have to reset the zipper on my sleeping bag, repair a broken tent pole, and clean the tent of snow—I am finally ready. Instead of an early start, I get off a half-hour later than previous mornings. Frustrated, I attack the first uphill with impetuous vigor, promptly slipping and spilling over onto my side. Not a great start to my morning (and my fourteenth tumble of the trip). I regain my feet, take a deep breath, and settle down. I'm not going to get anywhere by getting upset.

The climb up to the John Stearns Viewpoint is not easy. The deep snow of the last several days means that I spend very little time gliding and most of it trudging. Occasionally I hook a ski tip on a root or submerged branch, tripping me up and interrupting what little rhythm I'm able to establish. But I've been on the trail for several days now, and am starting to discover a method for making positive uphill progress, both physically and psychologically. I've learned that I need to focus on smaller, short-term goals. Instead of attacking an entire mountain—say, Ludlow or Stratton, or in this case, Burnt Mountain—I must take a more-myopic view. Put the blinders on, so to speak. Instead of focusing on the top, perhaps several miles distant, I now decide that I should try to shorten my outlook.

That birch tree up there, next to the short flat section. I'll get there first. Good. This allows me to take a breath. The next section is pretty narrow—I'll side-step it, so I don't hook a tip on the shrubs on the right, then shuffle beneath that stump and herring-bone the rest of the way up to the next flat section. There—nice work. Now comes a longer, gentler, uphill section. I'll glide along here until it gets steeper again, and then address that when I get there. And so on.

It appears to work. Even by simply keeping my gaze aimed slightly downward, I am able to trick my mind into addressing the present challenge of a short-term fifty-foot gain. By focusing on the immediate obstacle and surmounting multiple, continuous, easily achievable goals, I avoid getting bogged down with the long-term end goal of the summit. And before I know it, I am on top, far more cheerful, having surpassed a vast number of obstacles quickly instead of feeling exhausted after having worked hard for one large goal. The result is the same—arriving on top of the mountain—but the journey is far more enjoyable because of the psychological trick I've played on myself.

The lookout is nice, and the descent down the backside of Burnt Mountain is very pleasant. With watering eyes and numb nose, I pin my ears back and schuss down as fast as I can. Now this is skiing!

Emerging onto a plowed woods road that is clearly in use, I spot a skidder operating off to my east. I pause for a minute and pull out my map. The description doesn't seem to quite match the terrain, but after peering around I spot a blue blaze off to my right.

Following it, I quickly come to a three-way intersection. Left seems to quickly become a lesser-used snowmobile trail, while the right fork is a continuation of the plowed road I am currently on. With no blazes to help, I opt for the right, quelling rising frustration while consciously avoiding Robert Frost's mandate to take the "road less traveled." The map isn't much help, but my instincts say that "right" is correct.

The gravel road I am now following is not friendly to my skis. Uninterested in walking, I try to stay to the very margins of the plowed surface, making use of the one inch or so of freshly fallen snow from the night before, avoiding any of the recent tire tracks from this morning's loggers driving in to work. To my left is the dirty, rocky road and to my right, the snowbank, also peppered with dirt, rocks, and clods of debris. But I manage to stay clipped into my skis and only hit a couple of rocks. Eventually I spot another blue blaze, so I know I've taken the correct fork. The blazes direct me onto a snowmobile trail and then off it again into the backcountry for the climb up the side of Killington Mountain.

It's nearing evening and so, after crossing through another recently logged area, I start to look for a camping spot, finally deciding to camp near a steep gully with running water. A small group of young white pines grows nearby, and I flatten a spot in the snow within, using their protection to shield me from the breeze that has sprung up.

I start my stove using the routine I've become accustomed to. Removing it from its bag I can do with my gloves on. But getting the jet of the fuel bottle to nest into its nozzle in the stove requires me to take my gloves off. I do so, connect the two pieces immediately, and just as quickly put my gloves back on. But just this brief moment of exposure has resulted in leaden fingers, so I shake and beat my hands together for several minutes. Similarly, to light the stove I need to expose my fingers once again. If I don't flick hard enough and the lighter doesn't light on the first couple of tries, I pause again to warm frozen digits, until finally, the stove is lit and I can start boiling water. It's a slow process, but it's the only way I've found to get the stove going and dinner on the table.

I have no trouble downing it, savoring several pieces of summer sausage at the end. The greasy meat tastes good, and my fat-starved stomach appreciates the calories, few as they are. The fat from the sausage glistens in little amoeba-shaped splotches atop the soupy rice meal I've prepared. They look delicious. I must be burning thousands of calories more than normal; simply keeping warm out here takes a lot of energy. But, like many long-distance travelers, I've kept my meals on the small size to lighten the load in my pack. I plan to make up at least part of the calorie deficit every time I visit a town.

After eating, I crawl immediately into my tent to avoid the breeze. I am just settling down to do some reading about Knox when a voice startles and alarms me.

"Are you okay?"

What in tarnation? Who the heck is out in the woods at dusk with temperatures near zero and falling?

A little nervously I unzip the tent door and stick my head out. "Yes, I'm fine," I reply.

The faint outline of a man on skis stands thirty feet away from the tent. He leans on his poles amid the pines, away from the Catamount Trail. I remember spotting an old logging road there, overgrown and unused, as I cleaned my cooking pot. I'd thought nothing of it—Vermont's woods are saturated with them.

A thought comes to me.

"Is this your land?" I say. "I'm hoping to camp here for the night, if that's okay?"

He reassures me that it's not his property. He doesn't care where I camp.

"I was just skiing down and spotted your tent. I wanted to make sure you weren't stuck up here."

"No, no, I'm here voluntarily," I assure him. "Thanks for checking in."

His shadow, now even blurrier in the fading light, waves good night and he continues down the mountain.

I re-zip the tent, still a little discomfited by the encounter. What are the chances of him running across my camp? It doesn't keep me from falling into a dreamless sleep, however. All the excitement of the day has exhausted me.

John Becker, remember, was only a boy of twelve in 1776 during Knox's expedition. He had his own nighttime surprise, quoted in detail here for its humor. "Long before daylight we were on the move," he begins. "I had the trouble of managing an extra pair of horses . . . in consequence of the service in which we were engaged." Imagine a twelve-year-old driving four horses towing a heavy wagon loaded with a large cannon through the half-light of a winter's dawn—an imposing and extraordinary image. No boy would be charged with such a daunting task today.

But times were different in the eighteenth century. Stamping his feet and blowing on his hands in the cold winter morning, one can imagine him staring at the shadowy outlines of the animals in front of him as he listened to the wagon wheels creak and the horses snort, perhaps a little overwhelmed with his responsibilities.

"The road was dreary, the darkness great, and I anything but comfortable during the morning drive," Becker recalls. In conditions such as these, even an experienced man's imagination might start to blossom with fantasies. Becker at twelve was certainly no grown man. Watching his own breath explode in the crisp air, the bizarre must have seemed all too possible.

Their location did nothing to squelch his growing fears. They were nearing the site of a battle of the French and Indian War. "We were approaching the bloody pond and the scene of some terrible slaughters. My imagination peopled every bush with ghosts. In the pond hundreds of those slain in the battles [of the war] were carelessly thrown, the hurry and distress of the hour permitting no other receptacle for the dead." With growing nervousness, he "anxiously turned my ear to listen to the sounds of the voices behind me, which came along in melancholy intervals, and would then be lost for apparently an interminable period." Any unexpected noise or vision, no matter how inconsequential, would have certainly frightened his impressionable mind.

Sure enough, the unforeseen occurred.

"While I was thus in spite of myself giving way to the most unpleasant feelings, my leading horses, which had been jogging along on a pace quite inconsistent with my views of propriety, made a sudden halt and fell back upon the pair next the sled." His mind now rampant with fears, he "remembered an old superstition that dogs can see ghosts, and I now fancied that horses might have the same facility . . . I made liberal use of my whip." With alacrity, "the horses leaped over something which seemed to be in their way, and went on at a full gallop for some distance." Willing to let them flee for a time—he was as scared as they were—he "at length succeeded in arresting their flight and began to bawl lustily to those who were far away in the rear." Scared as he was, he likely could do little else.

Startled by his yelling, the men trailing his wagon responded.

"After making the woods resound with my halloos, I had the satisfaction of hearing a reply. My father came swiftly up, when I informed him of what had occurred." And, as with so many other things that go bump in the night, the truth was far more mundane than the illusory. "What should the cause of my anxiety prove to be, but a drunken soldier, who had, in some unaccountable way, fallen asleep on the road, overcome by fatigue and intoxication."[18]

One cannot be sure, not knowing how cold this particular morning was, but it was perhaps fortuitous that Becker discovered this man when he did. To be drunk and asleep outdoors in a New England winter is dangerous indeed. Nonetheless, Becker must have been relieved when daylight finally arrived and the ghosts of his imagination retreated with the dawn.

I again vow to rise before dawn. With no repairs or delays expected, I want to finally make an early start. I feel that I need to make more distance each day than I've been able to do thus far, given the existing daylight. If nothing else, it will improve my morale.

This desire for steady progress is an aspect of my temperament that I've always been aware of subconsciously but have never faced directly. Whether the delay is steep uphills through deep snow, dawdling in town as I take advantage of civilization's offerings, or a lack of natural light, I am frustrated by setbacks that prevent me from traveling. This ski trip seems to have crystallized the sentiment and forced me to face it as no other trips have done before. Of course, hiking and paddling trips have their own setbacks, including daunting mountains and challenging whitewater. But nothing makes a human being feel as helpless as wallowing through waist-deep snowdrifts in the freezing cold, with no end in sight. Especially if progress can be made for only eight hours a day.

Adding to my frustration is the fact that, no matter how exhausted I am at the end of the day, twelve hours is far too much time for sleeping. When I crawl into the tent at 6:30 p.m., in darkness, knowing that I won't see daylight again until the hands on my watch are showing the same position again the following morning, I can't help but feel dejected. All this time, and all I can do is write or read in short bursts, warming my hands between each paragraph or page to maintain circulation in my fingertips. Winter in New England is simply incompatible with human comfort and ambition—at least in the traditional sense.

Perhaps even worse is that all this free time means my mind has more of a chance to spin endlessly as I weigh the pros and cons of my future with Elizabeth, and the decision I must make. It doesn't seem to be helping. It feels more like torture as my thoughts crowd me mercilessly. Yes, I need to make a decision, but long, lonely nights in the snow don't seem to be as good a place as I'd hoped for making a balanced, informed, or even sane choice.

I am aware that even if it leads to longer stretches where my hands and toes are numb, in order for me to remain psychologically healthy, I need to travel farther each day. It's the only way I can remain sane. Hence, my vow to rise earlier, and why, at six a.m., I sneak my frozen boots into my sleeping bag with me. With temperatures dipping ever lower, I can no longer force my feet into my boots without first warming them against my chest. Elizabeth had recommended sleeping with them in my bag at night, but I've chosen to ignore that advice. They smell too bad and take up too much room. Fifteen minutes later I clamber out, ready to jam my suffering feet into the boots, and then turn the stove on for breakfast.

It's still dark, and the surrounding trees barely show through the gloom. The cold at this hour seems to permeate every bone in my body. I shovel down my instant grits and cheese—it's too cold to even consider lingering over the meal. But in spite of the temperature, I'm thrilled to be up and about. An early start like this will give me extra time on the Trail, hopefully enough to make the progress I need to maintain a sunny disposition.

The Trail, too, finally complies with my plans. While the first several miles out of camp are through the backcountry, the grades remain rolling and gentle. It hugs the flanks of Killington at a fairly low elevation, meaning that I avoid the deeper drifts found higher up. The light flurries now falling only bolster my mood. Few can remain impassive in the face of the Vermont woods dusted with freshly fallen snow, and I am no stoic. The beauty around me spurs me on, swishing my way happily in and out of gullies as I progress northward.

A line from Becker sticks with me from my reading the night before. "The dependence we were under to each other for assistance in case of accident," he reflects, "made it necessary for us to move in a body." As they battled freezes and thaws, breakdowns and thin ice, and myriad other frustrations and setbacks, they could look to each other for aid and support. If an axle broke or an ankle twisted, help was immediately available. Towns lined their route, allowing for periodic stops to restock with food, supplies, and medicine. By traveling together (albeit in several smaller groups, for speed), they were able to rely on each other as a first line of defense against accident or mishap.[19]

I, on the other hand, am all alone. While I too have towns that I can periodically access along my path for food, supplies, or help, if something goes wrong between stops, I am truly on my own. The cell phone I carry works only occasionally, and while Elizabeth knows my approximate timeline and location, she only expects to hear from me every three to four days. With deep snow, thick woods, and subzero temperatures, three to four days is likely too long for a rescue to be anything but a body recovery.

This knowledge only invigorates me. The danger, the risk, excite me. Self-reliance is perhaps the trait that I pride myself on above all others. As a dedicated outdoorsman and adventurer, it certainly needs to be among my characteristics. By heading alone into the Green Mountain State's forests during winter, with only a backpack and my wits to sustain me, I am able to challenge my physical and emotional endurance in ways that few other settings offer. My safety net is awfully frail when I'm shivering and stamping my feet in the dark amid several feet of snow, miles from the nearest road or house, with no cell-phone service. If something goes wrong—I freeze a fingertip or toe, cut or burn myself, twist an ankle, hit a tree skiing, fall in the water, anything—I am a long way from help. Potentially far enough away that even a small accident could turn fatal. And that's exactly how I want it.

For, if I don't try it, how will I know? How will I know if I can endure temperatures dipping into the double-digit negatives? How will I know if I am capable of handling the challenges that inevitably arise on the trail, such as deep snowdrifts or a wet sleeping bag? And beyond handling them, overcome them in such a way as to grow and thrive?

For it's not about crossing through the snowdrift or dealing with a spilt water bottle; those specific challenges are not something people face in their everyday lives. Instead, for me, they are representative of life's broader challenges. Can I confront physical and emotional adversity in an outdoor setting, only to persevere and flourish? If I can, as I am starting to find out by the seventh day of this trip, then I can prevail over the other challenges that life throws in my path. By facing and conquering these very real and tangible trials, I can be confident that life's other, often more abstract, challenges are also surmountable.

And so I embrace being alone in the frigid woods, confident in my abilities to conquer any obstacle.

But this line of reasoning also leads to another question, one that I mean to answer in my time out here. If I am capable of this kind of self-reliance, alone in this hostile winter environment, do I need the support of someone like Elizabeth at all? Or, on the other hand, is this reasoning fatally flawed, replete as it is with its sense of hubris? In embracing "rugged individualism," as the storybooks would call it, am I potentially ignoring a more fully rounded life with a partner at my side, especially someone I love as much as I do Elizabeth?

Weighty thoughts, all of them.

As I ski along the base of Killington, making excellent progress and warm with the exertion of it, I am hesitant to address my own questions for fear of what my answers might be.

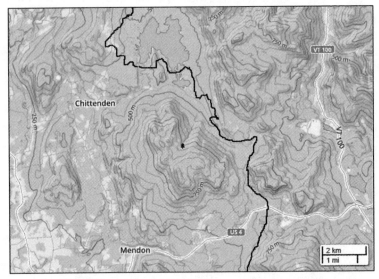

The Catamount Trail from Route 4 to Mountain Top Inn & Resort

5. Humbled by Thoughts of My Own Insignificance

North of Killington, one of Vermont's major east–west roads traverses the state. I come out onto Route 4 only to be hit with a cacophony of noise, dirt, and speed. Cars and trucks race over the asphalt, dark splatters of mud, oil, and filth reaching far past the snowbanks lining the pavement, stretching their tendrils of brown into the woods on either side. The trees themselves seem to hang their heads in disgust, their tops bowed toward the road in apparent submission.

It's an experience I do not enjoy, so I strip my skis from my feet, quickly cross this symbol of modernity, and reenter the woods on the far side. I ski hard for the first couple hundred yards in an effort to leave the scene behind. I'm not out here to watch interstate commerce roar by.

Knox in 1775 continued to wait anxiously for temperatures to drop so he could easily cross the Hudson River fords with the heavy cannons, but it took longer than anticipated. To distract himself in the meantime, he ventured on a little excursion up the Mohawk River near Albany.

"We came to the falls, so famous in this part of the Continent & known by the name of the Cohoos falls," he wrote in his journal. "Those stupendous falls, inferior to none except the Grand one of Niagara, are form'd by the whole body of the Mohawk River falling at one pitch from a perpendicular of eighty feet." Awestruck, he summed up the scene succinctly. "It is the most superb & affecting sight I ever saw." The description of these falls forms one of his longer journal entries (clearly he had some time on his hands), and is certainly his most illustrative. It's testament perhaps to both his awe of their beauty and the fact that for much of the journey he found little time to expound upon his travels. "The beams of the sun reflected on the whole Icy Scene around," he elaborated. "Vast Icicles of twenty feet long and three or four feet thick hung in pendants from the neighboring rocks, which were form'd from the rain & melted snow falling from the neighboring heights, & a very severe frost coming up which arrested the Water in its fall, this ornamented the scene in a very particular manner." He then gave a rather unique analogy, one perhaps not ever used before or since. "The water falling from such a height gave the water the look of milk. It look'd like one vast torrent of milk pouring from a stupendous height."

Nonetheless, he returned from the short side trip "not a little humbl'd by thoughts of my own insignificance."[1] I recognize the sentiment; it's certainly one I've felt in the presence of nature's remarkable beauty and raw power.

I am now skirting the southwest side of a small hill here in 2015. Despite its low elevation, the summit looms steeply over me, its face dotted with small cliffs and boulders seemingly poised to crash down on the unsuspecting traveler. Large-diameter oaks and maples dot the landscape, intermingled among the groves of beeches. All three species embrace Vermont's acidic soils and seem to thrive on its rocky slopes as they have for eons.

The woods are a wonderful place for embracing one's own insignificance, as Knox noted, bearing testament to the fact that humans are a very, very small drop in the oceanic vastness of earth's timeline. I take a breath and pause to admire the icicles creeping down the rock faces to my right. Unperturbed by my presence, they hang in icy silence. I hope they'll be here long after I've passed.

In this day and age, that's not a sure thing. Climate change looms precipitously over the human race as I ski through these Vermont woods. Humans are polluting at record levels and greenhouse gases are at all-time highs. Glaciers are melting, ice packs shrinking, and oceans warming, rising and dying at increasing speeds. Headlines now seem to warn daily of an increase in both size and frequency of forest fires, drought, hurricanes, and other natural disasters. Millions of species face extinction. Snowfall is decreasing, winters are growing shorter, and average global temperatures are rising. The Catamount Trail as I see and experience it now may not exist in just a few short decades. That's a scary thought.

But at this moment, I don't matter much to these woods. Passing through under my own power, I leave only the twin tracks of my skis in the snow before I'm gone. I am simply a fleeting phenomenon, leaving a brief shadow of my visit, but no lasting or permanent impact.

So it is with our lives. We are born, exist, and die, mattering little in the grand scheme of the universe—certainly, at least, in the context of our individual social, emotional, and psychological challenges. I sometimes like to look up at the stars at night, as millions of others do, and imagine the vast distances involved. When put into that context, it is very clear that our earthly problems, like my own troubles with Elizabeth and our future, matter not one whit.

I find it to be an incredibly comforting feeling. By realizing that my existence is unimportant, it reminds me that I am free to live it as I desire. It puts all decisions into perspective: Does this really matter in the end? No. In geological time, our species' time on the planet is but a blink. My life span is like that of a firefly in the galactic night. Long after I am dead and gone, nature will assert its power and all my worry and striving will have changed nothing. Regardless of whether or not I eat Fruit Loops or Wheaties for breakfast, opt to drive a Ford or a Chevy, or choose a career in business or the outdoors, the scene before me will endure in some guise. And when I am long forgotten, people will pass by here, enjoying the beauty as I am now.

Smiling to myself, I move on. It's best to enjoy life for what it offers and not put too large an emphasis on things that, after all, matter very little in the grand scheme of things. Now, if I can only remember this as I sort through my own personal decisions.

I am following not only the blue plastic blazes of the Catamount Trail but also the painted white blazes of the Long Trail. The two paths briefly overlap through here, and I have the pleasure of knowing that I traversed this very section of trail in 2007 when I thru-hiked the Long Trail. That was the first long-distance trip I undertook on my own. Little did I know that eight years later I'd be retracing my steps, now on skis and on a different trail, with thousands of trail miles under my belt in the interim. If only I'd known then that I'd be back. In a way, it's comforting to know that I had no idea then where I'd be eight years hence. For if the outcome is a foregone conclusion—if one knows the future, it's as if one is driving down a well-known road, perhaps the daily commute to work. Every twist and turn, gas station and corner market, stoplight and road sign, are imbedded in one's consciousness, so much so that we often arrive at work with no memory of having gotten there. We forget to experience the magical sensation of arriving at a goal with the knowledge of it already being within our grasp.

And so while it's warming to think that I'm back in the woods in the same place I was eight years ago, retracing part of a route that I took at the age of nineteen, it's infinitely more pleasurable to know that back then, I had no idea I'd be returning someday. The joy of the past eight years has been in the discovery of my life's journey, not in already knowing its path.

Smiling to myself, I realize it's time I focused on making progress. While tripping is a phenomenal place for reflection and thought, it sometimes comes at the cost of efficiency. I realize that I've slowed down considerably while deep in thought. Shaking off the reverie, I tuck into the trail. I'm ready to make some time!

By January 5, 1776, Knox's caravan had arrived more or less intact in Albany. Including their travels across Lake George, they had come barely one hundred miles, even though upon setting out, Knox had hoped to arrive in Cambridge by this time. Disappointment and disillusionment could not have been far off, yet Knox was not a man to let setbacks get him down. Instead, he was the type to focus on his successes. In the face of inclement weather, several sinkings of both boats and cannons, and unseasonable warmth, he had successfully navigated sixty tons of artillery across inhospitable terrain. The Albany townspeople further buoyed his spirits with their awestruck welcome.

"The next day we entered Albany," wrote a teamster. "Our appearance excited the attention of the burghers. They were accustomed, it is true, to seeing fine artillery, as some well-appointed [British] armies had been encamped within the city [during the French and Indian War]. But this was the first artillery which congress [*sic*] had been able to call their own, and it led to reflections not in the least injurious to our cause."[2] Joyous at the sight of the revolutionary caravan, Albany's inhabitants turned out en masse to show their support and admiration.

Knox returned the compliment, taking time to pen a letter to Lucy and discussing his own observations of Albany and its inhabitants. "The people of this city, of which there are about 5,000 or 6,000, are, I believe, honest enough, and many of them sensible people,— much more so than any other part of the government which I've seen. There are four very good buildings for public worship, with a State House, the remains of capital barracks, hospital, and fort, which must in their day have been very clever." Not all of the residents were thriving, however. "The women and children suffer amazingly at this advanced season of the year." Knox went on to make a bold prediction for the future of the city. "Albany, from its situation and commanding the trade of the water and the immense territories westward, must one day be, if not the capital, yet nearly to it, of America."[3] Perhaps he was overly impressed by his reception there, for time has not validated his prophecy.

General Schuyler also showed his support and admiration for Knox's work thus far. Writing to Washington, Schuyler noted that "the uncommon mildness of the weather for several days past" was the cause of the delay. "One frosty night if not deferred too long, however," he reassured the general back in Cambridge, "will put everything in order."[4] Until then, Knox and Washington would just have to wait; river crossings were simply not feasible with the warm temperatures.

I, on the other hand, am enjoying the cold temperatures that Mother Nature is serving up on a daily basis. Once I get moving for the day, I find the frigidity a blessing. By keeping the snow cold and crisp, there are no crusts or transformed snow to impede my way. Instead, each step and glide flies smoothly through delightfully light powder. With six inches of fresh snow on the ground and more falling, the trail could not be lovelier.

I have to clamber gingerly in and out of several small gullies that bar my way, babying my hip flexors as I do so (they've begun to act up on me again). Eventually I find myself on a VAST trail and turn right, immediately entering a forest of blue and black tubes running every which way. Their crisscrossed network lines each side of the Trail, reaching their seemingly haphazard tendrils of piping from tree to tree at about waist height. Signs tacked to the trees announce that I am on the property of A. Johnson Company. I've stumbled into the midst of a massive sugaring and logging operation, the tubing a technological improvement over the traditional metal buckets that collect sap from the trees.

I'm flooded with memories of numerous springtimes spent as a youngster in the woods surrounding my grandparents' house in Middlebury, Vermont. Spring is the only time when maple syrup can be made—in order for the sap to flow, freezing nights and warm sunny days are required—and every spring we'd drive north to visit Gigi and Gramps, my father's parents. Fighting the traffic flowing north from Boston, we'd finally reach the quiet, open roads across the mountains. We'd pull into their driveway late at night and my brothers and I would rouse ourselves sleepily from the backseat of the minivan to head to bed, pausing only to be enveloped by Gigi's welcoming arms. She'd always greet us in the same way, standing by the front door with her arms raised high overhead and a massive smile spread across her face. It's an image that will remain with me forever.

Dad wasn't the only one who refused to be pent up due to the weather. Perhaps he inherited it from Gramps, because the next morning, after a large breakfast of buttermilk pancakes, sausage, fruit salad, and last year's maple syrup, we'd head out to the sugarbush (the stand of maple trees that provide the sap). With someone driving the pickup truck on the woods roads around the property, the rest of us made trips to and from the taps and buckets nearby, transporting the sap to the holding tank mounted in the bed of the truck. Gramps was a lot of fun to be with in the woods. He'd tramped this same area for decades and knew every tree, track, nook, and cranny. What's more, he liked to share what he knew; a day in the woods with Gramps was a learning experience equal to none found in the classroom.

We each carried a five-gallon bucket to hold the sap, and in my younger years, I was unable to fill it much more than half full before struggling back to the truck to dump it into the tank. No doubt as

I stumbled across the uneven, snowy ground, I spilled a fair amount as well, but neither Gigi nor Gramps seemed to mind particularly.

After filling the holding tank, we'd drive to the sugarhouse nestled down the hill from the main home. A rustic building with dirt floors, it was more of a shelter than a true structure. Its frame was built partially with saplings cut nearby. Inside was the evaporator, the large flat pan where the sap is boiled down into syrup. Maple sap has a typical natural sugar content of 2 to 4 percent, but syrup is 66 percent sugar, so significant boiling needs to occur to achieve the required concentration. This takes time, which means the typical sugarer spends a lot of time watching the sap boil. This includes watching closely to make sure the level of sap remains high enough to prevent burning the pan, continually stoking the fire to maintain high heat, and siphoning off syrup from one end as the desired concentration is reached, among other chores. It also provides a fair amount of downtime, where one simply watches the sap boil.

A popular pastime among those not too particular about achieving commercial-grade syrup is to add hot dogs or eggs to the pan. Nothing tastes better than a maple-infused hot dog on a cold March day as you stand over the boiling pan, enveloped in maple-scented steam. For us kids, hot chocolate and Gigi's homemade chocolate-chippers and Joe Froggers molasses cookies made the rounds while the adults would pass around a bottle of something stiffer. Fortified with spirits, someone would begin a family story. My father is one of five brothers, and between Gigi, Gramps, my dad, and the four uncles, we have some prodigious storytellers in the family. Sitting in the corner, munching on a cookie and sipping hot chocolate, I would let the maple vapor and family history waft over me. Maple sugaring and family have become inextricably intertwined in my being. Rarely have I felt closer to my family than at moments like these—probably the earliest origins of my love for the New England landscape and all it has to offer.

A low rumbling gradually intrudes upon my reveries, growing too loud to ignore. I round a corner of the road and stop to watch a skidder moving logs from a pile onto a logging truck. Since sugaring only occurs during a few months of the year, and many commercial sugarers actively manage their sugarbush by removing competing species of trees from the stands, logging operations often go hand in hand with the syrup business. I wave at the operator as he backs up to let me pass. He nods in acknowledgment, barely pausing in his work.

The snow-covered woods road I am skiing on ends abruptly in a snowbank. Paved and plowed road stretches in front of me, and a blue emblem on a tree assures me that a road-walk is in order. I take off my skis and begin to trek down the side of Wildcat Road, staggering slightly as my legs get used to walking instead of gliding. My slippery boots don't help my balance, but I manage to stay upright, and after ten or fifteen minutes I am able to re-don my skis as the Catamount Trail turns back onto a VAST trail to my right.

I duck-walk up a steep hill easily; snowmobiles have packed down all the new snow, and in spite of the grade, it's fairly easy going. Once at the top, however, I am treated to a long, gradual descent. Snow is falling once again, and as I speed through the trees I squint my eyes in an effort to see. The hard flakes pelt my face with little stings; with the cold temperature, moving fast is a chilling experience. But I enjoy the speed and schuss my way through the freezing woods. It's good to be moving!

The cold night that Knox needed finally occurred on January 6, and the caravan was at last able to move forward. Leaving Albany necessitated yet another river crossing. The horse and oxen teams moved slowly across the Hudson ("without apprehension," wrote Becker optimistically), not wanting to jar the newly thickened ice with too much stamping of hooves, yet also hoping to cross the still-weak ice swiftly and efficiently. The townspeople watched, cheering the men as each team successfully made the crossing.

General Schuyler immediately wrote George Washington that "this morning I had the satisfaction to see the first divisions of sleds cross the river. Should there be snow all the way to Cambridge, they will probably arrive there about this day [next] week."[5] While Albany was a city of thousands, excitements like this rarely interrupted the long Northern winter, and locals had turned out in droves, some even paying the teamsters for the privilege of helping the expedition.

It was fortuitous that they had, for once again, fate must have felt, to them, cruel. In spite of the colder temperatures, as the heavy wagons crossed the ice, they left grooves in the surface. While townspeople cheered for each successful teamster, succeeding sleds only deepened these grooves, such that the last sled once again broke through the ice, "notwithstanding the precautions we took, & in its fall broke all the Ice for 14 feet around it." This was yet another setback for Knox which "retarded the dispatch which I wish'd to use in this business."

Frustrated, he somehow got the other sleds the rest of the way across the ice, and "then I went to getting the drown'd Cannon out, which we partly effected, but by reason of the night's coming, could not do it entirely."[6] With the cannon still submerged in the Hudson, that night must have been a maddening one for Knox.

The next day Knox woke early and headed back to the river at first light. "[We] were so lucky as to get the Cannon out of the River, owing to the assistance the good people of the City of Albany gave," he wrote the next night in his journal, "in return for which we christen'd her—The Albany."[7] In spite of the accident, it must have been heartening to know he had the full support of the local inhabitants.

This would be the last accident of the sunken-cannon variety, and Knox would take the lessons learned there to heart—not only concrete ones, such as taking precautions to prevent future sinkings and to enable easy recovery in the case of ice breaking, but also perseverance in the face of obstacles, the importance of maintaining an optimistic outlook, and the value of using local help in case of disaster. Later in the war, Knox crossed another river with artillery, this time the Delaware River with George Washington, in what would become a far more celebrated achievement than the Hudson crossing.

Knox would put to use all of the lessons he had learned during the Fort Ticonderoga march just a year later, in the 1776 holiday attacks of Trenton and Princeton. General George Washington, having faced defeat after defeat in the intervening months between the Ticonderoga march and Trenton, was backed against a wall. He needed a victory to show his soldiers, the colonists, Congress, and the world that the Revolution stood a fighting chance of success. Otherwise, all of their efforts would be for naught.

He developed an audacious plan to attack the British garrison in Trenton, New Jersey, on Christmas Day. Seemingly protected by the frigid Delaware River—the waterway was already bobbing with ice—those in the garrison no doubt felt safe for the time being. But Washington had other ideas. A surprise winter attack would involve complicated logistics, and a river crossing would add even more risk to the enterprise. Factor in a brewing winter storm, and the mission seemed to have little chance of success. But Washington knew he had an experienced winter traveler on his staff, so put Henry Knox in charge of managing the crossing of the army.

Making use of the famed Marblehead fishermen to help pilot the boats to be used in the crossing, Knox expertly supervised the loading and organization of men and equipment. In the pitch black (the army was crossing at midnight to avoid enemy detection), with snow and sleet pelting their faces, it could not have been an easy or pleasant task. "The night was as severe a night as ever I saw," remembered one soldier.[8] But Knox knew his work, and soldiered on.

Finally afloat, the sailors slowly worked their way across the river, threading and punching their way through the ice. Slowed considerably by the weather, the dark, and the ice, and already behind schedule, Washington and Knox knew there was no turning back. Did Knox remember crossing Lake George amid snowy conditions as he slowly traversed this new body of water? There can be little doubt that he did. One can only imagine the thoughts boiling in his head as he set forth with cannons on yet another winter march.

"[We] passed the river on Christmas night, with almost infinite difficulty, with eighteen field-pieces," Knox later wrote to Lucy about that night on the Delaware. "The floating ice in the river made the labor almost incredible. Perseverance accomplished what first seemed impossible," he elaborated. Indeed, pure stubbornness must have driven them, for by four a.m., the main body of the army had crossed the Delaware River.[9]

The episode was not without some humor. Washington is supposed to have used an empty beehive on the banks of the Delaware as a seat, passing his orders on to Knox, who, with his booming voice, would broadcast the commands loudly enough to be heard above the hubbub of the storm.[10] James Wilkinson later remembered the value of Knox's vocal cords. "The force of the current, the sharpness of the frost, the darkness of the night, the ice which [was] made during the operation, and a high wind, rendered the passage of the river extremely difficult, but for the stentorian lungs and extraordinary exertions of Colonel Knox."[11] A loud voice is a valuable trait.

Later, during the crossing itself, Washington supposedly noticed that Knox's weight was impacting the stability of his boat. "Shift your tail, Knox, and trim the boat," Washington allegedly called out, to much laughter.[12] Given all that Knox had done for Washington, it's likely that he said it with a smile on his face and affection in his voice.

Once across, the men regrouped and began their march on Trenton. A steep hill barred the way, and Knox used the lessons learned from dragging artillery over the Berkshires the previous winter to manhandle these cannons up the hill. "The challenge must have reminded Knox of the trip from Ticonderoga," writes one historian. The whole march toward Trenton is reminiscent of the Ticonderoga trek (in condensed form).[13]

The army reached Trenton shortly after daybreak. The battle itself was a fairly brief affair. The garrisoned British and Hessian soldiers, surprised—and perhaps a little hungover from Christmas festivities—put up a spirited albeit brief resistance. The artillery that Knox had struggled so mightily to get across the river proved to be a decisive factor in the attack. Positioning his cannons to sweep the streets of the town, the Hessians were prevented from making any sort of coordinated charge or stand. In the end, more than nine hundred Hessians were taken prisoner at the cost of four American dead and eight wounded (and two more frozen to death). It was a decisive victory, proving once again that Knox was a capable and clever artillerist and leader.

Knox would re-cross the Delaware, without issue and amid thickening ice, several more times in the coming days as the army continued its maneuvers and secured another victory in nearby Princeton. Even without news of his success in New Jersey, Knox's star in Congress continued to rise. On December 27, 1776 (before news of the victory had even reached Philadelphia), Knox was appointed brigadier general of the artillery of the Continental Army.[14]

My speedy descent off the unnamed hill just north of Route 4 in central Vermont gradually slows, and I finally turn onto a cross-country ski trail. I am now entering the Mountain Top Inn & Resort's trail network, the first of several resorts the Catamount Trail crosses. Although I enjoy the well-kept network, I'm more interested in whether or not I will find some hot food at the Rikert Nordic Center (the guidebook doesn't mention whether or not they provide this service).

The trail crosses a small dam where I'm forced to take my skis off and trudge. Then, dodging across a plowed road, I reenter the woods briefly. Finally, a field appears in front of me. Across it, the large buildings looming on the hillside tell me I've made it to the resort. Now, to find some grub! I skirt the edge of the forest and cross another paved road before spotting the ski lodge and rental building. Maybe they have coffee or muffins or some other delicacy inside.

Stripping my skis off (they decide to come off easily this time), I nod to a resort guest in the parking lot and clamber up the ramp to enter the building. After just six days in the woods, it already feels weird to be using something as civilized as a structure. But I also have this on-top-of-the-world feeling. I'm in the midst of doing something that the people I see around here would likely never dream of doing. I can't help but take on a slight swagger as I open the door and enter, blown back slightly by the power of the heat rushing out to greet me. I embrace it, and duck into the building with all of its warmth.

Standing in the dim light and letting my eyes adjust, I'm suddenly aware of the distinct odor emanating from my body and clothes. I feel the stickiness of days-old sweat on my skin, my clothes clinging to my body. But as my frost-nipped cheeks feel the warmth and I catch the aroma of food, I choose to ignore the effect I might be having on my neighbors. I need to put some fuel in this furnace.

I pass a red-hot woodstove and glove rack, and notice a comfortable-looking couch which has my name all over it. First things first. Not only is there a carafe of hot coffee on a nearby table, but the menu hanging from the wall tells me there's a short-order griddle. And the smiling cook behind the counter means I'm first in line.

"You're just the person I want to see," I tell her, grinning. "I'm hungry!"

"Good!" She smiles back. "What can I get for you?"

Not a picky eater on even the worst of days, I simply start at the top of the menu.

"Could I have a chicken club—and a tuna melt? Please? And a muffin while I'm waiting? And a cup of coffee? Please!" Then, spotting the asterisk at the bottom of the list, "And can you put bacon on both those?"

"Sure thing," she laughs. "Looks like you've worked up an appetite. Where have you been skiing?" she asks as she rings me up.

"I'm doing the Catamount Trail," I explain. "Started a week ago, and have made it this far on my way to Canada."

"You're making good time!" she says, impressed. "Let me get those sandwiches started for you."

"Do I talk to you about paying for passing through the resort?" I ask, as she starts to assemble ingredients. I plan on being conscientious about talking with any resorts or trail networks I travel through (especially if they have food like this one), but I hope they'll let me through gratis. The Catamount Trail passes through six or seven places like this one, and it could get a little pricey if they all decide to charge me for a day pass. It has always seemed to me to be good form on the part of these resorts to support thru-users with free passage. Even on trails like the Appalachian Trail, which sees thousands of hikers a year, most fee sites that the Trail passes through allow thru-hikers to enter for free, or at a significantly reduced price. At the very least, I've always thought, we're good advertising.

She apparently agrees with me. "You're just passing through?" she asks, and then, after my nod, tells me, "Then this one is on us."

"Thanks," I say. "Thanks a lot!"

I head toward the woodstove and settle into the couch. My quads and knees will be stiff later, but for now, I'm thankful for the warmth and softness.

Just as I settle in, a kid of perhaps six and what appears to be a teacher or instructor of some sort enter and sit in the chairs next to me.

"Let's see that finger," the instructor tells the child.

He dutifully takes off his glove and shows the finger to the instructor. "Do you think it's broken?" he asks, wiggling it around and flexing it with no apparent pain. Clearly the kid had vocalized some sort of pain outside and the instructor felt impelled to bring him inside to check it out, although it's obvious to all of us that he'll be fine.

"No, I don't think so. Maybe just sprained," the instructor says, hedging. She's faced with that age-old challenge of convincing the kid that he's fine while simultaneously not making light of his "injury."

"It reminds me of something I saw on TruTV," the kid says with pride. "A guy was break-dancing and dislocated his thumb."

I smile at the instructor in sympathy. Oh boy.

"Were you break-dancing while you were snowshoeing?" I ask the kid, who giggles at the image.

Then he suddenly turns reflective. "It may be tough for me to go on my iPad now," he says dismally. To that I can only shake my head. I'm only twenty-seven, but the phrase *Kids these days* passes through my head immediately.

My order is up and I make short work of it, wolfing down both sandwiches. Then, before I can think too much about it—my father always warned me against this as a child, when standing at the top of a cliff jump or starting a tough ski run: "Whatever you do, don't think about it; just do it!"—I pull my jacket back on and exit the building. With a full belly (and damp clothes, since everything defrosted indoors), I cross the remainder of the open field and reenter the woods.

Time to make some more miles.

Stopping by the woods on a snowy day.

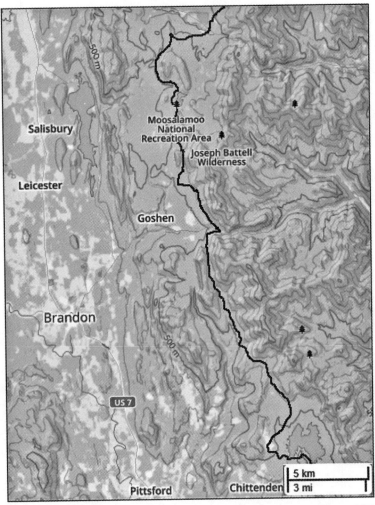

The Catamount Trail from Mountain Top Inn & Resort to Route 125

6. I Go to a Solitary and Painful Bed

Near the turnoff of the groomed trail and out of the Mountain Top Inn & Resort's trail system, I meet two men skiing in the other direction, with day packs on.

Spotting my own large backpack, one of them begins the conversation with "Are you Zach?"

"No," I tell him, "I'm Sam," with an obvious question in my eyes.

Laughing, he explains. "I probably should have introduced myself, or commented on the weather or something first. There's a kid named Zach who got in touch with the Catamount Trail organization. He's having trouble with a delaminated ski, and since we were heading out here, we were told to keep an eye out for him."

We chat some more. It turns out they are skiing for three days but stopping at inns and B&Bs each night. "The cushy way," describes the second one. They congratulate me on my progress thus far and wish me luck for the coming miles. Nice fellows, although one of them is wearing some sort of earmuff headpiece that I can't help but judge him a little bit for. Oh well. We all have our weaknesses, I guess. I myself have a tendency to overindulge in anything that's chocolate and coconutty, like Mounds bars or German chocolate cake. His just happens to be fuzzy in addition to decades out of fashion.

Knox had finished the final crossings of the Hudson River near Albany, but the river was not his only hurdle in the city. Before even leaving the town he was forced to renegotiate agreements with all of his wagon drivers. Since the journey was taking far longer than originally planned, they wanted more money, and they weren't going to move until Knox and General Schuyler promised it. A Mr. Palmer, who was a head wagon driver, met with Schuyler and proved to be a hard bargainer. Schuyler offered "18s. 9d. and Palmer asking 24s. per day for two yoke of oxen." (In layman's terms, Schuyler was offering 18 shillings and 9 pence (12 pence to a shilling) per day, while Palmer wanted 24 shillings per day.) Schuyler, apparently a tough negotiator himself, refused to waver, and so "the treaty broke off abruptly and Mr. Palmer was dismissed."[1] New wagon drivers would be needed.

At first glance, it would seem unpatriotic and miserly to be fighting over a couple of shillings when Washington was in need and the fate of the country was at stake. But we must remember that this was their livelihood. Surviving in the North Country in the eighteenth century required working a combination of jobs. These drivers were likely farmers, lumberjacks, potash makers, syrup producers, hunters, trappers, fishermen, and myriad other professions. They also would have taken on a variety of other odd jobs as needed and as were available. Few of these occupations paid well, and all were hard work (which still mostly holds true in the twenty-first century). The men who owned the draft animals knew that their well-being and perhaps very existence was tied to the success and health of their animals. A few extra shillings might mean healthier and more plentiful fodder for their animals, food for their own families, or other essential items. It was—and remains—incredibly challenging to eke out an existence in Upstate New York, and these men were simply trying to survive. Something similar is taught in search-and-rescue organizations today: Before even considering an attempt to help someone else, make sure that you yourself are safe and well taken care of.

Regardless, no agreement seems to have been reached between Palmer and Schuyler, so they had to comb the nearby countryside for new oxen and horse teams to replace those that were leaving. Becker notes the terms of the agreement upon leaving Albany. "We received drawings as such, one and four pence a mile, and when we were detained by breakages or other accidents, and laid by for repair, we received 15 shillings a day."[2] By the time Knox was leaving Albany, dozens of new teams had been hired on the new terms, and the caravan was able to move out with the cold snap.

Once past the final crossing of the Hudson River, new negotiations occurred, this time between wagoners. "Some of the party here bought out, from some of their friends," notes Becker, "the right, as they termed it, of carrying over the eighteen pounders." He doesn't state specifically whether an increase in pay was tied to the heavier cannons, but presumably there was. Or perhaps patriotism and bragging rights alone were enough incentive. Either way, "it was considered a good speculation," he noted.[3]

Before continuing south, Knox "got several spare slays [*sic*] [and] also some spare strings of horses, in case of any accident."[4] Through trial and error, misfortune and setback, Knox was learning lessons and taking precautions that would serve him well throughout the rest of the war.

Leaving the inn's boundaries, I rejoin a VAST trail and glide along smoothly. While the wide, graded, and well-packed trail is not an iconic backcountry ski trail, I enjoy my time on it just the same. It's exhilarating to make good steady progress with no obstacles or impediments. Parts of the Catamount Trail have already frustrated me with their incessant blowdowns and hard-to-spot blazes. It's a real pleasure to let my mind wander (you'd have to be blind to stray from a VAST trail) and simply put the miles behind me.

Naturally, Elizabeth enters my thoughts. While the sheer physicality of the Trail these past few days has left me less time to do much deep thinking, she perpetually hovers on the fringe of my consciousness. And today, the memory of her physicality takes over. She's a pert five-foot-seven and naturally buxom, with a trim, athletic build. When she's not taking the medical world by storm, she enters running races, her growing trove of trophies testifying to her ability to compete at a high level. It's not the trophies that turn my head (either now, or back in college); it's her mind, her laugh, her zest, and yes, her body. I miss her now—those winter nights when, curled up by the woodstove, I'd bury my face in her hair, inhaling the scent of her, the essence of her, the togetherness we felt. Alone in our house in the woods, firelight flickering across her face, and her heart slowly pumping next to mine. Her touch, her taste, the sensation of her skin beneath my fingertips. I can feel the —

I can feel the fact that these thoughts are getting me nowhere. At least, not here, not right now. I try to force the blood back to my numb fingertips from wherever it was headed, elevate my thoughts from the explicit to the darkening sky, and start to look for a campsite.

But the Trail begins to descend gently, and I start to gain speed. Looking ahead, I see that it grows more precipitous still. I continue to gain velocity and squint my eyes in an effort to see through the blowing snow and rushing air. The Trail here follows a sort of natural gully with sides higher than the middle. Small beeches and birches line the sides of the gully, their tops arching inward. To try to stop or turn off the trail now would be suicidal at the speed I'm moving, and the Trail itself is too packed down and icy for me to be able to stop.

Instead, I swerve from edge to edge, desperately trying to keep some semblance of control. To make matters worse, fist-size rocks dot the trail, kicked up from the ground beneath by passing snowmobiles. I feel like I'm right on the edge of disaster. Without question I've now lost the ability to stop. I whoop and holler the whole way—what a ride!

The Trail finally flattens out and I manage to eventually slide to a halt. It's a good thing no snowmobiles were heading toward me on that slope; I certainly wouldn't have been able to stop, and it would have been a tight squeeze to get around them. Ostensibly, I vow to myself not to do that again, but in the back of my mind, I know I'd repeat the performance given the chance. Moving that fast on just the precipice of catastrophe—it's ecstasy. The speed takes over, the danger just exhilarates, the potential consequences fade. I'm addicted. Addicted to risk, addicted to peril. God, it feels good.

Near the bottom the Trail comes to a junction with another VAST pathway. I ski off between the two forks into a low hollow near a small stream and set up shop for the night. This is my first night on trails used for something besides foot traffic, and I'm a little apprehensive that a curious snowmobiler might spot me and ask some questions. I'd rather not have that conversation. Snowmobilers and skiers have a long and uneven history of shared trail use, with skiers often stereotyping snowmobiles as simply loud, obnoxious polluters who don't respect nature, while from the other side, skiers are portrayed as tree-hugging elitists who are not only exclusionary and snobbish, but also a danger on the trail. The truth, as is typically the case in these kinds of debates, is somewhere in the middle. No individual fits all the stereotypes, and many buck them completely. But a freezing night in the middle of the woods seems an inopportune time to hold this type of debate, so as I set up camp, I make the conscious decision to try to avoid any interaction. Not surprisingly, as I set up my tent and stove behind a hummock, a dull rumble becomes a throatier roar, and a headlight appears on the trail far above me. I turn off my headlamp and let him pass before resuming my chores, intent on keeping a low profile.

Dinner is eaten at twilight, and by the time I crawl into my tent to write in my journal, it's dark. I want it this way. Over the last day or two, I've continued my experiment with rising earlier and stopping later, in an effort maximize my travel time during daylight hours. I've been finding that not only am I not particularly tired after only seven or eight hours on the trail, but time is hanging heavy on my hands. I seem to be sleeping fitfully (more than perhaps can be accounted for by my "two-sleep" intermission). When I crawl into my tent around six or six-thirty and don't get out until six-thirty or seven in the morning—well, that's a lot of time on my back (or side or stomach).

So, what to do?

I should ski more, seems to be the answer. For not only is time beginning to feel stifling in the tent, but I'm also feeling frustrated by the fact that I can only make progress during those eight hours of the day. In the summer one can hike from six a.m. until eight p.m. and have plenty of light to do it by. But with the sun rising after seven, I've been having a tough time getting on the trail much before eight, and when nightfall comes at five, I've been quitting at four or four-thirty to at least begin my evening duties in natural light. This just hasn't been cutting it; I've been feeling hampered and handcuffed. So today I stayed on the trail until nearly five p.m., and vow that I'll continue trying to get up earlier.

I have another good reason to get up a little earlier tomorrow: I'll be seeing Elizabeth. I talked with her briefly on the phone at Mountain Top Inn, where I had service, and confirmed our plans to meet tomorrow. She'll pick me up at the Route 125 crossing and we'll head into Middlebury, where we'll stay with my grandmother and enjoy a home-cooked meal, artificial heat by way of a furnace, and a warm, comfortable bed (not to mention a hot shower for me, desperately needed at this point). After a week of living in the snow, I couldn't be looking forward to it more, which of course doesn't help my sleep problem.

Knox, too, was missing his wife. During the Ticonderoga jour-ney, as they would throughout the war, the two of them kept up a lively correspondence. Knox sent Lucy periodic updates throughout, telling her about everything from the towns he was passing through to the challenges and delays of the journey. Knox even passed along lessons learned and musings on life. "It is, as I always said, misfortunes that must raise us to the character of a great people. One or two drubbings will be of service to us," he penned in 1776 upon the evacuation of New York, just months after having arrived in Cambridge with the cannons.[5] A surprisingly even-keeled and clear-minded judgment from one who had staked his life and livelihood on the revolutionary cause.

But it was not his maxims that Lucy looked for when she opened his letters. Knox always included tender sentiments and described a deep longing to be back with his Lucy. A love match when many marriages at the time were not, it is clear from Knox's writings that only the strongest sense of duty was keeping him from racing to her side. Good friend Nathanael Greene described the duo as "extravagantly fond of each other, and I think [they] are perfectly happy."[6]

This was a nontraditional couple in the eighteenth-century colonies in another way: Lucy was an outspoken young woman from a good Bostonian family, and she was not afraid to speak her mind. In an age when so many wives were overshadowed by their husbands' careers and lives, Lucy asserted her own right to a role in their life together. "Consider yourself a commander in chief of your own house, but be convinced . . . that there is such a thing as equal command," she reminded Knox in a letter in 1777, presumably in response to a missive of his that had crossed some line.[7] Lucy was not going to be some petticoat-ed ornament for Knox to show off. She would live her own life, too.

Years later, another friend remembered a humorous incident of disagreement between the two, and how it was resolved. "It was understood by [Knox and Lucy's] friends that their mutual attachment had never waned. It was, however, well known that they frequently differed in opinion upon the current trifles of the day," he began the reminiscence. Knox often deferred to his wife, the friend recalled, and "in those petty skirmishes . . . showed his generalship by a skilful retreat. On one occasion, at a very large dinner-party at their own house, the cloth having been removed, the General ordered the servants to take away also the woolen cover, which madam with an audible voice prohibited." No doubt all the guests waited with tensed muscles, hoping the awkwardness would smooth over or somehow disappear. Knox, true to form, both defused the situation and let his wife emerge victorious. "This subject of the under cloth," he announced to the company, "is the only one on which Mrs. Knox and I have differed since our marriage." The comment produced, as intended, "a general merriment."[8] Lucy would have her way. Husbands the world over might take a page from Knox's book in expert marital diplomacy.

Separated briefly before they were wed in 1774, Knox wrote a heartfelt note to Lucy. "Every particle of heat seems to be eradicated from the head or else entirely absorbed, in the widely ranging fire emitted from the heart," Knox effused. "To tell you how much I long to see you would be impossible—do, my good girl, let me hear from you some way or other."[9]

Upon enlistment, Knox had moved in with the army surrounding Boston in Cambridge, and Lucy stayed nearby in Watertown, Massachusetts. Writing him in the summer of 1774, she told Knox that he was "always in my thoughts, whose image is deeply imprinted on my heart . . . I love [you] too much for my peace." Knox, for his part, found his enlistment equally a challenge. "I wish to render my devoted country every service in my power," he affirmed to her. It was only the call of duty that "separates me from thee, the dear object of all my earthly happiness."[10]

I wake early, due both to my resolution and my excitement at seeing Elizabeth. Knox was longing for Lucy last night in his 1775 letters. I'm now experiencing pure longing this morning as I climb out of my sleeping bag. I love her—I'm *in* love with her—and more than anything, I just want to see her and hold her and give her a nice, long kiss. The simplicity of the feeling momentarily clarifies things in a way I've not experienced in a while, and lends a pep to my morning step. Not to mention that Route 125 and Middlebury will also more or less mark the halfway point of my journey, a milestone indeed.

But stepping outside the tent in the predawn darkness, I find I cannot fit my boots onto my feet. They are frozen rock-solid. Cursing softly, I crawl back into the tent with them and shiver in my sleeping bag as I hold them against my chest. After fifteen minutes they feel marginally softer, and I reemerge. It takes a lot of grunting and hopping about on one foot, but I finally manage to force them on, my toes going instantly numb. Already frustrated, I mutter to myself, "Screw breakfast," and simply pack up my tent and set off. It is already 7:30 by the time I hit the trail.

The VAST trail extends nearly all the way to Route 73, and I make good time. Skiing gradually warms up my feet, so by the time I walk across the pavement I can sense most of my toes. "Don't need all ten toes anyways," I chuckle to myself, my mood having risen as the sun and exercise warmed me. "Losing one or two won't hurt." But I make a mental note to myself to check the weather when I get to Gigi's. Every day seems to bring colder and colder weather.

Past 73, the trail reverts to a backcountry track, but, to my surprise and pleasure, I am following fresh tracks. An early riser seems to have pioneered this section while I was sparring with my frozen boots. Pulling hard now, I vow to myself to catch up to them before I reach Blueberry Hill Inn and the next cross-country ski trail network.

The trail descends gradually through a hodgepodge of hardwood trees, gullies, and several stone walls. The sun has warmed things up enough that I shed a jacket after I take a quick snack break. Then, as I round a corner, I spot a figure out in front of me. He is trudging along slowly, and as I close in on him, I holler out a greeting. It's always best to announce oneself from afar, I've found, so as to minimize the chance of startling someone. It's surprising how easy it is to sneak up on someone in the woods.

"Oh, hi," he responds. Clearly struggling, he is merely plodding along, going through the motions. I don't chat for long—he is clearly not interested in conversation—but I stay long enough for him to tell me that his fiancée is out in front of him somewhere.

"Good thinking," I tell him. "Give her all the hard work of breaking trail." He doesn't think I'm funny, so I hurry on past.

Sure enough, fifteen minutes later I catch up to her. She is moving slightly quicker than her fiancé, but is also clearly struggling to negotiate the twisting and narrow trail. She attacks it with an entirely different temperament, however. When she hears me approach she turns and looks at me with the wide-eyed innocence of a five-year-old.

"Where are you coming from?" she asks.

"Massachusetts," I tell her. "Thanks for breaking trail."

Her eyes go wider, big as silver dollars now, and her voice takes on the tremulous wonderment one normally reserves for far more miraculous circumstances than a thru-skier like myself who has been skiing for just a week.

"An end-to-ender! Wow!" She draws out the *Wow* as she mulls over what I've done. Then, before I can say anything, she starts off on a rushed, jumbled soliloquy about her own trip.

"I'm doing it in sections," she begins. "I've only got four more to go, then I'm done. I hope I don't get sixty-nine."

I must look a little confused because she shakes her head a trifle, piqued at my ignorance, and then unnecessarily explains the juvenile humor.

"You know, sixty-ninth on the end-to-ender list. You know, because, well, it's sixty-nine. My friend's a schoolteacher and she just finished last year, the last to do it, and she got sixty-seven, and she said it was a good thing, because being a teacher, she just couldn't get sixty-nine." She giggles sophomorically at her repeated reference to the sexual position, then takes a breath.

Quickly, before she can begin to launch into another asinine monologue, I extricate myself.

"Perhaps I'll see you at the inn," I say. We're within a couple of miles of it now.

"Yes," she marvels. "We dropped a car there. *He's an end-to-ender!*" This last, yelled to her fiancé, who by now is standing right next to her. He winces and nods, clearly not hard of hearing, but perhaps well on his way.

I politely say my good-byes and ski off.

"Try the soup," she yells after me. "It's really good!"

I wave my hand in acknowledgment and ski on.

No wonder the fiancé was way back there, I think. He must be a saint. I'm sure she's a wonderful woman, but that was a hell of a way to begin a conversation with a stranger.

I enter the Blueberry Hill Inn trail network by crossing a narrow, rutted dirt road, passing by a wooden hand-routed sign that reads PARALLEL PARKING ONLY. (Only in Vermont, I reflect.)

I hear a low whistle in front of me. Soon after, a dog bounds out of the woods just to my rear. He jumps out of the deep snow and onto the packed-down cross-country track and then begins to bark at me as he runs back and forth across the tails of my skis.

I don't speak dog very well but his request is obvious. He's barking "Track!" at me, telling me to step aside for the faster traveler.

"Nice try, bud," I tell him over my shoulder. "I only step aside for humans."

He barks some more, then gives up and races around me through the deeper snow. Once back in the track, now to my front, he turns and faces me to bark some more as if to scold me for not following common ski trail courtesy. I make a face at him. After a moment, his righteousness affirmed, he bounds ahead to his owners. The audacity!

I reach the open fields surrounding the inn just before noon. Blueberry Hill Inn is the definition of a picturesque Vermont B&B. Set in the hills of the Green Mountains and facing Lake Champlain, it's truly an idyllic setting. Maintaining their own network of ski trails in the winter, there is also snowshoeing, skating, and a sauna. I smile as I near the buildings—Elizabeth and I stayed here a year ago last December, in 2013, hoping to be able to ski, but the weather didn't cooperate. We were two of only four people at the inn.

I remember pulling in and turning the car off. As we sat in the small parking lot with the rain drumming on the roof of the car, I turned and looked at Elizabeth, sitting next to me. She smiled back, happily, and I knew that, despite the weather and lack of snow, despite the apparently dismal conditions and dreary appearance, we were going to have a wonderful time.

And we did.

We got soaking wet on a walk through the woods. As we came out from the trees and saw Lake Champlain dimly through the rain and mist, Elizabeth asked me, "You know the best part of Vermont?"

It's an old joke between us, and I answered for her, "The view of the Adirondacks."

She grew up across the lake on the New York side, in the foothills of those same mountains. We have both come to love Vermont during our time together here, but she still likes to tease me that New York is better.

After a hot shower and some time in the sauna, we enjoyed a couple of beers in what I can only describe as a greenhouse.

That evening we ate a picnic dinner spread out on our bed. Hoping for nicer weather, we had planned on enjoying it outside somewhere, but with the rain still coming down, there was no chance of that. Being indoors didn't stop us from enjoying sausage and cheese on a variety of crackers and bread, along with several different spreads and various fruits. Warm and sated, we lounged in our room and just enjoyed being together. My heart is full with that memory as I approach the inn now, several years later.

Instead of going right to the main building, I head toward their outdoor center. Stepping inside, I'm blasted by heat. For the second time in two days I'm able to strip off most of my layers, this time spreading them out to dry. Route 125 is only seven miles away, and I promised Elizabeth I wouldn't arrive too early. She wants to ski back toward me and meet me in the woods, so I take some time to relax first.

Grabbing a couple of cookies from the assortment of refreshments on offer, I sit back in a chair. It's Saturday, and NPR's *Wait Wait . . . Don't Tell Me* is playing softly on a radio nearby. I sip a cup of coffee, munch on the chocolate-chippers, and periodically inch closer to the crackling woodstove to better absorb its heat. Soon my clothes are dripping on the floor, and what now seems to be my permanent odor is wafting through the air. I don't care. It feels good in here.

It doesn't seem to be a busy day at the inn. An occasional skier pokes his nose in and nods at me, but for the most part, I'm left to my own devices. Chuckling occasionally as the wags on the radio go through their routine, I try the bowl of soup that was recommended to me. It's as good as advertised.

An employee stops in and we chat briefly. She is quickly followed by the betrothed couple I met on the trail. As the woman enters she is mid-sentence, talking a mile a minute. Her fiancé follows, and for their entire time in the hut, he doesn't speak a word. It's clear who is in charge. She offers me a place to stay when I make it up to Stowe.

"You will probably want a chance to dry out and warm up again when you get there. We can also make sure you get to the grocery store and wherever you need to go. We've got plenty of room," she assures me as she hands me her phone number. "Just call when you get close." It's a kind offer to make to a stranger, and I begin to rethink my initial impression.

They leave eventually and the center returns to silence. I begin to get antsy, so after a second bowl of soup and another cookie, I start to re-don my gear. My inner thighs have begun to chafe, so I smear some ChapStick on them in hopes that it contains enough petroleum jelly to help with the friction. I feel a little goofy, but it's all I've got.

Leaving the inn, the trail meanders gently along the edge of a road before weaving its way through some foothills toward Route 125 and Middlebury College's Bread Loaf campus. Excited to see Elizabeth (and to spend the night indoors), I continue at pace over the gradual trail. It's well tracked out and I am making excellent time as I reach the fields abutting the road. Looking across their windswept expanse, I spot a small figure in the distance, skiing toward me. I would recognize her graceful form and pumping arms anywhere: Elizabeth!

Knox, too, was moving along with relative ease in 1776. After the challenge of crossing Lake George in overloaded boats amid stormy weather, negotiating the Hudson and Mohawk Rivers with multiple crossings on thin ice, and frustrating delays due to warm weather, he was finally making progress. Neither sinking boats nor submerged cannons would stop him now.

This didn't mean there weren't any more delays, however. During the final crossing of the Hudson, one cannon-laden sleigh ran into trouble. "A tongue of one of the sleds, which was loaded with a smaller gun, struck and perforated the side of a very handsome pleasure boat," wrote John Becker. "[It] made a breach in it of rather a ruinous character. The driver seemed to have no alternative but to keep moving; he drove fairly over it, and the boat was made a complete wreck."[11]

There was not much Becker or Knox could offer the boat's owner in the way of consolation or repayment. "The idea that congress [*sic*] would pay all the damages was the only sympathy that we had then time to bestow on the owner. Whether congress responded to the sentiments of our corps we never learned."[12] Given the financial struggles of the fledgling government to simply pay and outfit the army, it seems unlikely that the boat's owner was ever reimbursed.

Knox was traveling with the caravan again, "first [seeing] all the Cannon set out from the ferry opposite Albany," before moving ahead to Claverack, no doubt to scout the road and look for provisions and lodging.[13] Without question he was thrilled to be finally traveling smoothly, without the Hudson barring his way.

Soon, however, Becker and the wagon train were once again delayed. "We made the best of our way to Claverack," he wrote, "and there the breaking down of a sleigh detained us two whole days. The dependence we were under to each other for assistance, in case of accident, made it necessary for us to move in a body."[14] It was a logical and reasonable modus operandi. Knox had clearly learned another lesson about mutual support, even if it did ensure that the train moved at the rate of its slowest common denominator.

With the lake and the river crossings behind him, Knox had surmounted some of the largest obstacles of the trip. Now, however, as he and the caravan prepared to leave New York and enter Massachusetts, they were facing a new challenge. Claverack is nestled in the foothills of the Berkshires, marking the start of the taller peaks—the next impediment to tax Knox's abilities.

As Knox crossed the Massachusetts border, his thoughts must have increasingly dwelt upon his wife. Pregnant with their first child, she was waiting for him in Worcester. The baby was due at the end of February, and he must have felt the need to be by her side. Later in life, Knox would write Lucy a letter detailing similar emotions to what he was likely feeling now. "[I] go to a solitary and painful bed—painful from the reflection that the companion of my soul is at a distance and that I am deprived of the blessed solace of her arms."[15]

After a week of solitary nights, I take Elizabeth into my arms with a bone-crushing hug and plant a sloppy kiss on her lips.

She pulls back slightly and looks me full in the face. "I missed you! A lot!" She's grinning widely at the joy of the reunion, love shining in her glistening eyes as she comes in for another kiss.

"I did too. An awful lot," I finally tell her, our mouths finally separating but our arms still around each other, the vapor from our breath mingling between us. "It feels good to put my arms around you and feel you in the flesh!"

She looks me over, then exclaims worriedly, "Your face—it's so red and dry."

"Well," I answer, "it's cold out here." I smile to let her know I'm fine.

"You poor thing," she empathizes, taking my cheek in her gloved hand. "Let's get you inside and warmed up."

Then, sensing that things have gotten too saccharine, she reverts to our old teasing ways. Donning an expression of mock accusation that would make an old-timey stage actor proud, she teasingly glares at me. "I knew you'd be early! We agreed not to meet until four!" Then, the ultimate accusation, "You ruined my workout!" She had been planning on skiing several miles south on the trail toward me.

She's kidding, of course. What she's really telling me is that she loves me and she's happy to see me.

"Well, you go on out for a ski," I tell her jokingly. "I'll just go sit in the car with the heat on high and wait. Don't worry about me."

She lets out the peal of laughter I know so well and love so much. We both know she has no intention of going anywhere as she comes in for another kiss.

"I'll have to get my workout some other way," she whispers when we break apart once more, giving me a wink.

"Yes, ma'am," I tell her. "It would be my pleasure."

We turn back and ski across the fields toward the parking lot. Elizabeth and I live less than an hour away to the east, so it was an easy trip for her to get here. We chat the whole way, Elizabeth updating me on her past week, me, telling her about my recent adventures. It's nice just to be near her.

After we climb into the car, she turns it on but doesn't shift out of PARK. Taking my hand, she whispers, "I'm glad you're safe. I've been worried about you."

"Oh, I've been okay," I reassure her. "I'm being careful and staying warm."

Which is mostly true, I think, remembering my careen down the steep trail and recent fights to maintain circulation in my toes in the mornings.

"Good," she says. "And I love you. A lot."

"It's really good to see you," I tell her. "Thanks for coming to get me. And I love you too. A lot!"

It's true. Looking at the side of her face as she pulls out of the parking lot, I'm overwhelmed by how lucky I am—to have a beautiful woman in my life who cares for me, who watches out for me and picks me up at a cold, snowy trailhead. I can't help but love this woman who is filled with such empathy and consideration, and who understands me, and my need to be out in these wintry woods. When I've lain awake these past few nights, between bouts of sleep, my thoughts have often turned to her. Every night I've wished that she was lying there by my side, keeping me warm, both physically and emotionally. Somehow, in the middle of the woods in the middle of the night, with dark trees looming overhead, snow falling softly around me, and the cold seeping into every crack and crevice of my body, it seems awfully tough to imagine a rewarding and fulfilling life without her love and support.

I take her hand as we drive toward Middlebury. She gives it a squeeze and flashes me a quick grin.

"I love you," I tell her again.

Pulling into Gigi's driveway, I am unsurprised to find it, and the nearby roadside, full of cars. Elizabeth turns to me with an inquiring glance.

"Didn't know that we were having a get-together," she said. "I thought this was going to be just the three of us."

"You know Gigi," I remind her. "Any excuse for a party."

We walk up to the front door, me still slightly bowlegged as I try to minimize the chafing on my thighs, and enter into a symphony of warmth, hubbub, and delicious smells.

A chorus greets us.

"There they are!"

"Sam! You're still alive!"

"Got all your digits?"

"Looking awfully skinny, Sam—better make sure you eat a lot tonight."

Uncles, aunts, and cousins are within, laughing and chatting. I wave my hello to all and then make a quick escape to the finished basement. I desperately need a shower before I can be considered even remotely presentable. Elizabeth can fend for herself among my rambunctious relatives.

It feels wondrous. Hot water streaming down my face. My back itches from the heat, and ecstatically, I scratch long and hard. The water burns my face and seems to scald my feet, but I don't even consider going near the knob. What a pleasure.

As I dress in the clean, cotton clothes Elizabeth has brought for me, I'm startled to find that my feet don't work very well. The sudden warmth and softening have made them very sensitive, and I hobble around the basement as I spread out all my gear—sleeping bag, tent, clothes, backpack, and the rest of it—across furniture and hanging from exposed pipes to dry. An examination reveals several blisters on the bottoms of my toes and one on a heel, but none are large. My feet are just tired.

Back upstairs, dinner is about to be served. A large pot of steaming pasta, homemade meatballs and sauce, a large salad, and fresh bread are all spread on the kitchen counter. I find Elizabeth and follow her through the buffet, heaping my plate high. Then we turn to the long table in the dining room and sit down.

For as long as I can remember, meals have been a central part of a visit to my grandmother's. As a family, we traveled from our home in Massachusetts several times a year for a visit. Inevitably, as is now the case, there was always a big crowd. While my father strayed slightly from the nest and settled outside of Boston, many of his brothers stayed in or near Middlebury, where they still live with their families. So gathering a group together for a meal has never been hard.

As a youngster, my cousins and I were always put at the "kids' end" of the table. There, we could chatter to our hearts' content while munching on steak, pork, or whatever other delicacy was being served.

We'd kick each other under the table, see how long we could hold a finger in the flame of a candle, and put hot wax in our hands just to feel the slight burn. Giggling and goofing off, we loved it. Then, after formally asking Gigi, "May I please be excused," one by one we'd race off to the basement to play billiards, tag, or Ghost in the Graveyard, or we'd all watch a movie together. With anywhere from two to ten other cousins all near the same age at any given gathering, it was a child's dream.

Now, I have no interest in being excused (although I do step away for a couple of minutes to answer the landline and talk to my father; he's abroad for business, but remembered to check in on me while I'm here). My aunts and uncles are too much fun, and I wouldn't dream of leaving the table. As I scrape up the remnants of sauce with my last crust of bread, I'm chuckling hard enough that it's tough to chew. All of my uncles are excellent raconteurs, but Uncle Dave is in a class of his own. A master of sound effects and facial expressions, he's narrating something about a tractor and a chicken that happened to him the other day. Choking down the last of my dinner, I sit back and laugh uproariously along with the rest of the table as the tale comes to a climax.

And suddenly, I'm reminded. I look around the room, at everyone who is here, and think *If I go to Utah, I'm going to miss them.* I'm going to miss my family. Utah is awfully far away.

It's a sobering thought, and I can feel the heartache already.

As if sensing my seriousness, Uncle Dave turns to me.

"It's been cold out there. Your gear is warm enough?"

"Oh, I've been fine," I tell him, smiling. I don't want anyone to be worried.

"Well, temps have been hovering around zero the last couple of nights, and it's supposed to get colder. Negative digits tonight, and negative teens tomorrow," he warns me. That's news to me; I wasn't aware that it had been that cold, or that it was going to get even colder.

"I think you should stay here for an extra night or two," he says. "Let this pass through. It's dangerous." He's not making faces or sound effects; in fact, he looks more worried than I've ever seen him before.

Surprised but not alarmed, I try to reassure him.

"I'm prepared. I've got warm clothes and gloves. My boots are good. My sleeping bag is excellent. I'll be okay."

"Well," he said, "just consider it, for my sake. I don't want you to get into trouble. These temperatures are not something to mess around with. Besides," he lightens his tone, "the Super Bowl is tomorrow night. That's a good excuse—you don't want to miss that!"

I laugh. "No, I wouldn't want to miss that . . ."

But I know I won't be sleeping here a second night, nor watching the Super Bowl. Cold or no cold, I have miles to make.

Elizabeth and I stay up until nine p.m. before I finally wish everyone a good night. It feels like midnight after my early nights over the past week.

After brushing our teeth, we crawl into bed in the basement, dodging the hanging gear throughout. As I fall asleep I wrinkle my nose. It smells like well-marinated week-old roadkill down here.

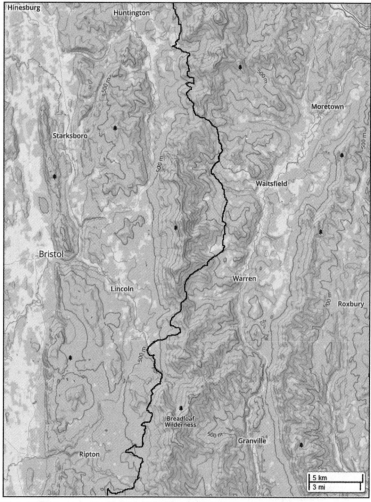

The Catamount Trail from Route 125 to Camel's Hump Road

7. All the Kingdoms of the Earth

The basement of Gigi's house is perhaps my favorite place to sleep in the world. It's cool, quiet, and absolutely pitch dark. I am traditionally an early riser, except when I'm in her basement. There, with no windows or doors to the outside to announce the sun, even my early-rising gene takes the morning off and I'm able to sleep to the ripe old hour of eight, or sometimes even eight-thirty. It's a real luxury.

True to form, I stumble up the stairs near eight a.m. and blink rapidly as my eyes adjust to the morning light. I've followed the smell of sizzling meat up to the first floor, probably what brought me to wakefulness. There's nothing like the smell of fresh-cooked bacon and eggs in the morning, especially when it's made by your grandmother. I think of Knox's sense of home and family, built around a particular place. I feel it now as I embrace Gigi in her kitchen and wish her good morning before joining Elizabeth, already at the table.

The eggs and bacon are complemented by homemade muffins, sticky buns, fresh blueberries, yogurt, and orange juice. Elizabeth and I agree that it's a feast. But, alas, all good things must come to an end, and we eventually have to hit the road. It's time to go skiing again.

Gigi doesn't appear to have the same worries as Uncle Dave, although I am also confident that she doesn't quite appreciate all the nuts and bolts of a long-distance winter sojourn like this one. Or perhaps she has more faith in me. She just shakes her head dubiously as we leave.

"Well, are you having fun, honey?" she asks.

I assure her that I am, and that seems to be enough for her. Which, after all, should be enough for anyone. If you're not having fun, just what the hell are you doing?

Of course, this often seems to qualify as Type 2 fun on the Brakeley Fun Scale. Whereas Type 1 fun is when you enjoy yourself both while you're doing it as well as later on when you remember and recount it (beach party or wedding), Type 2 fun is where it might not be that enjoyable during the event, but it's still fun to talk about afterward (think, roller coasters or scary movies, or things like the Catamount Trail—tests of physical endurance that may cause pain and exhaustion while doing them, but you're proud of accomplishing after the fact). Type 3 fun is when something is neither fun during nor after the event (maybe the hike you went on with your family with the allegedly stupendous view at the top but it downpoured the whole time and you had to turn around halfway up because of Great Aunt Sally, who had to be carried out).

What is it about expeditions like this one that have always compelled those with a certain temperament, like mine? Especially in this day and age, when our whole planet has already been explored and mapped, and I could probably see the Catamount Trail live via a Google Earth satellite from my desk, without risking my life.

I think about Knox, who, without a new nation and the lives of so many countrymen and -women in the balance, would likely never have volunteered to be out here. Let alone call it "fun." But he lived in a different time, and nowadays, these kinds of endurance expeditions continue to call to more and more people. In fact, for some of us, the luxurious comforts of modern life only push us harder to escape them. I think it's because those of us who are lucky enough to be drawn to wilderness adventure (and have the resources to acquire the skills and gear to venture on them) have a deeply human desire to discover who we truly are, deep down inside, by testing our resilience.

Every adventurer—be it rock climber, alpinist, long-distance hiker or paddler or skier or swimmer or whomever—knows the same thrill that I do when I push my body to its outermost limits. The thrill of living as close to the edge as possible in a merciless and relentless environment that is unfeeling and all-powerful. Testing our wits and our ability to survive, and even thrive, in extreme and perilous situations. We're reaffirming our capacity for achievement, not only physically but mentally as well, and reveling in the feeling of not only mere existence, but success amid discomfort and deprivation.

And so while it may not be the same type of fun as drinking beer and watching the Super Bowl, there is no way that I'm taking an extra night in town. I need to be back in the woods, no matter the conditions.

It doesn't take long to drive back up to the Catamount Trail. We stop in briefly at the Rikert Nordic Center. In answer to my query about whether we have to pay, the attendant behind the counter waves his hand dismissively.

"You're skiing through? Enjoy!" he says, then pulls out a map. "The trail winds back and forth through here a bit. If you take this trail here"—he points to a spot—"you'll save some time. It's much shorter."

I just smile. "I'm not in any hurry."

Elizabeth has brought her skis and will join me for the first couple of miles before turning back for the car.

As we enter the woods, I think back to one of our first dates, also in the cold and snow.

We were freshmen in college, and one weekend decided to go hiking. Selecting a peak called Mount Moxie—as much for its name as anything else—we set off. The parking lot was mostly bare, but as we gained in elevation, the snow got deeper. It was covered in a thick crust, just strong enough to hold our weight. Some of the time. Just when we felt like we were getting the hang of it, we'd punch through and sink in up to our knees.

It was incredibly frustrating. And tiring. Yet Elizabeth seemed surprisingly even-keeled. As I got madder and madder at the conditions, she just kept pushing along. Not wanting to call off the hike before we got to the top, I trudged along, too, all the while fuming inside. It was easily one of our worst dates. We still occasionally talk about it, and I laughingly remind Elizabeth of it now.

"Yeah, you were not happy," she recalls. "It's amazing I stayed with you after that. Who knew I'd fall for a grumpy old man."

She's eight months younger than I am and rarely lets me forget it.

"Not anymore," I tell her. "I'm the picture of optimism now."

She snorts in disbelief. "Yeah, right!"

"Listen to this," I say, and begin to tell her about the silly morning routine I've established. "The last couple of nights it has snowed at least a bit overnight. So, as I crawl out of the tent, it all falls off as I bump it. I like to take on a British accent and narrate my exit each morning. Something like, 'The recently hibernating yeti now emerges from its wintry lair. Hungry after a long winter's nap, it peers around for prey.' What do you think? Pretty good, right?"

She shakes her head. "You're crazy. If anyone heard you, they'd lock you up."

It's nice to have someone to talk to.

We eventually lapse into silence and I study her technique. She has a quicker, more up-tempo pace than I do (my heavy pack accounts for this, of course). She also manages to not get off balance at all; while I occasionally overbalance and need to wave an arm or shoot out a leg to maintain equilibrium, she seems to always stay centered over her legs. Without question, she looks far more graceful than I. Something to strive for.

The Trail follows the cross-country trail system briefly before breaking off. Then it meanders over and around low hills and eskers, crossing wet marshy spots and dry alike. The sun is shining through the bare beech and maple branches, but only manages to give the illusion of warmth.

Finally we come out onto a snowmobile trail. It's nearly eleven a.m., and Elizabeth turns around here.

"Well, I guess this is good-bye," I say.

"Oh, knock it off," she responds. "Don't get sappy. I'll see you in a week!" This is one of the reasons why I love her: her solid common sense.

I laugh and agree. We share a good-bye kiss and I watch her ski back the way we came, picking up speed now that she doesn't have my lumbering form holding her back. It's a beautiful thing to see.

Alone, I turn down the snowmobile trail and come to the Natural Turnpike. A wide road that is clearly used often by snowmobiles, it takes advantage of a natural cleft in the mountains to wend its way between two cliffs. The road's width and gentle grade belie the towering ridges nearby, and I crane my neck upward as I pass through, amazed. The sun is shining and no breeze ruffles my hair. Something about the stillness and silence around me amid the soaring heights on either side triggers an inner nerve ending. It's the visual equivalent of eating chocolate—that utter and overwhelming sensory pleasure as it melts across one's tongue—and I revel in it as I ski through the notch. While Vermont doesn't have quite the iconic formations or vast landscapes of, say, the Grand Tetons or the Grand Canyon, it does feature geology that's just as intriguing, in its own way; you just have to look a little closer.

The remainder of the afternoon is spent crossing fields and following woods roads in between dodging a house or two. I enjoy a quick descent through some young trees before reaching South Lincoln Road. Here, I get a little turned around. I try first one possibility then another, but can't seem to find where the Trail starts on the east side of the road. A field a hundred yards wide separates the street from the nearest trees upon which to put a blaze, and no blue stands out against the gray background to beckon me onward. After two false starts down tempting woods roads, I give up and spend a half-mile on the road, walking around to where the Trail crosses Masterson Road.

Back on the Trail, I continue to make my slow way through the ten inches of fresh snow on the ground. I pass an abandoned cabin, quickly losing myself in a daydream about its history and potential malevolent inner goings-on, which I manufacture out of whole cloth. Could a family of cannibals have lived here? Or perhaps this was the site of a gruesome kidnapping and murder. Who knows! Few things are as inherently creepy as a broken-down, abandoned structure when you're alone in the woods.

Finally coming out onto the main road over Lincoln Gap around 3:30 p.m., I opt to spend the night on this side of the mountains. I'm breaking my own rule of when to stop, but it's a long slog up this side, and according to the map, a longer slog down the other, and I'm conscious of trying to find water.

I head off-trail to my left and settle in for the night near the head of a small stream located in a beech sapling grove. The wind is not insignificant—another justification for halting before climbing too high—and I huddle behind a hummock as I cook rice and potatoes for dinner. It's not the spaghetti and homemade sauce of last night, but the warmth does my stomach good.

Snuggling into my sleeping bag, I enjoy for the first time in several days its dry warmth. The condensation and moisture have been building up steadily, causing it to stick together and making it difficult to unfurl. Each night my sweat and breath combine with moisture built up from my body heat, melting the snow around me. This is all absorbed by the bag, causing it to become damper and damper each night I spend on the trail. The night before last felt almost untenable. But, after a night drying out in the warmth of Gigi's house, all is downy and fluffy again. What luxury!

And good timing, for it's gotten colder. I write in my journal in short spurts, my hands and pen inches from my face. After a few sentences, I shove my hands deep down into my crotch to warm some life into them, then back up for a few more sentences, and back down between my legs. My upper thighs are unimpressed with this routine, but it's the only way to maintain feeling in my fingers.

Finished, I lie quietly, listening to the wind whisper through the branches overhead. Snow drifts up against the side of the tent, murmuring as it passes over the fabric. Everything else is silent.

I think about what I've written, of the two imagined scenes I've just described in my journal. In one, my uncles and aunts are together, watching the Super Bowl and laughing and joking as they pass the guacamole around. And in the other, Elizabeth is over at a friend's for the evening, watching the big game herself. Later, she returns to our empty house and settles down for the night alone.

"What do you want?" the wind and snow seem to be whispering to me, just outside the tent flap. I slip into sleep with the refrain echoing in my head. *What do you want? What do you want?* I wish I was closer to answering.

The next morning, I skip breakfast. There's a cold wind blowing through my camp, and I simply can't bear the thought of shivering here while waiting for the oatmeal to cook. Instead, I gear up and start the climb to Lincoln Gap. A steady gradient, it nonetheless flies by. Unplowed roads are my meat and potatoes now, and the climb warms me up. (Uncle Dave will tell me later that it dropped to fifteen below last night, not including wind chill.)

Last night's temperatures remind me of another of the first trips that Elizabeth and I took together. It was the spring of our freshman year, 2007, and we had just begun dating. We decided to traverse New England on a road trip, stopping along the way to hike and explore. It would also serve as an introduction to family and friends, as we planned to stop at each other's childhood homes.

We decided to camp out the first night. It was March in New Hampshire, and while the days were sunny and warm, the nights remained cold and snow still peppered the ground. We set up our tent, ate dinner, and crawled in. Elizabeth, already far more experienced in these matters, had brought her warmest sleeping bag. I, noticing the sunshine and not thinking about the chill of nightfall, had my summer-weight bag with me. Elizabeth, of course, had warned against this, but I thought I knew better. I shivered all night long and woke stiff and sore, my muscles knotted and eyes baggy. It was my first realization that perhaps I should pay more attention to Elizabeth; she clearly knew more than me, and would teach me and look out for me, if only I would let her.

Now, on the Trail, the blazes turn me north from the top of Lincoln Gap. I pause and look back over my progress. The road cut allows a narrow view through the trees, and I can faintly see the nearby Champlain Valley between blowing clouds of snow and fog. Up this high, it's pretty—but also brutally cold. I quickly begin to shiver and so continue onward.

I reenter the thick trees along the side of Mount Abraham. My pace slows considerably as I navigate steep gullies, narrow openings, and deep snow. Struggling with the obstacles keeps the blood flowing. Most of my body remains warm, but I occasionally have to beat my hands together to restore circulation to my fingertips.

With trees creaking and groaning around me, I finally begin to descend. I enjoy a couple of nice turns (albeit frigidly cold ones—on days like this, it's nice to be going uphill). Then I ski out onto a road and walk to the fifth hole of the Sugarbush Resort Golf Club. Here I find a small lightning shelter where I pause to cook some breakfast. It's not really protected from the breeze whipping across the open fairways, but at least it's out of the snow. I shiver and swing my arms and wait for the water to boil, wondering just what the hell I am doing out in weather as cold as this, on a freaking golf course, of all places.

Knox, too, was facing cold weather and steep hills as he continued on, turning westward from Claverack. The Berkshires (as the
Appalachian Mountains in Massachusetts are called) now faced him,
mountains running the height of the state. Before his caravan reached
their base, Knox went on ahead and climbed one of the taller peaks,
hoping both to scout the way through as well as perhaps spot his
own "noble train" with this bird's-eye view. "We might almost have
seen all the Kingdoms of the Earth," he wrote upon his return from
the adventure.[1]

There is some disagreement among historians as to the exact route
they took through the mountains. It is at this part of the journey that
the contemporary records and journals start to dry up and historians
have been forced to do a little extrapolation, drawing their own conclusions. As Bernard Drew points out, "There is no contemporary
account from any South Berkshire source as to Knox or the noble
train of artillery passing through. It was winter. People stayed indoors.
The Patriots didn't announce their intentions, fearful of Tory treachery. They were in a hurry. Some of the crew may have lingered for a
meal or night's rest . . . but there's no record."[2] Knox himself simply
states that they "went 12 miles thro' the Green Woods to Blanford,"
but doesn't describe the road they took, if any.[3]

North Callahan argues that the men forced their way through
untracked woods. "Here was difficulty almost unequaled on the
whole trip. The present inhabitants insist that there never was a road
here, and that it would be utterly impossible for a road ever to have
been in such an ominous confusion of mountains, precipices, chasms
and deep valleys which were interspersed with rivers, lakes and dank
swamps."[4] A picturesque description, but certainly terrain that would
be incredibly challenging for a cannon-laden wagon.

Drew disagrees, however. He states that there had been a road there for decades, wide enough to permit wagon travel, and offers ample contemporary accounts of other travelers to back up the assertion. In fact, he argues with evidence, General Jeffrey Amherst improved the road in 1758, enough to move an army across it during the French and Indian War.[5] Knox took advantage of this road, whatever its condition, as he moved through the region in 1776.

For the second time in as many days, I am a little turned around. After leaving the lightning shelter on the golf course, I traverse across the fifth hole and onto the sixth before reaching a wide-open expanse of white. Windswept snow covers the fairways and greens. Trees and other potential blaze-holders all fell long ago to the course builders' chain saws and bulldozers, so I am facing a blank panorama of gray and ivory snow. Where the Trail goes is anyone's guess.

Uncertainty on the trail is one of the many blessings of tripping. It's why I leave so much of the planning up in the air. Where will I camp tonight? What is the trail like up ahead? Will I be able to get into town to resupply? That's the joy of following a trail: not knowing what's coming, what the next bend will bring. But not even knowing the location of the next bend just annoys me. I'm a little frustrated as I scan my surroundings, looking for any hint of blue blaze.

I make my way downhill, angling across the open space and fall line while staying uphill of the clubhouse and associated buildings. Blundering blindly ahead, I finally spot a blaze on a distant tree. However, a stream splits the hole in two. This being a golf course, a small bridge crosses it to permit golfers and golf carts access to the green.

The way is barred, however; a tree has decided to fall directly across the bridge. Of all the things that might require me to remove my skis, it's a tree in the middle of a golf course. Between getting confused and this irksome blowdown, I quickly decide that golf courses are the Devil's playpens. I slip in between the branches and over the trunk, re-don my skis, and continue on, leaving the Devil to his wicked games.

The Catamount Trail merges with the Mad River Path past the golf course, and I begin to make good time. Clearly a popular hiking trail, I practically fly over the terrain. Thick spruces and firs soar overhead, their branches protecting the trail beneath. The snowpack is far shallower here, further abetting my strong pace.

Wending my way in and out of the evergreen stands and around a beaver pond, I finally reach Route 17—the road that cuts through the Appalachian Gap of the Green Mountains, (or "App Gap," as it's known in this age of abbreviation). The trail spits me out next to the Mad River Barn Inn & Restaurant. Although I peer hopefully through the window, it's too early for them to be open. No hot meal for me.

My guidebook tells me that I should parallel the road northwest for nearly a mile before finally crossing it, but after a circumnavigation of the Mad River Barn, I can't find a blaze or trail anywhere. Faced with bushwhacking or hugging the road, I reluctantly ski along the road on top of the snowbank. I'm forced to dodge a plow's spray and avoid chunks of ice and salt, but I eventually re-merge with the Catamount Trail proper.

Back on clean snow by the Battleground Condos, the trail enters the woods again, and this time will stay there for a while. The stretch from Route 17 northward is one of the more-remote sections of the Catamount. As I make my way along and gradually up a woods road, the profusion of tracks tells me it's a popular backcountry ski location.

As I continue deeper into the forest, however, these tracks gradually die away. Soon just a few ski tracks lead me onward.

I pass an older couple (one of whom, in response to my description of my journey, tells me, "Maybe in my next life"), but after that interaction, the woods are all mine. A solitary being traveling slowly through the towering hardwoods, I feel small, insignificant, and totally secure in my place in the world. This is where I'm meant to be.

A passage from John Knowles's famous coming-of-age story suddenly surfaces in my memory. It's been a long time since I read *A Separate Peace*, but one short section has stuck with me. Gene, the main character, is running one morning, with his friend Phineas watching. "After making two circuits of the [track] every trace of energy was as usual completely used up," describes Gene. "My lungs as usual were fed up . . . my knees were boneless . . . my head felt as though different sections of the cranium were grinding into each other."

He's clearly exhausted. Then, something changes.

"For no reason at all, I felt magnificent. It was as though . . . the aches and exhaustion were all imagined . . . and an accession of strength came flooding through me. Buoyed up . . . I lost myself, oppressed mind along with aching body; all entanglements were shed, I broke into the clear." Gene is experiencing the runner's high, a second wind, and any endurance athlete knows the feeling well. It is truly a magnificent feeling, of ultimate power and ability.

Trippers feel it, too, as they get into the groove of a trip, and I feel it now as I traverse these silent woods. A week or two into a trip, the "tripping mind-set" turns on. You forget about the cares, the considerations, the entanglements of your other life and feel as though you could go on forever, traveling slowly across the country. "You found your rhythm, didn't you, that third time around. Just as you came into that straight part there," Phineas tells Gene after Gene finally stops.[6] It's such an overwhelming experience to find it that it's even visible to the observer. And so it is on a trip. Everything else seems to melt away—the aches and entanglements—and the trip becomes the thing, the only thing that matters. It's as if I've finally put the blinders on and can at last ignore all the other distractions that pull me away, just pin my ears back and truly experience the adventure.

I stop at a small bridge briefly, where the Trail turns off the main woods road, and eat a snack. The tracks diverge here, most staying on the main cut. My route turns left and uphill and is far less traveled. With gentle flurries once again falling, most traces of any usage soon disappear. It's easy to feel like I'm the only one for miles around, as well I might be. This is what I imagined the Trail would be like, what I like to picture Knox traveling. Surrounded by an untouched winter paradise within the Vermont wilderness, with snowflakes settling dreamily around me and not a sound to break the stillness, I feel like I might literally be in heaven.

The cold, of course, brings my sentimental musings to an end. Packing up the wrappers from my granola bars, I sling my pack up and onto my shoulders, beat my hands together a couple of times, and start to climb. The ascent quickly warms me—a good thing, since the night promises to be another frigid one.

As the afternoon wears on and the sun sinks into the reddening west, I start to consider my options. I'm still climbing what is now the flank of Camel's Hump, one of Vermont's most iconic mountains. If I keep going, I'm unlikely to find a reasonable water source, as the trail stays in the upper elevations for a while. I also consider the cold and whether there might be any advantage to trying to stay slightly lower. Finally I just whisper "Screw it" and keep skiing. I'll end up where I end up.

"Skiing" ends up being a bit of an exaggeration, however. The Trail climbs steeply, and as I near the ridge, all vestiges of previous use peter out. With the snowpack deep, and getting deeper, I end up trudging for much of the remainder of the day, duck-footing occasionally on the steepest sections. I often need to thrash a ski once or twice to force the tip out so that I can take a step forward. It's exhausting work, and I begin to sweat steadily.

I set up camp amid some small white pines. It's a "dry camp," and I'm forced to melt snow for water to cook and drink. It's also absolutely frigid, and my drying sweat only exacerbates matters. I shiver as I put up the tent, but feel more secure once camp is squared away and dinner is bubbling on my stove. Again, I feel like the difference between security and peril is a very thin line.

Finally, having eaten and performed my chores, I zip up my sleeping bag. Shivering there for a while before I gradually warm up enough to settle down, I sum up the day and night in my journal with one word: "Cold."

The next morning I go through the now-standard process of taking the first fifteen minutes of wakefulness to hug my frozen boots to my body. The next fifteen are devoted to trying to get them on. It works, but just barely. Breakfast is a hurried affair in the faint light and then I'm skiing, desperate to get the blood moving in my body and feet. (Later, I find out the temp reached 17 degrees below zero on this day.)

All morning I move slowly. Very slowly. I cover six miles in the first six hours, slogging through knee-deep snow in the upper elevations. The Trail is a series of steep ascents and descents, all of which require patience and care to maneuver. The Trail is steep enough through much of this section along the side of Camel's Hump that any uphill requires me to duck-walk. I carry no skins with me, so am forced to either spread my stance wide to prevent slippage, or, in extreme cases, side-step. Duck-walking (or herring-boning, as some call it) is slow going, exhausting, and—after a time—a bit painful, too. For a man of my flexibility (read: highly inflexible), it's challenging to spread my legs and point my toes wide enough to gain purchase. My groin starts to ache and my knees to complain, and by the time I stop for my lunchtime snack, my legs are thoroughly annoyed with the terrain. Chuckling wryly to myself, I vow to bring skins the next time I decide to ski this trail.

Particularly frustrating are the number of blowdowns I encounter along this section. A simple tree trunk across the Trail is easily negotiated, but when you add in a number of branches sticking out in all directions, things suddenly become more complicated. It's easier to remain on my skis so I don't sink any deeper, but by doing so I need to laboriously maneuver each foot around myriad branches, checking to make sure my tips and tails make it through the openings. I often get hung up as a stray limb grabs at my ski or my backpack, and each struggle breaks me out of my skiing groove.

I also manage to lose the Trail for a half-hour as I near Camel's Hump Road. A large snafu of blowdowns has removed all trace of trail and blazing, and I stumble in and around large maples and oaks in an attempt to stay on the route. Inevitably, I lose it, and am forced to ski back and forth in wider and wider arcs away from the mess, casting about for a sign of the Trail. Eventually, a spot of blue catches my eye, and I struggle back on course.

Sam Brakeley

My only consolation this morning is the snowpack. The extreme cold means that the snow remains as light and fluffy as ever, easily passed through with no transformation or crust to impede my way. I hoot for joy on the downslopes as powder shoots up into my chest and face with each turn, enlivened as I *schuss* my way through the snow and mountain air.

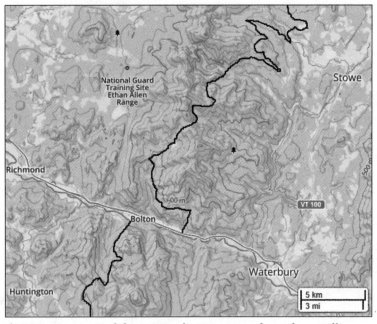

The Catamount Trail from Camel's Hump Road to Edson Hill's
Manor House

8. We Shall Cut No Small Figure

The afternoon proves to be more rewarding in terms of speed. Once past Fielder Road, the grades ease, the snowpack gets thinner, and I find that someone has broken trail for me. I move along quickly in the late-day sun, enjoying what little warmth it imparts. My new pole is holding up well (as is my old one); my boots remain warm; my skis, while scratched across the bottom in places from clambering over blowdowns, are in good shape; and all of my other gear is in operating order. It's a well-known expedition adage that most accidents and mistakes happen within the first week or so of a trip, when skills are rusty, routines unformed, gear unchallenged, and bodies green. Between snapped pole, spilled water bottle, and blisters galore, that held true for this trip as well. Now that I'm over that initial hump, I'm singing along. My gear all works, my pack is a svelte thirty-five to forty pounds (down from perhaps forty-five at the beginning), my body is humming, and my morale, high. Life is good.

Past the Camel's Hump Nordic Ski Area trail system, I find fresh tracks. Sure enough, I soon catch up to a group of three. After the standard explanation of my trip, they give me some advice.

"You should tell the Catamount Trail organization where you are! The two guys who are also doing it now have been giving them running updates, and people have been leaving trail magic—cookies and such."

That sounded pretty good. Trail magic is not uncommon along the Appalachian Trail where trail supporters leave everything from Oreos to soda along the trail for thru-hikers to enjoy. Some even go above and beyond, setting up a grill and passing out hot dogs or hamburgers. At one point in Tennessee on my hike in 2008, I was even invited into a couple's home for a waffle breakfast. If someone is doing the same along the Catamount now, I'd like to participate!

But with no way to give an update on my progress instantaneously (I own what is affectionately known as a "dumb phone"), I will just have to rely on luck and good timing if I'm to find some trail magic. I thank the trio for their advice and continue on.

The descent down to Duxbury Road is long and gradual, and I fly along, loving the speed even as I protect my face from the biting air with my gloves. It eventually turns into an unplowed road which I descend even faster before finally getting spit out onto Duxbury Road. Its half past four, and I'm nearly out of food, so I hike back into the woods and make camp. I'll go into Richmond tomorrow morning to resupply and get a hot breakfast while I'm there. Dinner tonight is rice mixed in with my last two packets of instant grits. Covered in cheese and hot sauce, it tastes delicious. Warmed by the thought of a hot meal cooked by someone else, I snuggle into my sleeping bag (already starting to get a little crusty from just two nights of perspiration and exhalation) and fall asleep.

My struggles going steeply uphill along the side of Camel's Hump would have been child's play for Henry Knox. Where I am now carrying a thirty-pound backpack, Knox was hauling literal tons of cannons. Combine those heavy loads with the steep hills of the Berkshires—and what in the best of circumstances would have been a poorly maintained road—and it's clear that Western Massachusetts's mountains posed no small obstacle for Knox's train of artillery.

Some of our understanding of what the caravan experienced must, of necessity, be inferred, but we can, with a fair amount of accuracy, envision just what it was like to cross the Berkshires.

North Callahan gives an evocative (and romanticized) description of what the journey was like. "The slender cortège of cannon-bearing sleds, their drivers shouting at the oxen and horses and cracking whips, passed between the two Spectacle Ponds, and then through a mountain pass . . . It was an Indian paradise, filled with fish and wild game—which were certainly more at home than heavy sleds with heavier cannons winding through the wintry depths."[1] The reader can easily visualize a bird's-eye view of the line of wagons snaking their way through the mountains.

Whips and yelling, however, were not always sufficient to force the heavy loads up the steep slopes. Oxen and horse teams were sometimes doubled or tripled up to drag the sleighs uphill, the outsized teams making several journeys up the same slope to bring all the loads to the top.

Ropes were also employed. Later in the war, Knox would attempt a similar stunt to move cannons toward Trenton after crossing the Delaware on Christmas Day, 1775, where steep hills barred their way. Historian Mark Puls describes their task: "Ropes had to be tied to trees and attached to the multi-ton cannons, and men grabbed hold of the lines in an effort to hoist the guns up the incline." Knox likely cut his teeth on the process during this earlier march, with Puls noting that "the challenge [in Trenton] must have reminded Knox of the trip from Ticonderoga."[2]

Making their way downhill was no easier. "To prevent runaways and the slashing of weighted sleds downhill upon the men in front, drag chains and poles were thrust under the sled runners, with check ropes anchored to successive trees along the way to hold back the sleds when necessary."[3] Progress would have been slow and tortuous.

Towns were few and far between throughout this stretch of the journey. So in addition to the trials and tribulations the Berkshires forced upon the drivers, they also would have been making camp in the cold, snowy woods each night (not conducive to a solid night's rest, as I can attest). The men must have pushed even harder, working to get through the mountains and reach the other side for the final leg of their journey.

Knox himself summed up this stretch of the march succinctly: "It appear'd to me almost a miracle that people with heavy loads should be able to get up & down such Hills as are here."[4]

Miracle or not, by January 11 the first division had left the woods and entered Blandford. They had passed the halfway mark somewhere upon entering the Berkshires, and were now more than 160 miles into the journey.

But if Knox thought that all challenges were behind him now that he was in central Massachusetts, he was sorely mistaken.

I wake early with visions of Richmond dancing in my mind. I pack up in the dark and leave my campsite without benefit of a headlamp—I am close enough to the houses on Duxbury Road that I don't want to alarm them with a dancing light in their woods. Thankful for the lack of dogs (or for the dogs' good sense to remain quiet on this frigid morning), I ski back to the Trail and then out to the road.

There is a break in the Catamount Trail from Duxbury Road in Duxbury to Pinneo Brook Road in Bolton. The parallel barriers of I-89 and the Winooski River mean that one is unable to ski between the two trailheads. Either a seven-mile road walk is required or, as I will do, a hitch. When I return from Richmond, I will get a ride to the north side of the river and continue my ski there.

But first I need to get into Richmond. Walking along the rural road in the dark, I am unsurprised when the first two cars pass me by without slowing. Hitchhiking in the dark is a futile cause; it too easily reminds drivers of horror movies. Even I, who often stop for hitchhikers as a pay-it-forward for future rides I might need, will not pick one up at night.

As first light is breaking, a beat-up truck with lopsided headlights pulls over for me. He only gets me to the Jonesville bridge but, nearly before I have finished clambering out of the cab and hoisting my backpack and skis from the truck bed, another car stops and takes me the rest of the way into town.

I hope to eat at a bakery called On the Rise. I worked in Richmond for a year soon after college and fondly remember stopping there for a beer, meal, or live music after work. It's been several years since I last visited, however, and I discover the business has changed hands, and names. An OPEN sign is lit up, and warm breakfast smells emanate from within, so I enter, leaving my skis and backpack leaning against the wall nearby. I am anything but picky on this cold morning.

It's clear that the place has just opened under the new ownership and is still going through some growing pains. I order at the register from the menu on the wall. A man with a lumpy face and dull eyes has to call the manager over twice in the process with questions about which buttons to push. I ordered from the menu, I can't help but think—and it's not even that extensive.

We finally get through it and he hands me a table number, even though I'm the only patron in the place. Standard operating practice, I guess. I wobble over to a wrought-iron table and chair and melt into it. Steam has already begun to rise off my clothes and I quickly begin to drip on the floor. My own unwashed scent soon begins to fight for prominence with the bakery smells coming from the kitchen nearby. I don't mind, though; it's just nice to be warm.

I call Elizabeth and let her know I'm alive. It's a quick conversation—she's on her way to work, and the call lasts barely a minute. A minute is better than nothing, I tell myself, and then immediately realize that it very well could *be* nothing. What if Elizabeth wasn't there to call? Or if she is only there to call, and that's it, because I've decided to stay while she goes. Will we be the same—will our relationship survive? And who will I lean on when I need love or support, if she's not there? Who will she lean on as she undergoes the trials and tribulations of residency and life in a new place, if I'm not there?

Suddenly I'm glad it was a short conversation, meaning I can still put off answering these questions. But for how long?

I leave a voicemail for my father, letting him know where I am, as well, and soon after, an older woman brings me my food.

"Cold enough for you?" she says by way of greeting. "My thermometer said fifteen below when I woke up." Then, placing the plates before me, "Here you go, honey. You must be hungry—enjoy!"

I am. I've ordered eggs, sausage, toast, home fries, and a platter of french toast. It disappears quickly, and I suck down the coffee my waitress is attentive about refilling, despite its blistering heat. Suddenly the idea of returning to the cold and elements seems highly undesirable, and the newspaper I've been flipping through very interesting. I can only read about the local sports teams for so long, however, and throwing back the last of my coffee, I rise and step back outside.

The grocery store is right around the corner, and I quickly resupply, then head to the side of Route 2 to get a hitch back to the Catamount Trail. It's not more than a couple of minutes before Spencer and his Sheltie Danny stop. Spencer is friendly, and Danny has that wide-eyed inquisitiveness that all Shelties seem to embody, and we have a nice conversation. Danny came at a discount—he has a broken tail—but seems content to rest in the backseat of the car. Although he did give me a look when I parked my backpack next to him when I climbed in, unimpressed with this sudden reduction of his personal space.

It's amazing to me how quickly a conversation can turn intimate between hitchhiker and driver (although of course some rides pass in utter silence). Something about the unwritten, unspoken contract we've both agreed to once a car pulls over—the driver to provide transportation, and the hitcher to provide conversation—seems to elicit the best in both. It's proof of an old adage that I will paraphrase (and perhaps butcher) here: The best way to develop a relationship with someone is not to do a favor or good deed for them but rather ask a favor of them. For example, giving a lift to someone in need of a ride.

And sure enough, as happens more often than I usually hope for, Spencer agrees to drive further out of his way to get me to where I am going. We even miss the turnoff due to a missing road sign, but

Spencer is more than happy to do a little problem-solving with me, and we eventually get to the trailhead.

Thanking him profusely, I pile out. Danny eyes me suspiciously as I grab my pack from beside him, but seems pleased that he's got the whole backseat to himself again.

The next seven miles of trail all overlap with the VAST system and I cruise along, belting out Elvis songs. Having surmounted the Camel's Hump leg of the trail, I am now nearing Bolton Mountain and the foothills of Mount Mansfield. It's nice to easily cover some miles between the two more-challenging sections.

Leaving the VAST trails while humming "You ain't nothing but a hound dog," I join the Bolton Valley Backcountry & Nordic Sports Center trail system and follow their trail signs to the base of Bolton Valley resort. The Catamount Trail skirts the downhill resort here in its climb upward, and I'm pleased to spot several downhill skiers as I near the buildings at the base. Now I know I am going to be going up, and quickly!

Having had good luck with prior resorts waiving my fees, I don't hesitate to stop in at Bolton Valley. Plus, I'm hoping that they may have some food or hot coffee (I'm already hungry again). Wandering through the front door, I stop and talk with Emily behind the register.

"Good morning. I'm skiing the Catamount Trail up to Canada and am passing through. Just checking in." I hope by not even asking about a pass, she'll let me on through.

She smiles at me. "Cool! All the way from Massachusetts?" She has a pair of striking eyes that immediately lock in on me. I simply nod, finding it hard not to stare at them as I talk to her.

"Well, good luck with the rest of the trip. Enjoy!"

That seems to be all, until a man—who it quickly becomes clear outranks Emily—steps out from an office behind her. "You'll need a day pass," he tells me. "Ring him up, Emily." He then turns back into his office. His eyes aren't nearly as enticing.

Emily rolls her lovely orbs at me. "Sorry," she says softly. Those are some eyes I could fall in love with.

"Oh, well," I tell her. "Just got my timing wrong, I guess."

The trek up the side of Bolton Mountain is continuously steep. But the trail is well maintained and has been broken before me, so I make solid time, herring-boning most of the way. A small cabin named Bryant Camp is perched among some spruces partway up, but I pause only briefly. It's fairly dingy and clearly well-used as an overnight shelter and smoke shack.

As I continue to get higher, I notice that the spruce trees are stunted and gnarled, and the air and flora take on an alpine feel—a first for the trip. The breeze picks up; I can hear it whipping through the tops of the trees. As the trees become shorter and shorter, the wind gets closer until it's ruffling my coat and nipping the tip of my nose.

Nearing the top, I catch up to my trail-breakers. Coming around a corner, I spot a man and his son pausing to add layers. Nodding my hello, I ski past them and soon after meet Jenn and Daniel, a couple. In front of them lies untrodden snow. They wave me on past but, with the added challenge of the untrammeled drifts in front of me now, we end up going at the same pace.

And fortunately so. The trees begin to spread out, and with a thick coat of rime and snow-bowed spruce branches, it's often hard to spot blazes. We end up tag-teaming the tough spots, the three of us spreading out amid the possible openings, searching for a slash of blue before hollering to the others that we've found the way. Although slow, it's rather pleasant searching as a team, and I enjoy my time with them.

The Trail finally begins to descend off the ridge and simultaneously opens up into beech and yellow birch. With wide-open spaces between trees and blazes now easily visible, we ski down with whoops of joy and delight. I make broad, swooping turns and attempt to practice my tele-turns. Still unstable even after all this time, I occasionally tumble head over heels in the deep, powdery snow, much to everyone's delight. Jenn, too, is still getting the hang of her skis, and Daniel chuckles at both of our antics as we struggle to regain our feet after yet another mistake. It is easily the best skiing of the trip.

I vow to myself to bring Elizabeth back to this place. She will love the steep terrain and snow-covered birches, the open shots descending off the mountain. I can already picture chasing her down this mountain for a day, her red cheeks and bright eyes enveloped in steamy breath, her peals of laughter reverberating across the valley. It's an image that brings a smile to my face. I realize this often happens to me: When I'm enjoying a spot or an experience, I immediately want to share it with her. It hasn't escaped me that I'm thinking of her so often out here, even in these little ways. I'm attached to her, I realize—really attached. In the way that only seven years together can do.

As I get closer to the end of the trip, it's beginning to crystallize for me—just how important this attachment, this history, this shared experience together is. And how much I look forward to a future of shared experiences as well.

After dropping down almost a thousand feet, the trail mellows out and begins to follow a stream out toward Nebraska Valley Road. Other skiers have accessed this terrain from there, so by the time we hit the pavement, the trail is well-traveled and packed out.

I wave good-bye to Jenn and Daniel as they climb into their car, then turn and do a double take as I spot another vehicle nearby. I know that car!

Skiing up to it on the shoulder of the road, I peer inside. Sure enough, it belongs to my friend Noah. He must be skiing where I came through—I must have just missed him! Chuckling, I leave him a note on the windshield, and then continue on.

My next waypoint is the Trapp Family Lodge network of cross-country ski trails, and it's easy going all the way there. I pop out onto their groomed runs through a stone wall and am soon met by a cross-country ski patroller named Ron.

"You doing the Catamount Trail?" he immediately asks me. It's likely my backpack gives me away, to anyone in the know.

I nod, hoping that he isn't a stickler about trail fees. It's also already 3:30 p.m., and I need to find a place to spend the night. I decide to take a chance on Ron.

"You wouldn't have any recommendations for a place to set up my tent for the night, would you? In the next several miles?"

I'm in luck.

"I skied the trail a couple of years ago with a buddy," Ron tells me. "Go to the cabin you'll see up ahead and talk to Mike. He may let you stay there—it's a warming hut more or less. He spends most nights there. Tell him Ron sent you."

"Great!" Pleased with this plan, I start to ski off.

"Oh, and don't bother skiing all the way out to the lodge," Ron yells at me as I leave. "They'll make you pay!"

I raise a ski pole in acknowledgment and continue on. That's music to my ears.

On my map, the Catamount does a brief out-and-back to the east, the only apparent purpose, allowing the Trapp Family Lodge to charge the thru-skier for using their trails. I see no need to subject myself to a second fee today, so while that does mean I skip a mile or so of very flat, groomed, official Catamount Trail, I know I won't lose any sleep over it. I don't even feel bad about not paying; after all, I made contact with an employee who told me not to worry about it.

Hurrying along the groomed trail through the increasing gloom, I finally spot the squat log cabin looming in front of me, larger than I'd imagined. Plenty of room for me.

But it isn't to be. I enter and meet Mike—clearly a quiet, introverted type. Not wanting to take a forward approach with him or impose myself, I begin a little hesitantly.

"I just met Ron out on the trails. He said you might know of a good place to spend the night." With a fire in the fireplace and a roof over our heads, I hope he gets my intended message: This cabin is clearly a good place to spend the night, and I want to be here.

But Mike just shakes his head.

"I don't know a whole lot about winter camping," he tells me. "But you can camp anywhere out there that you'd like, as long as you're off the trail so a groomer doesn't hit you."

Not exactly what I wanted.

I sit by the fire for a couple of minutes, warming my hands and feet while watching Mike continue his cleaning up for the day. They appear to offer snacks and soup here for cold skiers. It's too late for anyone else to be stopping in, so Mike is putting away leftovers and doing dishes. I can tell by his movements that he's not interested in re-opening containers and messing up the kitchen to feed me.

"Do you ever get lonely up here?" I ask him. It sure seems like a solitary existence—small talk with visitors during the day, but spending each night alone. I think I could do it for a bit, but winter is a long season in northern Vermont.

"No," he responds quietly. Then, as if introducing another person, "I have my guitar." I want to argue with him that a guitar isn't an antidote to loneliness. Actually, it might amplify said feeling. It just passes the time, like the harmonica of a solo cowboy out on the range. But I remain quiet.

After a bit, Mike sidles back over to me.

"I just remembered. There is another cabin a couple of miles away. It may be unlocked; you could spend the night there. I can give you directions if you'd like."

I don't need to be slapped over the head to get the message. I re-don my gloves and boots and head out, thanking Mike for letting me warm up. Oh well. I'll be just fine in the snow. As I leave, Mike is taping the day's money-take to his chest. He'll ski down, drop it off at the lodge at the bottom of the hill, and then ski back up for the night.

It's too late to be very particular about where I camp, so after about a half-mile of skiing, I detour off the groomed run and set up shop. It's a dry camp, so once again I have to melt snow for water for a hot drink and dinner.

As I sip my tea, I realize I'm not shivering. It's a warmer night than we've had in a while, and I'm smiling when I crawl into my sleeping bag. It's nice to be warm.

Knox, due to his own spate of warmer weather, was once again facing rebellious wagoners. Upon exiting the Green Woods and the Berkshires, Knox discovered warmer conditions. The wagoners, no doubt fed up with the changing conditions and incredibly challenging journey thus far, "refus'd going any further, on account that there was no snow beyond five or six miles further, in which space there was the tremendous Glasgow or Westfield mountain to go down." Knox was forced to bring all of his arts of negotiation and persuasion to the fore. As he notes in his journal, "after about three hours persuasion, I hiring two teams of oxen, they agreed to go."[5]

A receipt still exists, dated January 13, 1776, for work that one Solomon Brown performed for Henry Knox—apparently for the hiring out of these two new teams of oxen. The receipt states that he was paid "eighteen shillings lawful money for Carrying Cannon weighing 24C. 3 [approximately 2,800 pounds] from this Town to Westfield being 11 miles"—testament to the human toll of the march.[6] Tired, frustrated, and cold, the men must have begun to feel a real sense of futility for them to have begun to give up after so much progress.

Even during the long hard days of a march like this, however, fun can be had. John Becker describes a novel method he witnessed during a subsequent expedition north, toward Montreal. "I saw thirty men traveling in one sleigh," he describes. "Several short planks were placed across the sleigh, and on them the men stood up to catch the stiff breeze blowing from the south. These human sails carried them along at a rapid rate, and the horses, so far from feeling the weight behind them, were going at some speed so as not to be run upon by the sleigh." One can almost hear these men shouting for joy as they raced along—it must have been wildly enjoyable in addition to efficient. "It had a singular appearance," says Becker, "but was not without merit in idea and usefulness in its effect."[7]

Upon finally reaching Westfield, the marchers' spirits were buoyed by the supportive townspeople. As Knox had written to Lucy earlier during the march, "we shall cut no small figure in going through the Country with our Cannon, Mortars, etc., drawn by eighty yoke of oxen."[8] Sure enough, the citizens of Westfield turned out in droves. Becker notes that the marchers "were much amused with what seemed the quaintness and honest simplicity of the people. Our armament here was a great curiosity. We found that very few, even among the oldest inhabitants, had ever seen a cannon. They were never tired of examining our desperate 'big shooting irons.' "[9] For a small town in central Massachusetts, this was a lot of excitement.

Of course, the sleigh drivers were paid amply for the privilege of examining the artillery. "We were great gainers by this curiosity," wrote Becker, "for while they were employed in remarking upon our guns, we were, with equal pleasure, discussing the qualities of their cider and whiskey. These were generously brought out in great profusion, saying they would be darned if it was not their treat."[10] Clearly the caravan was not going to make any more progress that day, so Knox succumbed to the goodwill and celebration as well.

As everyone knows, every good celebration needs fireworks. Knox was carrying some very large fireworks with him, and was happy to oblige Westfield by firing off a gun. Apparently known as the "old sow," it was shot off several times "for the novel pleasure of listening to its deep toned thunders."[11] Clearly the "Tory treachery" noted by historian Bernard Drew was no longer on the mind of Henry Knox (if it ever was).

That evening the party continued at the local watering hole. Knox, surrounded by well-wishers who all seemed to introduce themselves by their local militia rank, was prompted to comment, "What a pity it is that our soldiers are not as numerous as our officers."[12] Fortunately, the comment was received with its intended humor (although, of course, as with every good joke, it contained a nugget of truth), and the rejoicing continued. One suspects that the caravan took a little extra time to pack up and start off the following morning. Some of the headaches must have been fierce.

I eat my oatmeal quickly on my following morning, anxious to set off. There are several towns coming up, and I hope to be able to stop in somewhere at least once for some hot food or coffee.

Perhaps it wasn't quite what the Catamount Trail creators had in mind at the beginning—leap-frogging from one eatery to another, always focused on the next non-oatmeal, non–instant pasta meal—but that seems to be how my mind is working right now. I can't help but believe that Knox felt the same way. His meals were likely as bland as mine, and I feel sure that he looked forward to each town he passed through—not just as a marker of distance covered, but for the hot meals they provided.

It's easy traveling to Route 108, mostly on groomed runs. I just make sure to keep an eye out for signs at each junction. In these Nordic trail systems, it'd be easy to get turned around and loop back onto yourself. At the state road, I'm disappointed to find no restaurant in sight. I look longingly in both directions, craning my neck in hopes that something will materialize: some garish neon sign or the brief scent of a fryer. Nothing. Not willing to take the time to hitch a ride, I hobble across the road and re-click into my skis on the other side. Damn—no fresh coffee for me. Maybe my next stop will have hot food.

But when I finally ski into view of Edson Hill's Manor House, it's clear that I won't fit in. A beautiful inn nestled in the foothills around Stowe, Edson Hill looks to be all that an exclusive rural Vermont inn can be. I look down at my dirty and frozen clothes, inhale a good dose of my own body odor, and shake my head. I'll have to pass this place by.

I turn to go, and then pause. You know what, I tell myself, what the heck! The worst that can happen is that I get turned around at the door. So I retrace my steps and lean my skis against a bush near the front. I'm just setting my pack down next to them when the door opens.

"Can I help you?" A slight man in middle age leans out through the opening. He's dressed neatly, his expression is unreadable. I can already tell how this will play out. He's cutting me off at the pass, aiming to not even let me in the front door.

"Yeah," I begin tentatively. "I was just hoping to step in for a brief—"

"Well, come on in then!" The man breaks into a smile that lights up his face. "Where are you coming from?"

"Massachusetts," I tell him, more readily now. "I'm skiing the Catamount Trail."

"Neat!" he exclaims, and his tone tells me he really does think it's neat. "I haven't met anyone doing that yet! Can I get you a cup of coffee?"

It's my turn to break into a smile. Frankly, it'd be hard not to—his warmth and exuberance are immediately contagious—but the offer of a hot cup of joe pushes me over the edge. It's what I've been hoping for all morning!

Carl introduces himself as we walk into the reception area and lounge. I sit down in a chair that, in the loving words of my father, looks to be worth more than I am. I settle in gingerly, hoping not to sully it too much, and glance around. A thick shag carpet covers the distressed wooden floor, leading up to a big fireplace. Horsehair chairs and couches dot the room and large paintings hang from the wall. Ella Fitzgerald plays quietly in the background. Trying to place the decor, I can only determine that it's a blend of the last five decades, with occasional touches of the nineteenth century. To my uninformed and undiscerning taste, it's perfect.

Carl had excused himself but returns carrying a silver coffeepot, steam emanating from its spout. As he sets it down in front of me, I notice two massive muffins next to the pot.

"There!" he says. "That should fix you up nicely. Now, tell me all about your trip while I light the fire."

In spite of my protestations (albeit, brief and disingenuous), he busies himself in front of the hearth and soon has a roaring blaze. He settles into a chair nearby, continuing to quiz me on my experiences up to now, asking about everything from camping out at night to navigation to the people I've met.

I sink deeper into the chair and try to share as much information as I can between sips of coffee and bites of muffin. It's hard to imagine that I almost didn't stop in. This is, without a doubt, the height of luxury.

I try my best to hold up my side of the conversation, too, asking him about the inn. It turns out that Carl is one of seven new owners who have recently bought the place. Carl is the on-site manager, and seems to have a fairly extensive background in hospitality (he's certainly taking phenomenal care of me). He even offers me the chance to take a shower, which I politely decline. I know I stink, but I decide that a shower is probably taking his generosity too far.

After a pot of coffee, the muffins, and perhaps twenty minutes of conversation, I finally decide it's time to take my leave. I'll fall asleep in this chair if I stay too much longer. Excusing myself and thanking him profusely, I rise. Carl ushers me out the door, refusing my offer to pay for my snack.

He waves from the doorway as I ski off, the very image of a Vermont innkeeper. This must be how Knox felt, I think to myself, as he and his men were plied with cider and whiskey in Westfield. And as it must have done for them, the true spirit of kindness and generosity reinvigorate me for the next leg of my journey.

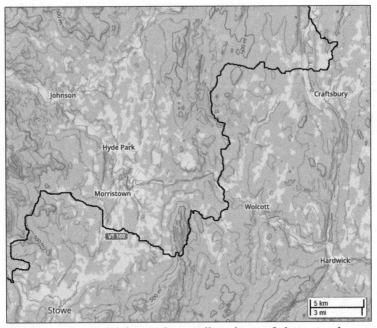

The Catamount Trail from Edson Hill to the Craftsbury Outdoor Center

9. We Could Go No Further

Leaving Edson Hill, I can't stop grinning. What a perfectly wonderful morning! I ski on their small trail system for a short while before turning off and slowing considerably as I begin to break new trail through eighteen inches of fresh snow.

The trail begins to turn east here, wending its way out of the Green Mountains and into the relative flats of Vermont's Northeast Kingdom. I ski through the Sterling Valley, enjoying its gentle beauty, and carefully poke my way across several streams and gullies. There are a few other people out here with me, and I nod my greeting and pass the time of day with a couple, but otherwise keep to myself. Temperatures have begun to drop once again, and as the day continues I focus more and more on myself; simply maintaining an adequate body temperature while at the same time avoiding any sweating seems to encompass all my thoughts.

Where the Trail meets up with a VAST corridor, I turn right, now heading due east. The landscape opens up and I begin to cross through windswept fields. A stiff breeze is building, and I keep up a steady pace to maintain circulation. Small drifts have blown over the groomed trail, slowing me down.

Here also, for the first time, the landscape begins to change significantly. Where most of the Trail up to this point has been through forests and mountains, I now find myself in wide-open farm fields. Occasional houses dot the skyline, and the foreground is interrupted by periodic telephone poles. But with fewer landmarks close by, it feels like I've slowed to a crawl. I inch across the fields, head bowed to the wind, listening to it whistle past my ears.

The afternoon is lightened by a moment of levity. I cross briefly through a pasture inhabited by several cows. As I negotiate the initial fence, they purposefully wander over to me, clearly curious. Once I'm inside, they maintain a respectful distance, following me as I traverse their territory. With their slightly gaping mouths, hay and drool hanging, they are the perfect image of idiocy, but I think I detect a faint light of intelligence in their eyes. I talk to them over my shoulder as I pass through, assuring them of my peaceful intentions. They in turn escort me to their far boundary, lowing softly, then stand and watch me as I ski off.

As five o'clock rolls around, I find myself in the midst of a golf course. Searching around, I finally settle on a copse of trees around a stream bottom. It's cold enough at this point that I need to stamp and beat my feet and hands continuously as I set up my tent and stove. Dinner is a speedy affair, shoveled down as quickly as thickly gloved hands will allow. Then into my sleeping bag and tent, where I gradually stop shivering as my body heat warms up the goose down. I whisper "Fore" as I drop off to sleep.

The caravan's next stop on the march was Springfield, Massachusetts, and here again they were faced with warming weather. John Becker notes that "we could go no further. The sleighing failed, and we had to leave our cannon lying ingloriously on the road side, in the mud." Once again, Mother Nature was throwing a wrench in Knox's plans.[1]

Also at Springfield, however, most of the teamsters employed up until this point appear to have returned home, including Becker and his father. John Becker's matter-of-fact tone seems to indicate that either he and the other New York teamsters were not prepared to go further than Springfield, regardless of weather conditions, or that they were unceremoniously told to return home, since their sleighs were now useless. One suspects the former, since Becker doesn't indicate any resentment.

It's not clear why this was the case. Having used these men for so long, why would Knox suddenly change? The New Yorkers had acquired hard-earned knowledge as they'd made their way this far. It seems like it would have been inefficient to suddenly change, requiring a new group to have to start at the beginning of the learning process. If it was simply that the snow had melted and wagons were now required, one can easily envision a circumstance where the New Yorkers remained employed aboard newly acquired (or transformed— removing the runners of the sleighs and replacing them with wheels would not have been unreasonable or uncommon) wagons.

Or was it simply the distance from home, as historian North Callahan suggests?[2] Springfield was a long way from Albany; perhaps the New Yorkers longed for their own families and firesides. But January was a tough month to make ends meet in the eighteenth century. Wouldn't Knox's offer of steady pay have been incentive enough for most of the men? Without stated evidence, however, it's hard to determine the exact impetus for the change.

In any case, at Springfield, Knox hired new teamsters to bring the cannons the final leg of the trip, to Cambridge. Having already traversed the rivers of New York and the mountains of Massachusetts, this final challenge must have seemed laughable. Based on the warm reception received at Westfield, one suspects that the local citizenry lined up with their wagons to help. It would not have been every day that an opportunity like that arose.

Becker and the other New York teamsters "returned to Albany in much quicker time than it took . . . to get to Springfield."[3] Without the burden of the heavy cannons, it must have felt like a pleasure cruise.

I am in a similar spot in my journey. Looking at the map the next morning while I wait for my boots to thaw, I'm pleased to note that only one substantial peak still bars my way. I'll cross high on the side of Elmore Mountain this morning, after which only a few mountain passes remain to be crested, each with a road crossing through them. They can't be that steep then, I tell myself as I struggle into my boots and stamp my feet. It's cold.

The water seems to take a little longer to boil this morning, but I'm finally able to make my oatmeal and get on the trail. It takes a long time for my boots to loosen up and my toes to warm, but eventually they do. The brisk wind and open fields between Route 100 and Elmore Mountain Road don't help my core temperature, but struggling through the resultant wind drifts does ironically restore circulation to my lower digits. My nose stays numb and cheeks wind-chapped and reddened, however, until I finally reach the shelter of the trees.

Climbing the side of Elmore Mountain goes slowly. The snow feels heavy, in spite of the temperature. I think it must be the wind, packing it in here so well. At least it's not steep.

Descending is much faster. I follow the access road out, zooming along the trampled corridor and creating my own wind while doing so. By the time I reach the bottom I can barely feel my cheeks and I know my whole face is cherry red. But also at the bottom is the village of Elmore, where I know I can find hot food. I also need to resupply.

I step into the Elmore General Store and immediately recognize that this is a place owned by kindred souls. It's a rambling building, three stories tall and painted white. The outside is plastered with posters for local events and services, and the inside consists of oddly angled aisles, barely wide enough to sneak two people past, and shelves stacked to the ceiling with goods. There's a section of groceries, a shelf of novelties and souvenirs, and a large section of miscellaneous. It's one of those "If we don't have it, you don't need it" kind of old New England stores, and while you may not be able to find it (whatever it is), all you have to do is ask and the proprietor will likely pull it out of some hidden corner. It's old and creaky, worn and beautiful. And it's warm and smells like hot food and ancient wood.

I put my pack next to two miniature grocery carts that are parked in a corner. I don't think they see much use. Then I immediately attack the donuts and coffeepot, only to find that it's nearly empty.

"I'll make you a fresh pot," says the woman who comes around the corner. "You look like you're hungry, too. If I heat up a pizza, will you have some? It's homemade on Elmore Mountain Bread crust."

She has a kindly face and introduces herself as Kathy. As I watch her easily navigate the coffee machine and gracefully move among the threatening-to-topple piles of merchandise and narrow aisles, it's clear that she takes pride in her establishment and her management of it. It's nice to find myself in such capable hands.

I quickly do my resupply from the shelves of mostly canned and prepackaged food. Trail bum that I am, I'm not picky. Perhaps a gourmand might hesitate over the Kraft Mac & Cheese or Knorr Pasta Sides, but not me. I round out the shopping list with Oreos, Fig Newtons, and a couple of boxes of granola bars, as well as oatmeal and peanuts. Stacking it all up on the narrow checkout counter, I am waved off.

"Just push it over here, out of the way for now," says Kathy. "I'll ring you up when you're done with that pizza. Here, the coffee is just finishing."

I grab a cup and two donuts and settle onto a stool in another corner, used by short customers for those high shelves. Dipping the donuts in the piping hot coffee, beset by the warmth of the building and with Paul Simon softly playing in the background, I am reasonably sure that I've found myself in another earthly paradise.

Her husband Warren enters from the back and introduces himself as well. He's heavy-set and much taller than his wife, but, like her, wears the compassionate expression of a person who enjoys people and his place among them.

"Would you like something higher?" he asks me, gesturing at my short stool. I am a little scrunched up in the corner, balancing my coffee between my knees, but quite comfortable.

"As long as I'm not in the way," I tell him, "I'm happy as a clam."

"Good," he says. "That's how we like our customers. Happy."

In response to their questions, I tell them the story of how I've arrived here.

"Hold on," says Kathy. "You stayed outside last night? It was twenty-two below!"

"Well, it was pretty cold," I allow. "But there have been a lot of cold nights. They're starting to blend together."

They both shake their heads in amazement and disbelief. I can tell they both think I'm a little crazy, so I try to turn the conversation to them, asking them about the store.

"We've been here for more than thirty years," Warren acknowledges proudly, looking around. For them both, it's been a labor of love. They're the center of the village, both literally and figuratively. The post office is within their building as well, and the only gas pump in town is out front. They are the hub of this small Vermont town, and they recognize and value their role in the community.

I ask them the question that popped up the minute I walked in. "Does anybody ever use those shopping carts?"

"Daily," Warren grins. "Kids love 'em."

A woman walks in and they both wander off to help her, greeting her by name as she closes the front door. I dip the last bite of my donut into my coffee and settle back to relax.

The woman grabs a loaf of bread and a can of something, I can't see what. But this is no brief, minute-to-spare, last-ditch-forgot-something shopping trip. She places her items on the counter and proceeds to chat with Warren and Kathy for the next fifteen minutes.

"I heard on the news that some woman got arrested for leaving her kid in the car. My folks used to do it when I was a kid, all the time. Wasn't a big deal. Now I never would. Why, I read a while back that some other woman had her car stolen with her kid still in it."

Warren chimes in. "My folks, could have been Fifth Avenue, New York, they'd give us some money to go get dinner and let us out. They'd go have a nice dinner themselves and come back and pick us up in two hours." Shaking his head, he laments those bygone days as countless others have before him. "Not anymore."

The woman eventually leaves. (Although not before I, silent up until now, am introduced to her and another customer by both Warren and Kathy with "He's doing the Catamount Trail." They coo in proper amazement. It seems I'm rapidly on my way to becoming a local phenomenon.) She is quickly succeeded by a delivery man, wheeling in a large stack of racks of bread. He too is greeted by name.

Kathy comes out with the pizza, which she slides into the hot rack. Gesturing at me not to move, she serves up two pieces on a paper plate, adding a plastic fork. Before I eat, Kathy insists that she take my picture standing next to the cook—a shyer-looking woman whose name I don't get and who immediately returns to the back.

Thanking Kathy profusely, I forgo the fork and gobble it down, going back for two more, then two more. Boy, does it taste good, and I tell her so.

"We're doing a hundred and twenty pizzas a week right now," she says with a smile. "Very popular. This spring, we're going to add a deck out back so people can sit out and look at the lake while they eat and chat."

I can only nod in response; my mouth is too full.

I finally feel sated and head up to the register. In addition to my groceries, I've eaten six slices of pizza, three donuts, and two cups of coffee. Kathy winks at me and rings me up for barely half of it. Then Warren comes up.

"Would you like some reading material?" he asks, proffering a newspaper.

I shake my head no and, protesting at their kindness, turn to go. A dog has appeared and decided to lie down in the aisle in front of me, forcing me to awkwardly clamber over her.

"Nice choice of a spot, dog," I say.

"She's been doing that for eleven and a half years," says Kathy. "I don't think she's going to change now."

Kathy wants a picture of herself and me and we pose in front of the store. It's still bitterly cold, so we do it quickly. Thanking her once again, I start to walk off down the road with a full belly and fuller heart.

"Don't forget us now," Kathy calls after me.

How could I?

In Springfield, Massachusetts, Knox was on the site of a future crisis for both himself and the young nation. Several years after the expedition, in 1777, Springfield would be selected by George Washington—upon the advice of Knox—to be the site of an arsenal. Knox traveled there for several days, scouting and planning. He was able to combine work with pleasure, for Lucy joined him there from the East and the two found time together in the midst of war before Knox was forced to return to the front in New Jersey and Pennsylvania. But as a result of that journey, and his recommendation, the Springfield Arsenal of the United States Army came into being, standing for nearly two hundred years before it was closed, in 1968.[4]

Ten years after its founding, it would also be the site of one of Knox's greatest challenges as secretary of war, one that schoolchildren still learn about today. Daniel Shays was a Revolutionary War veteran and farmer. Upon returning to his home from the war, he discovered that not only were debt collectors clamoring for payment on old debts—payment in hard currency that he did not have—but the Massachusetts government had increased property tax in its own effort to help pay for the recently finished conflict. Shays found that he was not the only farmer in this situation. Many were former soldiers and had not been fully paid for their participation in the war. At issue also were the Articles of Confederation, under which the government still operated, granting the states wide latitude on most issues and confining the federal government to a narrow role.

First attempting to resolve the issue through peaceful means, Shays and others in his situation petitioned their governments to issue paper currency to help increase the flow of money. These petitions were repeatedly denied. Protests broke out—at first peacefully, but then turning violent. Shays emerged as an organizer and then leader in these protests, eventually taking charge of 1,500 men and marching on the Springfield Armory. Another body of men under Luke Day was meant to meet up in a simultaneous assault on the edifice. Day, however, was delayed, and his message to Shays saying so did not make it through. Shays attacked anyway, but a brief barrage of cannon fire by the defenders left four of Shays' men dead and the whole force spooked. They fled north without firing a musket shot.

Knox was active throughout the escalation to the showdown, shuttling back and forth to Springfield, Boston, and New York. But his hands were tied; he didn't have the power to protect the armory under the Articles. He was forced to rely instead on Massachusetts militia. Massachusetts itself was unable to fund the effort and had to rely on donations from private citizens to pay its soldiers. The whole effort was a textbook example of why diffusion of power simply wasn't a feasible way of governing a nation.

While ineffective in its immediate goals, the rebellion stands out for its long-term effects on the formation of American government. The action solidified support for a stronger central government among America's leading men, and at least indirectly demonstrated to much of the country that the Articles were not an effective governing document.

"The powers of Congress," Knox wrote to Washington during the unrest, "are totally inadequate to preserve the balance between the respective states and oblige them to do those things which are essential for their own welfare or for the public good."[5] He recognized that only the federal government could rise above and do what was best for the entire populace, while simultaneously being strong enough to enforce it. "Our government must be braced, changed or altered to secure our lives and property," he wrote soon after, later submitting a detailed plan to Washington for the creation of a new government.

Sure enough, several years later, the Constitution was ratified, outlining a government very similar to the one Knox describes in his letter to Washington. Based on these communications, more than one historian has described Knox as "prescient."[6]

Leaving Elmore and the warmth of Warren and Kathy's store, I traverse some more fields before descending quickly on VAST trails to the Lamoille River. Crossing the river, the Trail skirts the narrow corridor between the water and Route 15 before rising quickly to pass through another maple-sugaring operation. It too is patterned with blue and green tubing, another up-to-date, high-efficiency operation. It makes me smile. I can't help but compare it to the bootstrap system Elizabeth and I have been using for the past couple of seasons.

When Elizabeth and I moved in together three years ago, we found a house set in the hills of Norwich, Vermont. Surrounded by fields and set against a backdrop of Green Mountain forest, it's a beautiful farmhouse in an idyllic setting. When that first February rolled around, I informed Elizabeth that we would be continuing the tradition of spring sugaring. A rural girl herself, raised in upstate New York, Elizabeth also comes from a family of sugarers, so she was fully on board.

Operating on a shoestring budget, we jury-rigged most of the required apparatuses. A fifty-five-gallon drum turned on its side formed our evaporator, with a large kitchen pan placed in a hole on the top acting as the boiling pan. We bolted a door on the side of the drum to allow us to feed wood into its interior, and stacked a couple sections of pipe on top of one another toward the rear as a smokestack. I purchased some used sap buckets at the local hardware store and was grateful for the gift of some more from a friend. We drilled thirty-five taps into the trees around the house that spring as a trial run, hung our buckets, and waited for the weather to turn.

We had a bumper crop that first year (sap creation is tied to the weather, as described above, and depending on the year, syrup production can vary significantly), and we spent many a happy afternoon and evening watching the sap boil. Elizabeth had enjoyed it when we boiled hot dogs in the sap; each bite held fond memories for both of us as we re-created childhood experiences. Beer and bourbon flowed, too, and we invited friends to come visit. Cozily sitting around the evaporator, we swapped stories and fed wood into the fire just as I'd done as a kid. It was a magical spring, and we'd slightly grown our operation in the ensuing years, making syrup for our friends and family just as our parents and grandparents have done for years.

A sobering thought comes to me as I cruise along the woods road through the tubing: With no sugar maples in Utah, this tradition will have to end if we are to move west.

In the midst of my reveries, I suddenly realize that I haven't seen a blue blaze in a while, and I've crossed through several intersections by this point. I turn back around and ski down to the last blazes. There's a hint of direction at the ensuing intersections and it's clear that I am firmly turned around.

At first the Trail is obvious, and I ski slowly uphill with a thick, black, three-inch sap tube on my right. Blazes are sparse but I spot a couple that tells me I'm on the right track. Soon, however, I enter a small clearing with three main trails branching off and several less-obvious paths striking away as well. Which is the correct one? The sugarbush has been thinned recently—sugarers routinely cut out underbrush and non-maple trees to ease travel and encourage sugar maple growth—and I can't help but suspect that some of the Cata-mount Trail blazes have fallen victim to their chain saws.

I choose one at random and follow it to another intersection, again with the same fan of trails branching away from me. Sugarers also are great trail builders, and ATV trails proliferate throughout their operations as they travel this way and that to access different parts of the sugarbush. Again, no blazes are visible, so I return to the original intersection, thoroughly frustrated now, and pick a second option. It too lacks blazes but feels better, traveling in a straighter line and in the direction that I think I'm supposed to be heading. With every stride my frustration grows. Mounting worry over whether I am in the right place or not is compounded by the fact that the afternoon shadows are getting longer, and I need a place to spend the night.

Losing a trail is different from being simply lost. If you are fully and truly lost in the woods, you've got some options. Head in one direction, or head downhill. Eventually, you'll hit a river, a road, and civilization. But looking for a trail—a concrete, finite line through space—is a far tougher proposition. Is it to my left? My right? In front or behind me? If I head in one direction, I may be working further and further from my actual goal without even knowing it.

Adding to the challenge is the fact that there are numerous other trails snaking through the woods, and my trail may or may not be marked to distinguish it from the others. It quickly becomes an exercise in futility and frustration.

Trying to quell my mounting anger, I soon pop out on a dirt road. Opening a nearby mailbox, I glance at the mail and discover that it's Jones Road. That's where I'm supposed to be, according to my map, but relief turns to frustration again as I ski along the edge of the road to the end. A VAST trail continues away from the plowed corridor, but I still see no blazes, and my guidebook tells me I'm meant to find a turn off Jones Road to the left, before the road ends.

I ski back and forth along Jones Road again, looking for any trace of a turn, but find nothing. With no better options, I ski to the end and take the VAST continuation of the plowed road.

For nearly half a mile I ski along with no sign of blazes. I grumble to myself about the family heritage of the mapmakers and guidebook writers, but vow to continue to ski on this trail until I find another landmark from which to get my bearings. With direction set, I make good time on the packed-out trail, eventually coming to a T junction. Another decision to make—one that will potentially take me even farther away from my desired route.

I'm in luck. Looking left, I spot a blue blaze. To my right, another. While the trail I am on is not the Catamount, somehow I've found it again. Shaking my head disgustedly but vastly relieved, I turn right, thankful to be on the correct path again. To this day I still have no idea about the actual route of the Trail through this section, but I'd found my way back to the blazes, and that's what matters now. Amid lengthening shadows, I set up camp near a small stream. As I fall asleep I vow to make up some of the distance tomorrow.

But while the next day brings slightly warmer temperatures, it also holds some new challenges of its own.

The first couple of miles along the east side of the Green River Reservoir are advertised on my map as groomed, flat VAST trails. The reality, however, is something quite different. Flat they are, but they're covered in a thick layer of untouched snow. This would typically mean slower going, except for the fact that it's obviously been several years since someone was last through here with a chain saw. Birches drape their branches across the path from both sides, hanging far enough over that their top branches are now frozen to the ground. Deadfall also crisscrosses the corridor regularly. Not only has no snowmobiler been through here recently, but it seems clear that no skier or hiker has bothered to come this way either.

I sigh as I fight through yet another draped tree. There is nothing to do but continue on, slow and unrewarding as it is. I force my way between the branches of a fallen beech, awkwardly straddling the horizontal trunk to cross it. Then I duck under another low-hanger, only to find a network of trunks on the other side that renders passage impossible. I struggle up the cut bank to the right and circumvent the blockage, but another one soon rears its ugly head. I bow my own and continue on.

I finally reach more frequently traveled terrain, where at least the blowdowns become rarer, although I'm still breaking trail through nearly two feet of snow. The day is cold and bright, but I continue to sweat. The Trail crosses through several fields, but with no wind, the snow remains light and fluffy. Resigned to my fate, I continue my slow plod throughout the morning.

Finally, around noon, I spot three dark shapes moving toward me across one of the openings. It's a trio of skiers, and I smile at them when they near. (After two weeks on the trail, I suspect they probably began to smell me about the same time I came into view.)

"Nice to see you guys. It's hard work, breaking this entire trail!"

They ask me about the trail in front of them, where I've just come from, and also about my own trip. They're impressed with my pace.

"You're really moving along," one tells me.

I just laugh. "It's cold out here," I explain. "Not much else to do but ski!"

Now making far better time, I follow their tracks all the way to Craftsbury. My mood improves remarkably as I sail along; nothing cheers me up like making good time.

It takes a little bit of problem-solving to navigate my way through town, but I soon find myself on the Craftsbury Outdoor Center's groomed trail network. It's a Saturday, and the weekend crowd is out in full force, taking advantage of the cold weather, good snow, and excellent skiing conditions. I garner more than one curious look as I ski along. Not many other people have an oversized backpack on.

"So you're doing it solo?" asks one woman, after I explain the backpack, and my trip.

I nod, and she tells me (in what feels like a bit of a *non sequitur*), "I'm so proud of you." Seems like an unreasonable emotion to feel about a stranger's journey, but I thank her anyway.

I pause with a small group at the top of a knoll, and one man does a double take.

"Where'd you get those skis?" he asks me.

"A fellow in Burlington sold them to me," I say. I'd bought them on Craigslist.

"That was me!" he exclaims. "I thought I recognized you! So you made it all this way on those skis," he continues softly, shaking his head in wonderment that his skis had made it here from Massachusetts. I thank him for the sale, as I had two months prior when I'd purchased them out of his garage. It is a small world after all.

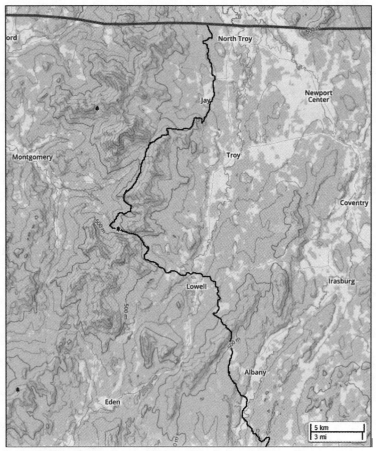

The Catamount Trail from the Craftsbury Outdoor Center to the Canadian Border

10. We Supped There Very Agreeably

I run into another acquaintance at the Craftsbury Outdoor Center base lodge. The mother of one of my friends is here, cheering on two of her other daughters in a ski race, and she spots me through the crowds around the building.

"Sam!" she yells. "What on earth are you doing here?!"

When I tell her about my expedition—for what seems like the umpteenth time in the past couple of weeks—she insists on buying me a piping hot bowl of chili. We find a corner in the packed lodge and sit down. She catches me up on what's been happening with my friend, whom I haven't seen in a while, and I regale her with stories from my trip. The chili doesn't last long—it's greasy and delicious—and I thank her for her kindness before bidding her good-bye. It's nice to see a familiar face.

I grab a sandwich and an apple for the road and then move away from the crowds. Finding a quieter spot, I pull out my phone and call Elizabeth.

"Hi, honey," she says. "I figured you'd be buried in a snowbank by now."

I laugh and assure her that I'm fine. We agree to meet in a couple of days; she has the morning off from work, so it will work well, and the northern trailhead of the Catamount Trail is only a couple hours from the house. She also makes me promise to let her ski a little bit, too. When she met me in Middlebury I was too early to the trailhead, and she'd barely gotten to ski. I promise to linger more this time, and we hang up with the pledge to see each other soon. I can't wait.

Skiing onward, the trail crosses the ice of Little Hosmer Pond. A not-insignificant body of water, I ski across it for a ways, following faint tracks and aiming toward a distant shore. The cold weather of late leaves no doubt in my mind that the ice is amply thick.

I start to imagine what it would feel like if I didn't follow Elizabeth to Utah. If she was never there to pick me up again. If she relocated across the country and moved on because I stayed here and she didn't. That at the end of the next trail, and the next, it would be a solo celebration with no one to share it with. And even if there were, it wouldn't be with her. My love. Lonely thoughts on a lonely and windswept expanse of ice.

For the remainder of the afternoon the Trail continues to be well tracked. I re-cross Route 14 and hug the foothills of the Green Mountains, skiing northward and parallel to the road. I have the sneaking suspicion I know where the trail is heading, and as I spot a hulking pile of tree trunks in the distance, it's confirmed.

I come out into a lumberyard for Goodridge Lumber, a company I know well. I've made the pilgrimage to Albany, Vermont—the town I'm now in—many times. Goodridge specializes in cedar lumber, which is extremely rot-resistant. I am a trail-builder throughout the summer months and, as one might imagine, prize that particular characteristic highly. So I drive up here regularly to purchase a load of cedar for the bridges, boardwalks, kiosks, and other lumber projects I build around New England. I smile as I navigate between the log piles.

"I'll be back for some of you," I tell the inanimate trunks.

They don't respond, but then again, I'm not expecting an answer. (And then again, if they had answered, I'd be more than a little nervous about the state of my own sanity. Perhaps that would be a sign that it was time to take a break from the trail.)

Emerging from the other end of the log yard, I am once again on a woods road. Stone walls line the sides and large, looming trees arch overhead. It's well graded and winds gently through the woods, much like the dozens of other woods roads and logging paths the Catamount Trail takes advantage of throughout its length. This one, however, is different from the rest.

I'm on the Bayley-Hazen Military Road. Construction on it first began just months after Knox would complete his own journey from Ticonderoga to Boston. George Washington, perceiving a need to access the Canadian front via land as well as water (the route to Montreal via Lake Champlain and the Richelieu River was already well-traveled and -fortified) ordered that construction begin on a road to aid and abet efforts in that region. Accordingly, in 1776 a path was blazed from Newbury, Vermont, on the Connecticut River to St. Johns, Quebec, on the Richelieu. Soon after, Jacob Bayley began construction to upgrade the trail to "road" status. He didn't improve much more than six miles of road, however, when fears of British retaliation forced the work to stop. Somehow, the fact that roads work in two directions—that while enabling the Continentals to attack Quebec, it would simultaneously facilitate any attack by the British south, toward the colonies—seems to have been forgotten in the planning process.

A more-concerted effort was rebooted several years later in 1779. Moses Hazen with several regiments of soldiers made better progress here, improving the track all the way past Albany, to Lowell and Westfield. The planning process seems to have improved in the intervening years, as well, for they installed a series of blockhouses along the new route to protect from invasion. Once they reached Hazen's Notch in Westfield, however, work was once again due to fears of British retaliation.

Unfinished, the road would figure only tangentially in the Revolutionary War. Following the conflict, it remained in use as a travel way for settlement and commerce between the Connecticut River and interior communities. Today, it's a footnote in Revolutionary War–era history, and has been mostly swallowed up by tarmac. Only a few portions, like the one I travel on now, remain nearer their original state.

The road wends gently upward. Fields now line either side of the path, but the crumbling stone walls remain, and even a few towering oaks and maples shade my path. Thicker undergrowth has also begun to take over, and I dodge some scrub brush on occasion. Dusk begins to fall and a faint dusting of snow drifts down from the sky. All is silent around me and, in the eerie half-light, I'm easily transported back to the time of the road's original construction. I can almost see the men and beasts slaving away to fell trees and remove stumps. It must have been incredibly taxing work.

I cross through a small neighborhood but soon rejoin a VAST trail. I hurry along, looking for a campsite. It's time to stop moving.

Crossing a small stream, I turn off the trail and thrash my way through the deep snow a ways before finding a small opening. This will work. As I do each night, I stamp out a flat spot with my skis before slinging down my pack and setting up camp. It's macaroni and cheese for dinner, followed by Oreos. Taste has truly stopped mattering by this point—I'm just hungry for calories. In my journal I write, "What a feast!" I mean it.

As I scarf down the cookies I hear the dull roar of a four-stroke engine. Beams of light cut through the night and flit across the trees. A trio of snowmobilers flow past on the trail, out for a night tour. As I drift off to sleep, snug in my sleeping bag, I'm lulled to dreamland by other engines occasionally breaking the silence. I can't help but think that the men who built this military road would have been quite startled to learn that it's now a recreational path for motorized use.

As Knox led his caravan over the final miles of his trek, some distinguished visitors turned out to congratulate him. Elbridge Gerry—at that point, a member of the Massachusetts Congress, but later vice president under James Madison—and John Adams, who was at that time a delegate for Massachusetts at the Second Continental Congress, came to visit.

Adams noted the event in his journal. "About 10 Mr. Gerry called me," he wrote on January 25. "We rode to Framingham where We dined. Coll. Buckminster after dinner shewed us, the Train of Artillery brought down from Ticonderoga, by Coll. Knox." Adams had lobbied hard in the Continental Congress for Knox's commission as full colonel of the nascent artillery regiment. No doubt he felt validated in his support of Knox. He left no other impressions of the visit other than noting afterward that they "rode to Maynards, and supped there very agreably."[1] Could the thrill of seeing the artillery—the knowledge that soon Washington and the forces surrounding Boston would have the means to evict the British—have heightened the flavor of his meal and aided his digestion? It seems more than likely.

From Framingham, Knox rode out ahead of the caravan. Now traveling along well-known roads through populated towns, the wagoners saw little excitement and did not need his direct supervision. So he set off for Cambridge and Washington's headquarters. Here, he was met exuberantly. In spite of all the setbacks, the sunken boats and guns, weather that was too warm or too cold or too snowy or too dry, despite poor roads, tall hills, and unruly wagoners, he had made it through. Historian Victor Brooks calls it "one of the most stupendous feats of logistics" of the war. It would be hard to disagree with him.[2]

Washington must have been ecstatic: He now had the artillery to attack British-held Boston. And Knox also must have been pleased, and not just for having accomplished his mission. Upon arriving in Cambridge he finally learned of his appointment to full colonel. He had his commission.

There was yet another reason for Knox to be pleased. Lucy had been anxiously awaiting his return, and their reunion must have been joyous. They had been married just a little more than eighteen months, and the separation had been their longest to date. Lucy, pregnant, was thrilled not only that her husband had been successful, but also that he had returned healthy and whole—not always a given in the eighteenth century (or the twenty-first, for that matter).

Washington invited the couple to dinner almost immediately, and they dined with the commander in chief and Martha Washington on February 2. Knox also presented his bill for the trip (though probably not over the meal) of 520 pounds, 15 shillings, and 8 3/4 pence. He would not be paid until 1779.[3]

Sam Brakeley

My last full day of the trip, I rise and shake the snow off my tent. I tossed and turned for much of the second half of the night. I'm worried about getting to Elizabeth in the time I've allotted, so I break camp in the dark and begin skiing when there's just enough light to see. Once I slog back onto the VAST trail, it's easy to see where I'm going.

The air is crisp this morning, and the cold, cutting. Outlined against the sky are a series of wind turbines. Their silence stands in stark contrast to the revolutions they are steadily arcing in the sky— fearsome structures standing tall and proud, yet incredibly sleek and minimalistic. Simple, yet magnificent in their awesome power. But then again, I've always admired turbines. There's a little Don Quixote in me, tilting at windmills.

The noisy snow machines of last night have long since gone to bed, so there is no one else awake to disturb my musings, or my steady progress, for which I am thankful. The group I was tailing yesterday appears to have made it this far, so I simply follow their twin marks. I wind in and out of a couple of river bottoms, but the trail remains relatively level, with only short inclines and declines, until Lowell.

In Lowell, I call Elizabeth, briefly confirming that I'm (hopefully) still on schedule to meet her the following day. I also talk to my father. He's glad to hear from me. By this point he, like Elizabeth, is inured to my wandering ways. He's given up both on trying to cure me and on bothering to worry unnecessarily. He knows I can take care of myself. But that doesn't mean he's not glad to hear my voice, and he catches me up on the family news. I finally beg off when I stop being able to feel my fingers. In the open space of the town's main street and fields, the wind is whipping.

I rejoin the Catamount Trail to the west of Lowell's sparse infrastructure and make use of VAST bridges to cross the Missisquoi River, before once again turning off the snowmobile corridor for narrower passage. The trail remains broken for me, although its previous users appear to have been headed toward me. A different group than my previous trail-blazers, I am none the less grateful for them. It makes my job easier, and with as much snow on the ground as there is, I'll take whatever I can get.

Eventually I emerge onto an unplowed road, packed hard by snowmobiles, to cross through Hazen's Notch. It's a slower but still steady ski up to the high point—where the Bayley-Hazen Road finally concluded in its improved state, due to fears of those pernicious British—but a phenomenally fast descent. I zoom past several snowmobilers headed in the opposite direction, raising my hand in salute. It's all I can do, for, with my legs spread wide for balance and my eyes squinted tight against the cold air and the snow that's now falling, I am mostly focused on not careening off the side into the trees. Although I'm a very confident downhill skier, I still haven't totally accustomed myself to these thinner skis with free heels, so it takes all my concentration to stay upright and on track.

It's a long descent and I whoop it up, enjoying the speed and the thrill, before the road finally mellows out. After slowing, I spot a small parking area on the right and turn here to follow the Catamount Trail back into the woods. I pass a small sedan with Quebec plates and sure enough, find that three skiers have once again broken trail for me. I smile with a little relief. I can almost certainly make my rendezvous with Elizabeth tomorrow, as long as nothing unexpected happens. I silently thank what I've come to think of as a version of my own personal group of pacers and trail-breakers and continue on.

This is my final long ascent, from the side of Hazen's Notch Road up to Jay Pass. It's now 1:30 p.m., and I'm feeling tired, but there's no question of holding back now.

The trail is not as easy as I'd hoped. After the well-packed surfaces from multiple skiers and snowmobiles, this section is much softer. The snow is just deep. Really deep. The Trail winds up and down over knolls and outcroppings—meaning that while the general incline is not too daunting, multiple short steep sections impede my progress. The trio in front of me plainly have skins, so, when the trail steepens enough, I still bumble through fresh snow either duck-walking or side-stepping. Their skis, complete with climbing aids, merely leave two parallel lines in the snow.

Despite the exertion and challenge (or perhaps because of it), I make sure to enjoy myself. This trip is coming to a close tomorrow, where I expect only easy traveling, and I treasure these last hours of my final afternoon.

As darkness begins to slowly descend, I pause and look to the west across the valley. Headlights from cars below cut soft arcs in the deepening gloom while a barred owl asks who's making dinner. I shake my head in response. We both know that it's going to be me.

And I serve up a feast for myself on this final night. I make several boxes of macaroni and cheese with some extra Cabot cheddar cut into it. I also have one sausage remaining—pineapple-flavored—and I toss that in there, too. I dust it with some instant mashed potato flakes and stir the whole mess together. It's hot and delicious and represents calories on top of calories. Just what the doctor ordered.

Crawling into my tent afterward, I shake out my sleeping bag. It now has seven days' worth of moisture again and is frozen into a ball after the day in my pack. But I peel it apart and slip inside. Soon enough, my body heat warms it to an acceptable temperature. It doesn't matter now; tomorrow night I'll be in between cotton sheets, snug with the woman I love.

In the damp warmth, I think back to my earlier discovery of the best way for me to make uphill progress in the face of a long and challenging climb: to take the mountain in bite-size chunks, breaking the larger, longer-term, and seemingly insurmountable goal into more-manageable and achievable ones. To ski to that birch up there, I just need to get up this little pitch, and then take on the next fifty yards of trail after that.

This trick doesn't apply to only physical pursuits, of course. If, psychologically, I can ignore the immensity of potential consequences and outcomes looming over me, maybe I can break my important decision into littler, bite-size chunks, too. To take it day by day and week by week, one step at a time, thereby perhaps finding myself suddenly months—or even years—ahead, well into a future I'm comfortable with. Although this isn't a decision in and of itself, it's comforting to decide upon a process with which to move forward.

And, suddenly, at long last, in my damp sleeping bag in my frozen tent, with my frost-nipped cheeks and beat-up feet, I feel secure in the knowledge that, deep down, I've always known the answer to my question. I know where my heart is now, where it has always been. One final night's sleep on this trip should bring my head on board, too.

Knox's mission was not yet complete.

Yes, he had brought the artillery from Ticonderoga to Cambridge. But, as the final cannons were dragged into town from Framingham,

Knox was still a bundle of activity. The purpose of the artillery was not just to look intimidating, but to be put to real use.

The British remained holed up in Boston proper. George Washington and the Continental Army had them surrounded, but, without enough artillery, they had no way of making an assault on their position. Washington was preventing the British from being supplied or reinforced from anywhere but via the sea (a costly endeavor for the British, considering that all foodstuffs at the time had to be shipped to the entrenched army from England). In truth, it was a stalemate. With Knox's cannons, however, the balance was about to be weighted in favor of the Continentals.

An additional piece of luck fell Washington's way when news reached his headquarters that the ship, *Nancy*, had been captured. She fortuitously carried thousands of rounds of shot for the cannons, meaning that Knox's slim round count was now generously supplemented. With dozens of pieces and more than enough ammunition, all that remained was to get the big cannons into position.

On the night of March 4, 1776, Knox and his men did just that. In the days leading up to this night, Knox had mounted guns on three sides of the city, in Roxbury, Lechmere's Point, and Cobble Hill. Under cover of fire from these three points, General John Thomas marched two thousand men toward Dorchester Heights, overlooking Boston Harbor and the British fleet. Working all night, the men dug entrenchments and mounted the new cannons so that by dawn, these guns were trained on the British fleet. The British were now effectively surrounded and cut off.

And flabbergasted. When the British officer corps woke on the morning of March 5, they were bowled over at the intimidating sight that greeted them. "Many of the soldiery said they never heard or thought we had mortars or shells," reported one colonist in Boston of the British reaction.[4] Not only did the new cannons from Ticonderoga surprise the British, but the speed with which they had been brought to bear was also greeted with amazement. "The rebels," noted General Howe, the commanding officer in Boston, "have done more in one night than my whole army would have done in a month."[5] It was a masterful stroke by Knox and Washington.

The British immediately commenced preparations for a counterattack. They initiated a bombardment of the new positions, but called it off almost before it had begun. Their guns couldn't be elevated enough to be effective. Their ground attack fared no better, for fate once again smiled her beatific smile on the upstart colonists. A violent storm hit the region as Howe prepared to set off, grounding the troop transports needed to move his men to the shores of Dorchester. The inclement weather bought Washington enough time to further entrench and reinforce the new positions on Dorchester Heights, convincing Howe that this too would be a futile endeavor. No doubt the Battle of Bunker Hill was fresh in his mind—assaulting uphill against entrenched positions is always a costly enterprise.

With his hands tied in Boston and both reinforcements and supplies delayed due to bad weather at sea, Howe was left with only one other option: evacuation. On March 17, St. Patrick's Day, the British evacuated Boston. Loyalists all, Lucy's parents and siblings went with them, never to return. Soon after, the Continentals marched in and took possession of the city. It was the first victory of note for the army, and an important one at that. It returned one of the hotbeds of independence to colonial control, demonstrated that the British could, in fact, be beaten, and proved to the rest of the colonies that there was hope for the new nation. Maybe this dream of independence from Britain could become a reality after all.

I wake early. Very early. I get to see Elizabeth today!

Filled with excitement and pushing back any fears about our future, I crawl out of the tent into the pitch dark. It takes an extra minute to force my boots onto my feet, but I move efficiently after that particular struggle, and am packed and ready to go before the sun is. I head off anyway, my bobbing headlamp beam leading the way for the first half-hour.

I move steadily up the final stretch of the ascent, reaching Jay Pass a little after seven a.m. The headlights of cars moving along Route 242 across the valley from me parallel my journey, the low-gear rumble of engines straining up the mountain pass accompanying their beams. All else is quiet except for my own labored breathing and the scratch of skis on snow.

The Trail emerges onto the road at a parking area at the top of the pass, where I pause to watch a couple of cars inching their way through swirling snow before continuing on. From here into the town of Jay, the Trail is well traveled. Clearly a popular day trip, it's wide and packed down. More importantly, it's downhill. I cruise, swerving around corners and dodging trees. With just a dusting of new snow on it, it's easy to follow. No chance of getting lost here.

I take a tumble three times in quick succession, bringing my fall total to thirty for the trip. After the third, I decide to take it slower; no sense in getting injured on the final leg. The gradient evens out soon after and begins to follow the contour of the hill. A couple of blowdowns bar the way, further moderating my speed, and I manage to stay on my feet the rest of the way.

A little after nine, I come to a small field, which quickly brings me to the back of a country store. Thankfully, I drop my pack on the porch, prop my skis and poles next to it, and totter inside. I skipped breakfast at my tent this morning, and am famished. It's time to eat!

The Jay Country Store is an updated, more tourist-y version of the Elmore Store, without, of course, Kathy and Warren. The man behind the register is clearly an employee, and no owners are in sight. The shelves are lower and the aisles wider, the floor less creaky, and the gifts and knickknacks, more prominently displayed. If there were any shopping carts, I feel confident that they would all be adult-size. But it will do just fine, since I spot a short-order griddle in one corner.

I make straight for it and order my favorite breakfast: eggs covered in cheese, sausage, toast, and home fries. Then I head for the rotating food warmer by the register and also purchase a premade breakfast sandwich (eggs, sausage, and cheese again, of course), as well as a cup of coffee and an oversized donut.

It turns out my early morning start means that I've got a lot of time on my hands. Elizabeth has mandated that I give her at least a mile or two to ski toward me before I meet her. If I don't let her exercise, she warned, she will turn around and drive back home alone, stranding me. So I set a hard-and-fast deadline of 1:00 p.m. for leaving the store. That should give her plenty of time to make some progress south from the border, toward me.

So I find a couch around the corner and settle in, spreading my jacket out on a nearby chair. I feel like a king. There's a newspaper on the table, and I read it front to back, pausing only to scarf down my breakfast. Then I grab another cup of coffee. Two magazines also found on the table come next, and I devour them almost as fast as my meal.

Sam enjoying a meal and oil-fueled heat at Elmore Store.

The man behind the counter gives me an odd look as I come up for a third cup—I've been here for a couple of hours now—but I ignore him. Lounging in a soft couch with hot coffee surrounded by oil-fueled heat is about the epitome of bliss at this point. I order a sandwich and chips from the griddle, just to show him I'm not done yet. It goes down just as quickly as everything else.

As I knew it would, my deadline rolls around eventually. I don my now-damp layers and step outside. It hasn't warmed up any, and after my long sojourn indoors, it feels even colder. But I grab my skis and walk across the road, rejoining the VAST trail on the other side.

I move very stiffly for the first half-mile or so as my muscles and joints get limber. The warmth and immobility have seized everything up, but eventually my body smooths out and I start to look less like I'm controlled by an amateur puppeteer.

It turns out that I still left the store too early; I'm moving too fast to give Elizabeth anything like the time she'll want on skis, so I force myself to a slower pace. After two and a half weeks on skis, I've shed my initial ungainliness and fallen into a smoother motion. While no one would mistake my technique for the pure, unadulterated grace of Elizabeth's, I feel confident in the comfortable efficiency and ease with which I now ski.

Finally, with no sign of her in front of me, I stop. I'm off the VAST trail now, and in the middle of an overgrown apple orchard, I can see the trail for a ways in front of me. I'll wait here for her, I decide, and as soon as I spot movement in front of me, I'll start skiing. That way I can fool her into thinking that I timed it correctly and didn't have to wait for her.

Five minutes go by. Then ten. Then five more. I keep anxiously checking my watch and doing the math, trying to decide what time she should be turning the corner toward me. I beat my hands and throw my arms in circles to keep warm, even do a lap or two back and forth over the last one hundred yards of trail. Still no sign.

Maybe she was caught in traffic? I know that can't be; northern Vermont has never had any traffic to speak of in its entire history. Well, maybe she got stuck behind a tractor? Common enough in the summer, but unlikely in the winter.

It's finally clear that she is significantly late and behind the schedule we agreed to. I check my cell phone, but there is no service. I give her five more minutes, then give up. I start forward, slowly at first, and then, picking up speed. Where on earth is she?!

Possibilities start racing through my head. Car crash? Bear attack? I half-laugh to myself as my alternatives become more outlandish, but my worries grow as I continue to see nothing in front of me. I race through a low cedar swamp along the last mile of trail before joining the VAST trail once again. She's more than capable of taking care of herself in the winter—hell, she was a guide for multiday snowshoeing and skiing trips one winter—but that doesn't mean I'm not worried that something may have happened to her now. Where the hell is she?!

On the VAST trail, I whip my head back and forth. And there, in the distance to the south, I spot her. She's just fine, and has clearly spotted me already, for she's skiing like a demon toward me. Before I know it, she's in my arms.

"This stupid trail," she pants. "Those stupid blazes."

It turns out that the Catamount Trail, until recently, simply followed the VAST corridor through this whole section, from Jay to the border. It was just recently partially relocated to go through the apple orchard where I waited, and the cedar swamp that I'd raced through. The new turn—to the right off the VAST trail, if one is heading south from the border, as Elizabeth was doing to meet me—is poorly marked. Furthermore, the old blazes down the VAST trail to the south have not been completely removed. So Elizabeth missed the turn and then was thoroughly confused by some rogue blazes further down. She'd been skiing back and forth on this quarter-mile of trail for the past forty-five minutes, trying to figure out where she had gone wrong, and is now thoroughly frustrated.

I'm just thankful it wasn't a bear attack. I give her another hug, then tell her, "It's cold out here! Let's get moving."

She's still upset with herself for missing the turn. "There it is, clear as day!" she says, when she spots it.

I acknowledge that when you're looking directly at the turn, there are some very obvious blazes. "But if you're coming at it from a right angle," I add, "it'd be easy to miss. Don't worry about it!" My reassurances do little good, and she can't let it go.

"That wasn't how our meeting was supposed to go. I was too pissed. Here," she says, suddenly decisive as she skis ten meters away from me, "let's do a do-over."

She turns around, sets her face in a smile, and skis back up to me.

"Honey!" she exclaims with outsized enthusiasm. "Here you are! I've found you! You're almost done! Congratulations!" She skis into my arms again, this time all smiles and giggles. I just laugh at her—what a goofy, wonderful woman.

We set off and the VAST trail takes us to the final road crossing. Elizabeth is moderating her pace—in spite of my days of practice, she is still far speedier than I, especially with no pack on her back. From there, it's just an easy ski along a tree line across a field. Skies are gray, as is most of the landscape, and the breeze is steady, but I am feeling pretty good. I'm at the northern tip of Vermont, having just skied the length of the state. My body and soul feel good—I'm proud of the achievement and how I've done it. And I'm with a woman I love dearly. It's hard to imagine life being much better right now.

Before I know it, we're at the end. We take the requisite pictures around the small granite monument.

Then I turn to Elizabeth.

"Well, what do we do now?" I ask, playing the straight man a little.

She giggles. "Well . . . let's go home. It's been lonely around the house without you storming around the place with your big feet." She turns more serious. "I've missed you. It'll be nice to have you back."

So we turn and head south.

She's right. It'll be nice to be back home.

Epilogue: My Dearest Friend, My All

Elizabeth and I are loading my gear into her car when an SUV with BORDER PATROL emblazoned across the side pulls up. The officer within sticks his head out the window.

"Anybody talk to you yet?" His tone is gruff and short and all business.

I can't help but think to myself that this is not the best way to start a conversation, but it's clearly not the right time to teach him a lesson in manners, so I manage to keep myself to a similarly succinct "Nope."

"Okay, well, what are you doing here? Did you go out to the border?"

"We're skiing the Catamount Trail," I tell him.

"Well, how far did you go? Did you go to the border?" he asks again.

He seems awfully fixated on this *border* of his, I think to my smart-alecky self. Out loud, I decide to egg him on a little.

"We skied right up to it—that's where the Trail ends. But I promise, I didn't put more than one leg across it."

He doesn't find me funny, which of course I knew from the start.

Elizabeth just rolls her eyes at me and the officer drives off soon afterward, seemingly satisfied that either we weren't causing any harm, or that I was a raving idiot. Or both. Either way, his business here was clearly finished. (As Elizabeth so frequently tells me, at least I make myself laugh.)

On the road after finally jamming my skis and poles into Elizabeth's small car, I convince Elizabeth to pull over at the first gas station we pass. Not only do I need to use the bathroom, but I could use a cup of coffee.

I enter the low-lying, ramshackle building to the tinkling of the bell on the door and find myself in the midst of a relationship-counseling effort. The old-timer behind the counter is lecturing the young woman perched on a stool nearby, and as I pour myself a large cup of joe, I listen in.

Gesturing dramatically and nodding his head whenever he makes a point, the man is trying to convince the woman that she should stay in the relationship she is currently in for the financial benefits. He starts listing off the perks: "shared rent, shared car, tax write-offs," tagging them off on his fingers one by one as he does so.

The young woman is unconvinced, and I agree with her. She can't be more than barely out of high school, but she seems to know that financial security is not the only basis for happiness and a successful relationship. As I'm leaving, however, instead of arguing theoretically on the importance of love in a relationship, she continues the monetary argument, explaining to the man just why she is financially solvent enough to make it on her own. If he's as jaded on love as his speech seems to demonstrate, I guess that's the only argument that will work with him.

Climbing back into the car, I look at Elizabeth. She's got her driving glasses on again and self-consciously glances at me before pulling out onto the main road. I've got it all, right here, I realize. Even that old-timer would be pleased with me. I've got both love and security right here next to me with this beautiful woman. After completing the trip, my head is on straight and my heart is true. Secure in my decision, I can look forward to the future with equanimity and hope.

Knox would have been equally ecstatic to be reunited with Lucy. But it was not in their near future to spend time together. As Lucy bounced around from one temporary lodging to another, she wrote to "my Harry" often, and Knox replied with long letters of love.

"Every particle of heat seems to be eradicated from the head or else entirely absorbed, in the widely ranging fire emitted from the heart," wrote Knox to Lucy early in their courtship. "To tell you how much I long to see you would be impossible."[1]

Lucy responded with ardor of her own.

"My dearest friend, my all, my Harry—where are you—are you safe—are you well? Would to heaven I could see you for one-half hour. Do you wish for your Lucy? Do you think of me? Do you ever shed a tear for me?"[2] Lonely and alone (and often pregnant—their sporadic liaisons were clearly productive), Lucy desperately wished to be permanently reunited with her husband.

But for Knox, duty called above all else, and after his spectacular success traveling from Ticonderoga, he became an integral part of Washington's army. Using the hard lessons he had learned in New York and Massachusetts as he dragged the artillery to Cambridge, Knox became a first-class artillerist. Washington testified to Knox's capabilities in a letter in 1778. "There is no department in the army that has been conducted with greater propriety," wrote Washington, "or to more advantage, than the one in which [Knox] presides; and owing principally, if not wholly, to his management."[3] Soon after, in 1780, Knox dragged five hundred sleighs loaded with equipment and cannons through deep snow in an attack on Staten Island, New York.

While repulsed, that the mission was even attempted was testament to Knox's abilities and Washington's faith in them.

Using George Washington as a role model and mentor, Knox also became a superb leader of men. Knox was friends with Washington, as few men were, but remained in awe of him throughout his life. "Every military character on this continent, taken collectively, vanishes before him," wrote Knox in early 1778, "and he is not only a soldier but a patriot in the fullest sense of the word. As it is impossible truly to describe a living Character, it must be left to posterity to do him justice."[4] Under Washington's direction, Knox, too, became a soldier and a leader. "He is a brave, sensible, enterprising man," wrote Dr. Benjamin Rush in 1777 of Knox. "I saw his behavior in the Battle of Trenton; he was cool, cheerful and was present everywhere."[5] Knox was impressing those around him on all fronts.

Knox continued to put on weight throughout the war and his subsequent career. "I never saw a (Kn)ox fatter in my life," punned a clergyman upon sighting Knox in a parade.[6] Another agreed, writing that, "When thinking, [Knox] looked like one of his own heavy pieces."[7] Lucy, too, continued to grow. Wrote John Adams's daughter to Abigail Adams, "I verily believe that her waist is as large as three of yours at least."[8] Yet in spite of their heaviness, they both continued to be full of energy and vivacity.

Knox's career would rocket throughout the war and beyond. Promoted from colonel to brigadier general of artillery in 1776, he went on to form the continent's first artillery and officer training school in 1779. He was present at Yorktown where he worked to establish siege lines and artillery positions to assault the British from land while the French blockaded Cornwallis from the sea. Upon the final installation of the batteries, Knox handed Washington a lit torch. Washington, therefore, touched off the first artillery shot of the besiegement, a testament to their friendship and Knox's humility, for no doubt he would have liked to do the same himself.

Knox's friend Nathanael Greene wrote to Knox around this time, wishing him luck, and saying that he "hope[d] you will not get in the way of a four-and-twenty pounder but will return to [Lucy] with whole bones."[9] Knox, of course, survived the victory at Yorktown, and did see Lucy soon after, albeit, once again, only briefly. In 1782 he was promoted to major general and, upon completion of the war and the retirement of Washington, became the senior officer of the army. To be inactive was never his way.

In 1785, he became secretary at war, where he served Congress and then Washington until 1794 (the position changing titles along with Washington's election to the presidency in 1789, to secretary *of* war). Here, he dealt mostly with Native American affairs (as well as navigating Shays' Rebellion, as noted previously). He finally retired from public life in 1794. Apparently the march from Ticonderoga had not dimmed his enthusiasm for snow and northern New England, for the family moved to Maine.

Knox had always had his heart set on a country estate, a la George Washington and other Virginians. Lucy had inherited some land in Thomaston, Maine, and it was here they decided to build their home. Naming it Montpelier, it was begun in 1794. "All my life hitherto I have been pursuing illusive bubbles which burst on being grasped," Knox had written in 1792. "Tis high time I should quit public life and attend to the solid interests of my family, so that they may not be left dependent on the cold hand of charity."[10] So Knox resigned his postwar position in Washington's cabinet and retired to Maine in 1795. While duty and business meant that he was still often summering in Boston, he would spend much of the remainder of his life at Montpelier.

Lucy was ecstatic. Finally able to set down roots in a home of their own, she would also now be able to stay close to Knox. She had been hoping for this for years, and it was finally a reality. No more would Knox's duties and obligations draw him away from her. Knox, for his part, was excited as well. "I long with the utmost devotion for the arrival of that period when my Lucy and I shall be no more separated," he wrote in 1779. "When we shall sit down, free from the hurry, bustle and impertinence of the world, in some sequestered Vale where the education of our children and the preparation on our part for a pure and more happy region, shall employ the principal part of our time in acts of love to men and worship to our Maker."[11] That period had arrived. "No man on earth separated from all he holds dear on earth, has ever suffered more than I have suffered in being absent from you whom I hold dearer than any other object," he would write to his wife during the war.[12] Now, they were together at last.

And hoping to have lots of children. Perhaps because he had so few remaining family members himself, he and Lucy aimed for a large family. (Remember, his father had left the family when Knox was nine, and his mother later died when he was twenty-one, leaving him with only one brother in the country, his two others being sailors and permanently out of touch.) Lucy would give birth to thirteen children in all, from 1775 to 1794. As noted earlier, however, only three would make it to adulthood. A variety of childhood diseases, so prevalent in the eighteenth century, would carry them off. Their deaths were the greatest sorrows of both Lucy and Knox's lives.

"Unfortunate, indeed, have we been in the loss of eight children, requiring the exercise of our whole stock of philosophy and religion,"

Knox would write to George Washington (prior to their loss of two more), also noting that, "We find ourselves afflicted by an irresistible but invisible force to whom we must submit."[13] The man who was so able and resourceful on the battlefield conversely seemed to find comfort in knowing it was out of his hands.

Lucy, however, appears to have been hit harder. As yet another child died years later, Lucy's "former wounds are opened afresh and occasion a pressure of grief almost too much for human nature." [14] Knox would write.

Perhaps in response to the tragedies, Knox threw himself into life at Montpelier. Fancying himself a paternalistic overseer, he offered up his lands to settlers. He envisioned a robust, bustling town with schools, libraries, churches, farms, and homes, and to this end, he established numerous industries in the region. Lumber mills, brick-yards, a limekiln, and various fishing, ranching, and farming enter-prises all bore the indelible stamp of Knox's initiative. It would take time, and while a few remained stillborn, eventually many of these ventures would begin to pay off.

All the while he and Lucy hosted myriad guests, as their ini-tial housewarming party foreshadowed. "On July Fourth, we had a small company of upwards of 500 people," Knox wrote to his son.[15] Later on, he hosted the entire tribe of Tarratine Indians of Penobscot County, who promptly overstayed their welcome, necessitating a dismissal after a weeks-long visit. Visiting dignitaries even made the pilgrimage, with Talleyrand and the son of the Marquis de Lafayette stopping by.

Over the years, Lucy's grieving for her lost children led to unstable mental health. Upon the death of son Marcus in 1782, Knox wrote to a friend that "my utmost attention and philosophy were necessarily exerted to calm the agitated mind of its wretched mother."[16] Later, after the dual deaths of two of their children in 1796, and the death of yet another the following winter, Knox wrote that their passing "is almost too great for the inconsolable mother who will go mourning to her grave."[17]

Lucy seemed to find solace not only in her remaining family, but also in games. Numerous visitors to Montpelier in the couple's later years commented on her obsession with cards, chess, and similar pursuits. "Madame Knox, who although very haughty, I find pleasant and sensible," noted one visitor. "Chess is now her mania, which she plays extremely well, only too often for my fancy . . . she is certainly the most successful player I have ever encountered."[18] The repetition of game after game seemed to temporarily numb the grief she felt from morning to night.

Knox for his part was indulgent of his wife's growing eccentricities. He seemed to know that she was overwhelmed and did his best to indulge her whims. With guests he "preferr[ed] to converse with those who were not engaged at play; and thus on foot walking from one circle to the other with his cheerful smile and affable speech did he make his guests happy, and himself beloved."[19] Knox, always the empathetic gentleman, thus protected his wife and her needs while still making all visitors feel welcome and at home.

Their lives, split between Boston and Montpelier, were settling down. Knox still had business in Boston and had a seat in the state legislature. But his heart seemed to be more and more in Maine, especially as some of his enterprises finally began to bear fruit. It was therefore untimely when, in October of 1806, a chicken bone became lodged in his throat. An infection quickly developed, and he died days later on October 25, 1806. He was fifty-five years old.

Lucy was inconsolable with grief. After the deaths of ten of her children, she had now been robbed of her Harry, as well. She became reclusive, eventually dying in 1824 at age sixty-seven. Henry Jackson Knox, their only surviving son, suffered from alcoholism and was in and out of debtors' prison for much of his adult life, before experiencing a religious conversion in his waning years. Their two surviving daughters, Caroline and Lucy, fared better, marrying a Maine senator and a lawyer respectively. They both lived in Montpelier periodically throughout their lives, but after their deaths it fell into disrepair, and was demolished in 1871. Knox's grave, on the property, was relocated several times as the property was sold and resold. A recreation of Knox's original Montpelier was built in 1929 in Thomaston, ME. It is now part of the Knox Museum and open to the public.

Tributes and testaments to Knox and the impact of his life abound, both during and after his life. "To praise his military talents would be to deprive him of half the eulogium he merits," wrote one upon meeting Knox. "It is impossible to know him without esteeming him, to see him without loving him . . . at present he belongs to the whole world by his reputation and his success."[20] Later, another described him as "a rock, a pillar of granite faith. Tidal waves and cross winds may shake others. But not him. He banishes doubt and fear by knowing precisely what he will do when the storm breaks and the trial by fire is on."[21]

While the general public no longer necessarily recognizes his name alongside those of Washington, Adams, Jefferson, and some of the other founding fathers, there is no doubt that this is where he belongs. First, as an essential cog in the Revolutionary War army, and subsequently, involved in both the initial confederacy and the first presidency as secretary of war, Knox left an indelible mark on this nation's history. "It is doubtful," writes one historian, "that many of the colonies would have supported separation from Great Britain if the army had been unable to free Boston from occupation. The victory led patriots to believe that the British could be beaten in the field and that freedom was attainable."[22] Certainly, without Knox's fifty-nine Ticonderoga cannons, the potential for that victory would have been greatly diminished.

Historian Mark Puls ends his excellent biography with a powerful description. "Perhaps it is best to imagine his booming voice piercing through the howling wind and falling snow, directing the shivering patriot soldiers," envisions Puls, "and remember a man who risked everything he had for the sake of freedom and his country."[23] Puls was writing of the crossing of the Delaware, but he could have just as easily been describing Knox's very first expedition, where he began his long and fruitful career: the trek from Ticonderoga, with his noble train of artillery.

And me?

I sit in the car, damply, listening to the radio and softly humming along. We've got the heat blasting hot air out of the vents and the seat heaters turned up high. The defroster is on, too, yet the edges of the windshield are still foggy with all of my moisture.

Elizabeth wrinkles her nose at me.

"You stink," she says. "Like, a lot."

I grin back at her. "I know," I respond.

Sam Brakeley

We sit in silence for a while longer. At one point I reach out and take her hand. We sit there peacefully—she, concentrating on the road, and me, staring out the side window at the landscape passing by.

I love these woods. I love the rivers, lakes, ponds, and streams of New England, the rocky forest floor and steep mountains. I love the open hardwood groves and thick evergreen stands. I love walking beneath the forest canopy and coming upon an old foundation or crumbling stone wall. I love the feel of New England, its threatening, snowy winters and its soft, welcoming summers. Even mud season in between. It all has its place.

I love the attachment I feel to this place. I know its ways, its interstates and back roads, and all the twists, windings, and ruts that come with them. I know its towns, big and small. I know the people, their quirks, their gruff exteriors and their true welcoming natures. Their passion and dedication to hard work, to making something of this place and their lives. The kindness and generosity of the Carls, Warrens, Kathys, and the others I've met along this journey. These are my people, for better or worse.

Especially my own people, my family. We're sprinkled across New England, in Maine, New Hampshire, Vermont, and Massachusetts. All within a couple of hours of each other. Nearby, supporting.

I think ahead to my next rendezvous—I'm meeting an aunt, uncle, and three cousins for breakfast at a favorite local diner. We'll eat short-order eggs and pancakes, slurp slightly burnt coffee, and it'll be the highlight of my week. Seeing them, laughing over old family stories and recent mishaps, and feeling warm and cozy in the embrace of people who I love and who love me back, is a feeling like no other. I can't wait.

Then I look over at Elizabeth. It's been a long two-and-a-half weeks without her, on the trail. Her love, support, and comfort have been a mainstay of my recent life, and I've come to rely on her strength and affection more than I sometimes like to admit. As I gaze at her, I feel even more strongly that I've made the right decision. This land—it's not going anywhere. The maple trees and mountain streams, mud seasons and fall foliage; it'll all be here whenever we're ready to return. The same is true for the people. The faces may change, but New England's character won't. I'll be able to slip seamlessly back into life here, whenever the time is right.

And my family. Both immediate and extended, they'll be here, too. Even with most of a country between us, they'll be wherever I need them to be, loving and supportive as always. Sure, the diner breakfasts may be fewer and farther between (which perhaps is best for all of our health—the body can only absorb so much short-order grease), but the laughter and the love will always be there, for me to access when I need it. My family is like that. That's why I love them.

I turn from the window and look at Elizabeth once more. She's staring at the road, but clearly her mind is elsewhere. Perhaps on the coming trials and tribulations of moving across the country to a new job, a new life. *She's family, too*, I think. And right now, she's the one who needs my love and support as she faces these new challenges. It's time that I returned some of the selfless love that she has provided me for so long.

This trip hasn't changed me. I didn't undergo some sort of magical transformation as a result, and I haven't found God or anything like that. It wasn't that kind of trip. (Frankly, none of my trips are like that; I'm not that kind of person.) But this trip has helped me to come to a decision that I should have known the answer to long ago.

Elizabeth shakes her head a little and refocuses her eyes, bringing her mind back to the present. She glances at me before turning back to the windshield, smiling as she does.

"I love you," she tells me.

I gently squeeze the hand I've been holding.

"I love you too," I reply.

What I leave unspoken now but will tell her later is this latest revelation: Yes, I'm going to move across the country with you. We'll start a new adventure, a new trip, a new experience in a new place.

Together.

Skiing with Henry Knox

Acknowledgments

This trip could not have been taken, this book, not written, without the help of numerous people, both close friends and family and acquaintances I met out on the trail. To all of them, I am indebted.

First of all, thank you to the numerous historians who have worked this subject before me. I am grateful for to their tireless research and countless hours in various libraries. They helped me to find sources and decipher sometimes confusing or contradictory accounts left by some of the participants of the expedition.

I'd also like to thank all the people I met on the trip. Whether aiding me with rides—deeply discounted—or free equipment or food, or just sharing warmth and hospitality, they are the people who make a trip special and unique. I appreciated your generosity greatly, as I'm sure countless others have, before and after me. The world is filled with kind and thoughtful individuals.

My family has been supportive of all my endeavors throughout my life, including this one. Here in this story I was able to share just a few of the many formative experiences I've had over the course of my life. My parents, my brothers, my grandmother and grandfather, and my extended family have all helped to shape who I am today, and they once again demonstrated their unwavering support by aiding me in this most recent adventure, in ways both big and small.

Thanks in particular are due to Erica and Hank, as well as to Sue and Ben, for their thoughts on earlier drafts of this manuscript. Their thoughtful critiques and pushes in new directions helped to fill out the stories contained within. Genevieve Morgan, my editor at Islandport

Press, provided perceptive, professional insight and direction where (and when) it was much needed. Thank you.

And finally, my greatest debt is to Elizabeth. Not only were you my chauffeur for both travel legs—a first—but you also came and found me on the side of Route 125 and got me to a much-needed warm bed and hot meal with family at the halfway point. You also helped to edit and inspire this story. And in spite of our differences and occasional disagreements (where you continue to be right all the time, of course), you've been a patient, loving, and imperturbable force in my life. Utah didn't work out the way we'd hoped it would, and much of that is without a doubt on me. You're an incredible woman and a truly good person, and I'm just thankful I got to have the time with you that I did. Thank you for your caring, your generosity, and for all the good times together. I still love you, and I can't imagine what life would have been like had I not shown you all the constellations I knew all those years ago (it's still three).

Notes

Historical Background of Henry Knox and the Ticonderoga Expedition

1. North Callahan, *Henry Knox: George Washington's General*, p. 18.

2. Nancy Rubin Stuart, *Defiant Brides: The Untold Story of Two Revolutionary-Era Women and the Radical Men They Married*, p. 17.

3. Callahan, *Henry Knox*, p. 10.

4. "Lucy Knox," History of American Women, www.womenhistoryblog.com/2009/04/lucy-flucker-knox.html, accessed September 26, 2016.

5. Stuart, *Defiant Brides*, p. 17.

6. Noah Brooks, *Henry Knox: A Soldier of the Revolution*, p. 8.

7. Brooks, *Henry Knox*, p. 8.

8. Callahan, *Henry Knox*, p. vii.

Chapter 1. No Trouble or Expense Must Be Spared

1. Callahan, *Henry Knox*, p. 37.

2. Francis S. Drake, *Life and Correspondence of Henry Knox: Major-General in the American Revolutionary Army*, p. 119.

3. Ibid., p. 119.

4. Callahan, *Henry Knox*, p. 35.

5. Mark Puls, *Henry Knox: Visionary General of the American Revolution*, p. 30.

6. Ibid., p. 30.

7. Ibid., p. 34.

8. Ibid., p. 32.

9. Drake, *Life and Correspondence*, pp. 128–29.

10. Callahan, *Henry Knox*, p. 38.

11. Puls, *Henry Knox*, p. 36.

12. Callahan, *Henry Knox*, pp. 38–39.

13. Puls, *Henry Knox*, p. 38.

14. Callahan, *Henry Knox*, p. 102.

15. Puls, *Henry Knox*, p. 148.

16. Henry Knox, "Diary of the Ticonderoga Expedition," p. 323.

17. John P. Becker, *The Sexagenary: Or, Reminiscences of the American Revolution*, p. 36.

18. Callahan, *Henry Knox*, p. 112.

19. Knox, "Diary," p. 323.

Chapter 2: It Is Not Easy to Conceive of the Difficulties We Have Had

1. Knox, "Diary," p. 323.

2. Ibid., p. 323.

3. Ibid., p. 323.

4. Callahan, *Henry Knox*, p. 43.

5. Ibid., p. 43.

6. Drake, *Life and Correspondence*, p. 24.

7. Puls, *Henry Knox*, p. 38.

8. Drake, *Life and Correspondence*, p. 24.

9. Puls, *Henry Knox*, p. 51.

10. Drake, *Life and Correspondence*, pp. 31–32.

11. Callahan, *Henry Knox*, p. 73.

12. Puls, *Henry Knox*, p. 136.

13. Callahan, *Henry Knox*, p. 46.

Chapter 3: I Almost Perished with the Cold

1. Knox, "Diary," pp. 323–24.

2. Bernard A. Drew, *Henry Knox and the Revolutionary War Trail in Western Massachusetts*, p. 155.

3. Knox, "Diary," p. 324.

4. Drew, *Henry Knox*, p. 156.

5. Ibid., p. 156.

6. Ibid., p. 157.

7. Becker, *The Sexagenary*, p. 26.

8. Ibid., p. 26.

9. Stuart, *Defiant Brides*, p. 23.

10. Drake, *Life and Correspondence*, pp. 28–29.

11. Ibid., p. 28.

Chapter 4: In the Manner of the Esquimaux

1. Becker, *The Sexagenary*, p. 27.

2. Ibid., p. 30.

3. Ibid., pp. 37–38.

4. Ibid., p. 38.

5. Ibid., p. 38.

6. Ibid., pp. 37–39.

7. Alexander C. Flick, "General Henry Knox's Ticonderoga Expedition," p. 132.

8. Becker, *The Sexagenary*, pp. 30–31.

9. Knox, "Diary," p. 324.

10. Becker, *The Sexagenary*, p. 31.

11. Ibid., p. 31.

12. Knox, "Diary," p. 324.

13. Becker, *The Sexagenary*, p. 31.

14. Flick, "Ticonderoga Expedition," p. 132.

15. A. Roger Ekirch, *At Day's Close: Night in Times Past*, p. 300.

16. Ibid., pp. 305–11.

17. Ibid., pp. 303–04.

18. Becker, *The Sexagenary*, pp. 27–28.

19. Ibid., p. 34.

Chapter 5: Humbled by Thoughts of My Own Insignificance

1. Knox, "Diary," p. 325.

2. Becker, *The Sexagenary*, pp. 31–32.

3. Drake, *Life and Correspondence*, p. 25.

4. Puls, *Henry Knox*, p. 40.

5. Ibid., p. 41.

6. Knox, "Diary," p. 325.

7. Ibid., p. 325.

8. Puls, *Henry Knox*, p. 74.

9. Drake, *Life and Correspondence*, p. 36.

10. Callahan, *Henry Knox*, p. 82.

11. Puls, *Henry Knox*, pp. 74–75.

12. Callahan, *Henry Knox*, p. 83.

13. Puls, *Henry Knox*, p. 75.

14. Ibid., pp. 78–79.

Chapter Six: I Go to a Solitary and Painful Bed

1. Callahan, *Henry Knox*, p. 48.

2. Becker, *The Sexagenary*, p. 33.

3. Ibid., p. 33.

4. Knox, "Diary," p. 325.

5. Puls, *Henry Knox*, p. 61.

6. Stuart, *Defiant Brides*, p. 16.

7. Ibid., p. xv (preface).

8. Drake, *Life and Correspondence*, p. 152.

9. Stuart, *Defiant Brides*, p. 19.

10. Ibid., p. 21.

11. Becker, *The Sexagenary*, p. 33.

12. Ibid., p. 33.

13. Knox, "Diary," p. 325.

14. Becker, *The Sexagenary*, pp. 33–34.

15. Callahan, *Henry Knox*, p. 289.

Chapter 7: All the Kingdoms of the Earth

1. Knox, "Diary," p. 325.

2. Drew, *Henry Knox*, p. 159.

3. Knox, "Diary," p. 325.

4. Callahan, *Henry Knox*, p. 51.

5. Drew, *Henry Knox*, pp. 91–92, 106.

6. John Knowles, *A Separate Peace*, p. 120.

Chapter 8: We Shall Cut No Small Figure

1. Callahan, *Henry Knox*, p. 51.

2. Puls, *Henry Knox*, p. 75.

3. Callahan, *Henry Knox*, p. 52.

4. Knox, "Diary," p. 325.

5. Ibid., p. 325.

6. Ibid., p. 326.

7. Becker, *The Sexagenary*, pp. 47–48.

8. Flick, "Ticonderoga Expedition," p. 134.

9. Becker, *The Sexagenary*, p. 34.

10. Ibid., p. 34.

11. Ibid., p. 35.

12. Ibid., p. 35.

Chapter 9: We Could Go No Further

1. Becker, *The Sexagenary*, p. 35.

2. Callahan, *Henry Knox*, p. 54.

3. Becker, *The Sexagenary*, p. 35.

4. Callahan, *Henry Knox*, p. 100.

5. Ibid., p. 246.

6. Puls, *Henry Knox*, p. 195; Callahan, *Henry Knox*, p. 245.

Chapter 10: We Supped There Very Agreeably

1. Massachusetts Historical Society, Adams Family Papers, "John Adams' Diary, 27 October 1775–13 October 1776," January 25, 1776. http://masshist.org/digitaladams/archive/doc?id=D25& bc=%2Fdigitaladams%2Farchive%2Fbrowse%2Fdiaries_by_date. php, accessed November 1, 2016.

2. Victor Brooks, *The Boston Campaign*, p. 210.

3. Callahan, *Henry Knox*, p. 56.

4. Puls, *Henry Knox*, p. 44.

5. Callahan, *Henry Knox*, p. 58.

Epilogue: My Dearest Friend, My All

1. Stuart, *Defiant Brides*, p. 19.

2. Puls, *Henry Knox*, p. 89.

3. Ibid., p. 125.

4. Callahan, *Henry Knox*, p. 132.

5. Ibid., p. 91.

6. Ibid., p. 59.

7. Drake, *Life and Correspondence*, p. 119.

8. Ibid., p. 102.

9. Callahan, *Henry Knox*, p. 179.

10. Drake, *Life and Correspondence*, pp. 108–09.

11. Callahan, *Henry Knox*, p. 159.

12. Ibid., p. 128.

13. Drake, *Life and Correspondence*, p. 114.

14. Callahan, *Henry Knox*, p. 285.

15. Callahan, *Henry Knox*, p. 348.

16. Stuart, *Defiant Brides*, p. 143.

17. Callahan, *Henry Knox*, p. 285.

18. Callahan, *Henry Knox*, p. 378.

19. Stuart, *Defiant Brides*, pp. 184–85.

20. Callahan, *Henry Knox*, p. 168.

21. Ibid., p. 384.

22. Puls, *Henry Knox*, p. 251.

23. Ibid., p. 257.

Bibliography

Books

Becker, John P. *The Sexagenary: Or, Reminiscences of the American Revolution*. Albany, NY: J. Munsell, 1866.

Billias, George Athan, ed. *George Washington's Generals and Opponents: Their Exploits and Leadership*. New York: Da Capo Press, 1994.

Brooks, Noah. *Henry Knox: A Soldier of the Revolution*. Memphis, TN: General Books LLC, 2012.

Brooks, Victor. *The Boston Campaign*. Conshohocken, PA: Combined Publishing, 1999.

Callahan, North. *Henry Knox: George Washington's General*. New York: Rinehart & Company, Inc., 1958.

Catamount Trail Association. *Catamount Trail Guidebook*, 9th ed. Burlington, VT: Catamount Trail Association, 2009.

Drake, Francis S. *Life and Correspondence of Henry Knox: Major-General in the American Revolutionary Army*. Boston, MA: Samuel G. Drake, 1873.

Drew, Bernard A. *Henry Knox and the Revolutionary War Trail in Western Massachusetts*. Jefferson, NC: McFarland & Company, 2012.

Ekirch, A. Roger. *At Day's Close: Night in Times Past*. New York: W. W. Norton & Company, 2005.

Flick, Alexander C. "General Henry Knox's Ticonderoga Expedition," *Quarterly Journal of the New York State Historical Association*, Vol. 9, No. 2 (1928): 119–35.

Knowles, John. *A Separate Peace*. New York: Scribner, 2003.

Knox, Henry. "Diary of the Ticonderoga Expedition," *New England Historical and Genealogical Register*, Vol. 30 (1876): 321–26.

Puls, Mark. *Henry Knox: Visionary General of the American Revolution*. New York: Palgrave Macmillan, 2008.

Royster, Charles. *A Revolutionary People at War: The Continental Army and American Character, 1775–1783*. Chapel Hill: University of North Carolina Press, 1986.

Stuart, Nancy Rubin. *Defiant Brides: The Untold Story of Two Revolutionary-Era Women and the Radical Men They Married*. Boston, MA: Beacon Press, 2013.

Websites

Adams Family Papers: An Electronic Archive, Massachusetts Historical Society. http://masshist.org/digitaladams/archive/doc?id=D25&bc=%2Fdigitaladams%2Farchive%2Fbrowse%2Fdiaries_by_date.php.

"Lucy Knox: Wife of Revolutionary War Patriot, Henry Knox," History of American Women. www.womenhistoryblog.com/2009/04/lucy-flucker-knox.html.

Image Credits

Unless otherwise noted: Brakeley, Sam. All 2015 Photographs: Copyright © 2015 by Sam Brakeley.

Image on page vi: (Accessed November 25, 2017 at www.archives.gov/files/research/military/american-revolution/pictures/images/revolutionary-war-018.jpg.)

Images on pages 28 and 29: Stuart, Gilbert. *Portrait of Henry Knox*. (Accessed November 25, 2017 at https://en.wikipedia.org/wiki/Henry_Knox#/media/File:Henry_Knox_by_Gilbert_Stuart_1806.jpeg.) Hoit, Albert Gallatin. *Portrait of Lucy Flucker Knox*. (Accessed November 25, 2017 at https://commons.wikimedia.org/wiki/File:Lucy_Flucker_Knox_Thatcher.png.)